Partners in Prosperity:
The Changing Geography of the Transatlantic Economy

Daniel S. Hamilton and Joseph P. Quinlan

Center for Transatlantic Relations
Johns Hopkins University
Paul H. Nitze School of Advanced International Studies

Funding for this project was made possible by a generous grant from the DaimlerChrysler Corporation Fund

Hamilton, Daniel S. and Quinlan, Joseph P. *Partners in Prosperity. The Changing Geography of the Transatlantic Economy.* Washington, DC: Center for Transatlantic Relations, Johns Hopkins University, 2004

Center for Transatlantic Relations
American Consortium on EU Studies
EU Center Washington, DC
The Paul H. Nitze School of Advanced International Studies
The Johns Hopkins University
1717 Massachusetts Ave., NW, Suite 525
Washington, DC 20036
Tel: (202) 663-5880
Fax (202) 663-5979
Email: transatlantic@jhu.edu
http://transatlantic.sais-jhu.edu

ISBN 0-9753325-5-4

Cover: Maps represent transatlantic foreign direct investment (FDI) flows. Original maps are reproduced in complete form in the Appendix.

Table of Contents

List of Figures

Chapter 5

Chapter 6

Chapter 7

Preface

The transatlantic partnership has weathered many storms, but over the past fifty years none was perhaps as turbulent as the transatlantic tempest generated by the U.S.-led invasion of Iraq in 2003. Lost in the headlines, however, is a current of change that may prove more enduring than the strains of the moment. Iraq was perhaps the most visible sign that over the past decade the traditional relationship between the transatlantic strategic and economic agendas has reversed. During the Cold War, European and American leaders strove to keep transatlantic economic conflicts from infecting their core political alliance. In the post-Cold War, post-9/11, post-Iraq world the challenge may be to keep transatlantic political disputes from damaging the world's most important economic relationship.

For years observers on both sides of the Atlantic have been accustomed to viewing Europe and America primarily as partners in peace and security. This aspect of the relationship remains important, yet in an era of globalization and transatlantic political travails it has become increasingly urgent to broaden this somewhat myopic view by underscoring the degree to which Europe and America are also partners in prosperity.

This volume examines the changing landscape of the transatlantic economy in a globalizing world. It extends and deepens the analysis offered in a shorter 2003 Center study by Joseph P. Quinlan. We were gratified by the tremendous response to that study, and to the encouragement we received to expand its scope. This volume tells how the transatlantic economy weathered the squalls of 2003; describes the ties that continue to bind both sides of the Atlantic; maps the increasingly dense web of investment, trade, and jobs that connect Europe's regions to America's states; traces the impact of Nafta and EU enlargement on transatlantic economic flows; tracks intercontinental "connectivity" in the new knowledge economy; and sets forth areas in which Europe and America continue to be global pathfinders.

On behalf of the Center for Transatlantic Relations, we would like to thank the DaimlerChrysler Corporation Fund for its encouragement and support of this project. Particular thanks go to Michael Duignan, Todd Jablonski and Nathan Simon for their spectacular research assistance. We are also grateful to Chantal de Jonge Oudraat, Esther Brimmer, Katrien Maes, and Jeanette Murphy for their help and good cheer throughout the project. Additional thanks go to Ernst & Young for permission to draw on data from their *European Investment Monitor*; to Telegeography Research Group—PriMetrica, Inc. for their data on interregional connectivity; to the Representative for German Industry and Trade for assistance with additional data on the German *Länder*; and to Peggy Irvine, Kirby Lithographic, and Cartisan AGS for their patience and skill in working with us to produce this volume and to develop some rather unusual maps of the transatlantic economy. Although we have benefited from the insights of many, we carry sole responsibility for the content of the text.

Daniel S. Hamilton
Joseph P. Quinlan

Executive Summary

- One of the defining features of the global economic landscape over the past decade has been the increasing integration and cohesion of the transatlantic economy. Globalization is happening faster and reaching deeper between Europe and America than between any other two continents.

- European and American economies and societies have not drifted apart since the end of the Cold War; they have become even more intertwined and interdependent.

- Despite the perennial hype about the significance of Nafta, the "rise of Asia" or "big emerging markets," the United States and Europe remain by far each other's most important commercial partners. The economic relationship between the United States and Europe is by a wide margin the deepest and broadest between any two continents in history—and those ties are accelerating.

- The years since the Cold War—the years when the fading "glue" of the Cold War partnership supposedly loosened transatlantic ties—marked in fact one of the most intense periods of transatlantic integration ever.

- The transatlantic economy generates roughly $2.5 trillion in total commercial sales a year and employs over 12 million workers in mutually "insourced" jobs on both sides of the Atlantic who enjoy high wages, high labor and environmental standards, and open, largely non-discriminatory access to each other's markets.

It's Foreign Investment, Stupid

- Transatlantic trade squabbles steal the headlines but account for only 1-2 % of transatlantic commerce. In fact, trade itself accounts for less than 20% of transatlantic commerce.

- Trade flows are a misleading benchmark of transatlantic economic interaction. Foreign investment, not trade, drives transatlantic commerce, and contrary to common wisdom, most U.S. and European investments flow to each other, rather than to lower-wage developing nations.

- Foreign affiliate sales, not trade, are the backbone of the transatlantic economy. In 2001 foreign affiliate sales amounted to $2.8 trillion, more than five times the $549 billion in total trade.

- When one adds investment and trade together to get a more complete picture, one sees that U.S. economic engagement remains overwhelmingly focused on Europe. The transatlantic economy is where the markets are, where the jobs are, where the profits are.

- Foreign affiliate sales not only dwarf transatlantic trade flows but also every other international commercial artery linking the United States to the rest of the world. In 2001, total foreign affiliate sales between the U. S. and Europe were more than double U.S.-transpacific foreign affiliate sales, more than three times larger than total transpacific trade flows, and more than four times larger than foreign affiliate sales between the U.S. and Nafta partners Mexico and Canada.

- Despite transatlantic tensions over Iraq, corporate America pumped nearly $87 billion in foreign direct investment (FDI) into Europe in 2003. That represents a jump of 30.5% from 2002 and was more than double the rate of growth in total U.S. investment outflows for the year.

- Europe accounted for nearly 65% of total U.S. foreign direct investment in 2003.

- Even though U.S.-German relations ebbed to one of their lowest levels since World War II, American firms sank $7 billion in Germany in 2003, a sharp reversal from 2002, when U.S. firms pulled some $5 billion out of Germany.

- Despite Franco-American diplomatic tensions, U.S. investment flows to France in 2003 rose by more than 10% to $2.3 billion, and U.S. affiliates more than doubled their profits in France to $4.3 billion. French firms were also among the largest European investors and largest foreign sources of jobs in the U.S.—Corporate France invested $4.2 billion in the United States in 2003.

- U.S. investment in Ireland alone in 2003 ($4.7 billion) was more than two-and-a-half times greater than U.S. investment in China ($1.7 billion).

- U.S. investment flows to Denmark between 2000 and 2003 ($4.1 billion) were nearly three times greater than U.S. flows to India ($1.5 billion).

- The $19.2 billion of U.S. investment in the Netherlands alone in 2003 was not far behind total U.S. investment in all of Asia ($22.4 billion).

- Europe's investment stakes in the U.S., on a historical-cost basis, exceeded $1 trillion in 2002, 20% more than America's stake in Europe. Europe's investment stake in the U.S. doubled between 1998 and 2002. Europe accounts for nearly three-fourths of all foreign investment in the U.S. No other region of the world has made such a large capital commitment to the United States. European firms have never been as exposed to the U.S. economy as they are today.

- Virulent anti-war sentiment across Europe did not prevent European firms from investing $36.9 billion in foreign direct investment in the U.S. in 2003. That represents a sharp rebound from the depressed levels of 2002, when European FDI inflows to the United States totaled $26 billion.

Europe and America: That's Where the Profits Are . . .

- Europe is the most important commercial market in the world for corporate America by a wide yet underappreciated margin. U.S. companies continue to rely on Europe for half their total annual foreign profits.

- Similarly, the United States is the most important market in the world in terms of earnings for many European multinationals. The annual earnings of Europe's U.S. affiliates has risen more than ten-fold since the end of the Cold War, from $4.4 billion in 1990 to $46.4 billion in 2003.

- Despite talk of transatlantic boycotts or consumer backlash due to European-American tensions over Iraq, 2003 was a banner year for transatlantic profits as measured by foreign affiliate income.

- U.S. foreign affiliate income from Europe surged to a record $77.1 billion in 2003, a 30% jump from 2002.

- U.S. affiliate earnings in 12 European markets (France, the Netherlands, Switzerland, Italy, Ireland, Spain, Belgium, Denmark, Sweden, Austria, Czech Republic and Poland) reached record highs in 2003. U.S. affiliate profits in France more than doubled. Profits earned in Ireland surged by 45%, in Italy by 40%, and in the Netherlands by 24.5%.

- 2003 was also a record year for profits of European affiliates operating in the United States. Despite the strong euro, European affiliate earnings of $46.4 billion easily surpassed earnings of 2002 ($32.23 billion) and 2001 ($17.4 billion), and the previous peak in earnings of $38.8 billion in 2000.

- British, Dutch, Swiss and Swedish foreign affiliates all enjoyed record U.S. profits in 2003.

That's Where the Markets Are . . .

- Corporate America's foreign assets tallied over $5.8 trillion in 2001. The bulk of these assets—roughly 60%—were located in Europe.

- Most of the top destinations for U.S. investment in the world in 2002 were European: the UK (1), the Netherlands (3), Switzerland (4), Germany (6), Belgium/Luxembourg (8) and France (10).

- Transpacific linkages based on trade are relatively shallow in comparison to the deeper transatlantic linkages rooted in foreign direct investment.

- The United Kingdom is the most important market in the world for corporate America. U.S. assets in the United Kingdom—roughly $1.4 trillion in 2001—were more than 50% larger than the entire U.S. asset base in Asia and almost equivalent to the combined overseas affiliate asset base of Asia, Latin America, Africa and the Middle East.

- The UK, not China or Mexico, was at the forefront of America's great overseas investment boom of the 1990s, attracting just over 20% of total U.S. FDI over the period. The Netherlands was second.

- Despite all the talk about Nafta and the "Pacific Century," over the past decade U.S. firms have ploughed ten times as much capital into the Netherlands as into China, and twice as much into the Netherlands as into Mexico.

- U.S. assets in Germany in 2001 of $320 billion were greater than total U.S. assets in all of South America.

- In 2001, U.S. affiliates accounted for 16% of Ireland's total output, 7.2% of the UK's aggregate output, and 6.2% of the Netherlands.

- Europe accounted for roughly 55% of the total gross global product of U.S. affiliates in 2001—$583 billion.

- European firms held some $3.7 trillion in U.S. assets in 2001, nearly 70% of the total.

- U.S. foreign affiliates in Europe achieved sales of $1.5 trillion in 2001—$5\frac{1}{2}$ times the $276 million in U.S. exports to Europe.

- Europe accounted for just over 51% of global U.S. foreign affiliate sales in 2001.

- U.S. affiliate sales in Europe were more than double affiliate sales in the entire Asia/Pacific region in 2001. U.S. affiliate sales in the UK alone ($428 billion) exceeded aggregate sales in Latin America.

- Even though U.S. affiliate sales in China have soared, they have done so from a very low base. Sales of $36 billion in China in 2001, for example, were on par with those in Sweden ($33 billion) and well below sales in either Germany ($240 billion) or France ($135 billion).

- Weak European growth means lost opportunities for Americans. Growth of just 3% in Europe would create a new market the size of the entire country of Argentina for companies and investors from the U.S. and other countries.

- Affiliate sales, not trade, also represent the primary means by which European firms deliver goods and services to U.S. consumers. In 2001 European affiliate sales in the U.S. ($1.4 billion) were over four times larger than European exports to the U.S.

- UK affiliate sales in the U.S. in 2001 were more than five times the amount of UK exports to the U.S. German affiliate sales in the U.S. were more than four times greater than German exports to the U.S.—a striking statistic for Germany, a country commonly thought to be a classic "trading" nation.

That's Where the Jobs Are . . .

- The bulk of corporate America's overseas workforce is employed in Europe, not in low-wage countries like Mexico, China or India. Of the nearly 9.8 million workers employed by U.S. foreign affiliates in 2001, roughly 43% work in Europe.

- The U.S. also "insources" more jobs from Europe than it "outsources" across the Atlantic. In fact, the U.S. enjoys a "million worker surplus" with Europe. In 2001 European affiliates of U.S. firms directly employed roughly 3.2 million workers, while U.S. affiliates of European firms directly employed just over 4.2 million U.S. workers.

- The U.S. insourced more jobs from Belgium, France, Germany, the Netherlands and Switzerland than it outsourced in 2001. U.S. firms employed slightly more workers in the United Kingdom than British firms in the United States.

- The transatlantic workforce directly deployed by U.S. and European foreign affiliates is massive, totaling over 8.4 million workers in 2001. That is three times the number of total workers employed by U.S. affiliates in Nafta partners Canada and Mexico (2.8 million). It is also well above total foreign employment of U.S. foreign affiliates in Asia and Asian foreign affiliates in the United States (2.3 million).

- Europe is by far the greatest source of America's insourced jobs. European firms employed roughly two-thirds of the 6.4 million U.S. workers on the payrolls of foreign affiliates in 2001. The top five employers in the U.S. are the United Kingdom (1.1 million), Germany (734,000), France (578,000), the Netherlands (571,000) and Switzerland (546,000).

- Figures tracking direct employment due to investment alone do not include indirect employment related to nonequity arrangements like strategic alliances, joint ventures and other deals. Moreover, affiliate employment figures do not include jobs supported by trade with Europe. Trade-related employment is substantial in many U.S. states and European regions. In total, and adding in indirect employment, we estimate that the overall transatlantic work force numbers some 12-14 million workers.

That's Where Trade Opportunities Still Lie . . .

- 2003 was a record year for transatlantic trade flows. Total transatlantic trade in goods grew by 7% to $395 billion in 2003.

- U.S. exports, supported by the weaker U.S. dollar, recovered from the two-year downturn in trade with Europe and grew by 4.8% to $150.6 billion in 2003.

- U.S. imports from Europe jumped 8.5% to a record $245 billion in 2003—despite a 20% appreciation of the euro against the dollar. America's trade deficit with the EU widened by 15% to a record $94.3 billion in 2003. Surging imports from Europe produced record U.S. trade deficits with Germany, Italy, Ireland, France and the Netherlands.

- Surging U.S. demand for European products in 2003 offset the dampening trade impact of weak European economic growth and a surging euro. Roughly 57% of total U.S. imports from Europe is considered related party trade, which means more than half of U.S. imports from Europe are affected less by exchange rates than by U.S. demand. 67% of U.S. imports from Germany, 59% of U.S. imports from the Netherlands and 54% of U.S. imports from the United Kingdom are considered related party trade.

- The U.S. current account deficit with Europe in 2003 reached an estimated $94 billion, up 9% from 2002.

That's Where Opportunities Are for States and Regions . . .

- The commercial relationship between the United States and some regions of Europe, such as Baden-Württemberg, Ile-de-France, or South East England, is greater than that between the United States and most countries in the world.

- Three German states—Hesse, Baden-Württemberg, and North Rhine-Westfalia—invested more in the United States in 2001 than they did in the entire European Union outside of Germany.

- Despite much talk of big emerging markets, three German states—Bavaria, Baden-Württemberg and North-Rhine Westfalia—have a higher GDP than the four Asian tigers—South Korea, Taiwan, Singapore and Hong Kong.

- The Pacific coast state of California is Europe's main commercial partner in the United States and is the sixth-largest economy in the world, just behind France and Britain.

- California alone exported some $20.4 billion in goods to Europe in 2003, an amount greater than total U.S. exports to OPEC.

- Texas ranked as the top U.S. state for European investment in general and for French investment in particular in 2001. Europe's investment stake in Texas topped $68 billion in 2001. There is as much European investment in Texas alone as all U.S. investment in Japan and China put together.

- European companies are the top foreign investor in 45 states, and ranked second in the remaining five states in 2001.

- The Southeast of the United States accounted for nearly 23% of total European investment in 2001 and ranks as the top U.S. region for British, French, Dutch, Swedish and Belgian investments. No other region of the U.S. benefits more from European investment.

- The Great Lakes region ranks second to the Southeast in overall investment attractiveness to Europe, and is the favored destination of German firms.

- The United Kingdom ranked as the number one European export market for 25 states in 2003. Germany was a distant second, ranking as the top European export market for 10 U.S. states in 2003.

That's Where Services Are . . .

- The service economies of the United States and Europe have never been as intertwined as they are today, notably in such activities as financial services, telecommunications, utilities, insurance, advertising, computer services and other related functions.

- Foreign affiliate sales of services on both sides of the Atlantic have exploded over the past decade. In fact, affiliate sales of services have not only become a viable second channel of delivery for U.S. and European multinationals, they have become the overwhelming mode of delivery in a rather short period of time. Nothing better illustrates the ever-deepening integration of the transatlantic service economy.

- Sales of services by U.S. foreign affiliates in Europe soared from $85 billion in 1994 to roughly $234 billion in 2001—a 175% increase, well ahead of the 64% rise in U.S. service exports to Europe over the same period.

- U.S. foreign affiliate sales of services in Europe—after being roughly equal to U.S. service exports to Europe in 1992—were more than double the value of U.S. service exports in 2001.

- Europe leads the way in terms of U.S. foreign affiliate sales of services, just as it does in global U.S. affiliate sales of goods. In 2001, Europe accounted for 54% of total U.S. affiliate sales ($432 billion), with Asia (a 20% share) and Latin America (13%), a distant second and third, respectively.

- Foreign affiliate service sales of $124 billion in the UK alone in 2001 were greater than foreign affiliate service sales in all of Asia ($87 billion) and Latin America ($54 billion).

- Sales of services by U.S. affiliates of European firms have also soared over the past decade. As Europe's investment position in services has expanded in the U.S., so have Europe's foreign affiliate sales of services. The latter totaled $249 billion in 2001 versus $86 billion in 1994, a jump of 190%, well ahead of the 83% rise in European service exports to the U.S. over the same period.

That's Where the Research Is . . .

- 60% of U.S. corporate research and development conducted outside the United States is conducted in Europe. R&D expenditures by U.S. foreign affiliates are greatest in the UK, Germany and France, in that order.

- European R&D expenditures in the U.S. are substantial and dwarf expenditures spent by Asian counterparts, namely Japan.

That's Where the Money Is . . .

- Europe is not only a critical source of revenue for blue-chip companies, it is also a key supplier of capital or liquidity for the debt-stretched United States, which presently must borrow over $1.4 billion a day to finance its current-account deficit.

- European investors purchased a record $169 billion in U.S. corporate bonds in 2003—52% more than in 2002.

That's Who Is Connected in a Globalizing World . . .

- Interregional internet bandwidth underscores the "thick" nature of transatlantic connectivity. Between 2001 and 2003 transatlantic internet bandwidth doubled, to more than three times that of North American connections to Asia and the Pacific, $7^1/_2$ times that between North America, Latin America and the Caribbean, and 87 times that of European connections to Asia and the Pacific.

Drifting Apart? Or Growing Together?

- In sum, the years since the fall of the Berlin Wall have witnessed the greatest period of transatlantic economic integration in history. Our mutual stake in each other's prosperity and success has grown dramatically since the end of the Cold War. Ignoring these realities is shortsighted and shortchanges American and European consumers, producers, investors, workers and their families.

Partners in Prosperity:
The Changing Geography of
the Transatlantic Economy

Chapter 1

The Changing Landscape of the Transatlantic Economy

Despite periodic episodes of stress and strain on both sides of the Atlantic, over the past half century transatlantic cooperation has been the key to international coalitions advancing security, prosperity and freedom for millions around the world. Yet much has changed in the United States, Europe and the world. Issues that stir dissent and debate on both sides of the ocean seem to multiply with each passing month. Headlines are dominated by transatlantic spats over the situation in Iraq, the campaign against terrorism and the unsettled Middle East; genetically modified food, climate change and the International Criminal Court; export subsidies, tax breaks and competition policies. All of these issues and more have converged to strain transatlantic relations.

Given current acrimony, it is tempting to ask whether the transatlantic relationship has entered its twilight, whether Europeans and Americans are simply drifting apart after decades of alliance and partnership. Answering that question, however, means being able to judge whether current transatlantic squalls are surface storms or whether they reflect deeper currents. We seek to analyze the micro and macroeconomic dimensions of this question in this volume.

We conclude that one of the most dangerous deficits affecting transatlantic relations today is not one of trade, payments or military capabilities but rather a deficit in understanding by opinion leaders—in and out of government—of the vital stake Americans and Europeans have developed

in the health of our respective economies. The political, economic and media errors that result from this deficit are shortchanging American and European consumers, producers, workers and their families.

The facts are straightforward yet rarely acknowledged. Despite the perennial hype about the significance of Nafta, the "rise of Asia" or "big emerging markets," the United States and Europe remain by far each other's most important commercial partners. The economic relationship between the United States and Europe is by a wide margin the deepest and broadest between any two continents in history—and those ties are accelerating. The years since the Cold War—the years when the fading "glue" of the Cold War partnership supposedly loosened transatlantic ties—marked in fact one of the most intense periods of transatlantic integration ever. This transatlantic economy generates $2.5 trillion in total commercial sales a year and employs, directly or indirectly, over 12 million workers in mutually "insourced" jobs on both sides of the Atlantic. These workers enjoy high wages, high labor and environmental standards, and open, largely non-discriminatory access to each other's markets.

Lost in headline stories about banana, beef or steel disputes are three critical facts. First, trade squabbles represent a miniscule amount—only 1-2 per cent—of overall transatlantic economic activity. Second, trade flows themselves are a misleading benchmark of transatlantic economic interaction. Foreign investment and foreign affiliate sales, not trade, drive transatlantic commerce, and contrary to common wisdom, most U.S. and European investments flow to each other, rather than to lower-wage developing nations. Third, when U.S. or European companies invest in the other side of the Atlantic, that investment usually generates greater transatlantic trade because the company's home base and its overseas affiliates are connected through intra-firm production networks. Such investments and the economic linkages they generate are fusing European and American societies together far more tightly than the shallow form of integration represented by trade flows alone.

Also absent from most reporting and analysis is the fact that global profits of U.S. and European firms are generated largely from the places where their investment roots are deepest—each other's markets. Europe remains the most important foreign source of global profits for U.S. companies whipsawed by one crisis after another in the emerging markets. U.S. companies continue to rely on Europe for roughly half their total annual foreign profits, and in fact 2003—a year of great transatlantic political turmoil—was a year of historic transatlantic profits. America, the world's largest debtor nation, also relies on Europeans for capital to fund its record external imbalances.

Transatlantic integration is also outpacing integrative flows between other continents. If one uses Tom Friedman's definition of globalization as farther, faster, deeper and cheaper integration at inter-continental distances, then it is advancing farthest, fastest, deepest and cheapest between the continents of Europe and North America. The networks of interdependence that are being created across the Atlantic have become so dense, in fact, that they have attained a quality far different than those either continent has with any

other. Many transatlantic tensions result less from the fashionable notion that our societies are drifting apart, and more from the growing evidence that they are in fact colliding. Often these frictions are so severe precisely because they are not traditional "at-the-border" trade disputes, but reach beyond the border and affect such fundamental domestic issues as the ways Americans and Europeans are taxed, how our societies are governed, or how our economies are regulated.

These examples are but the tip of the iceberg in terms of what is missing from the public debate on competitiveness, "outsourcing," and economic growth. The trade-oriented mentality of U.S. and European policymakers, the media and the public at large is fraught with danger in that it ignores the fundamental basis of global competition. Trade alone as a scorecard of international competitiveness is not only woefully inadequate, it is dangerously misleading as a guide to policy in a world in which global sales of foreign affiliates totaled $17.7 trillion in 2002, more than double world exports ($7.8 trillion). Unequivocally, foreign affiliate sales represent the backbone of the transatlantic economy, with foreign affiliate sales amounting to $2.8 trillion in 2001 versus $549 billion in total trade.

These issues go to the heart of globalization. If globalization is to proceed and flourish in the future, the U.S. and Europe will have to prove that they can deal with the challenges generated by the deep integration of their economies. If the U.S. and Europe fail to resolve such differences with each other, they are unlikely to resolve them with economies much less like their own. Because the United States and Europe have been at the forefront of a more integrated global economy, the possibilities—and potential limits—of globalization are likely to be defined first and foremost by the successes or failures of the transatlantic relationship.

Uneven Globalization

"Globalization" is one of the most over-used and least understood phenomena shaping our world today. There is a surfeit of rhetoric and a scarcity of fact. Globalization is so broad and vague, in fact, that it has come to be one of those catch-all phrases that can mean everything and thus mean nothing, that can obscure as much as clarify.

One key to understanding globalization is to recognize its tremendously uneven quality. Interactions between continents are certainly accelerating overall, but the breadth, depth and speed of those interactions vary considerably between various continents. "The extent, form, and pace of globalization is not uniformly spread across the planet," John Dunning reminds us, "nor across different value-added activities." Globalization is both widening the scope of multi-continental interaction to embrace more parts of the globe than before, and also deepening the intensity of such interaction.[1]

Neither the breadth nor the depth of such interaction is occurring at the same rate everywhere, however, which means globalization is "thicker" between some continents and "thinner" between others.[2] And if one bundles the various connections that bind the different continents in this world—foreign direct investment, global capital flows, internet connectivity, financial convergence—it becomes clear that globalization is "thickest" between the European and American continents.

The Economic Drivers of Multinational Strategies

A second key to understanding the impact of uneven globalization is to understand the economic dynamics that drive it.

"Economic globalism" evokes the image of a global marketplace in which goods, services and assets flow across national boundaries without friction, a seamless world market in which nation states have been stripped virtually of all powers. Reality is different. While formal barriers to trade, investment and capital flows have been substantially reduced over the past five decades, much liberalization over the most recent decade has occurred as much within regions as between them, and there are extremely strong cultural and political barriers preventing the development of a single, seamless world market.[3]

The key actor driving economic globalization is the multinational enterprise (MNE). The largest 500 MNEs account for over 90% of the world's stock of foreign direct investment (FDI) and conduct about half the world's trade.[4] And while trade is the benchmark typically used to gauge global economic engagement, international

[1] John Dunning, *Regions, Globalization, and the Knowledge-Based Economy* (Oxford: Oxford University Press, 2002), pp. 13-14.

[2] For more on the notions of "thick" and "thin" in a globalizing world, see the introductory chapter by Robert O. Keohane and Joseph S. Nye, Jr. in Joseph S. Nye and John D. Donahue, eds., *Governance in a Globalizing World* (Cambridge, MA: Visions of Governance for the 21st Century), p. 11.

[3] For an overview of economic globalization, see Jeffrey Frankel, "Globalization of the Economy," in Nye and Donahue, op. cit., pp. 45-71; Alan Rugman, *The End of Globalization* (London: Random House, 2000); and Thomas Friedman, *The Lexus and the Olive Tree* (New York: Simon and Shuster, 2001).

[4] Rugman, op. cit.; United Nations, *World Investment Report 2002* (New York/Geneva: United Nations Conference on Trade and Development, 2002).

production by MNEs through FDI has superceded international trade as the most important mechanism for international integration.[5]

"Foreign direct investment is 'globalization' in its most potent form," argues *The Economist*, and represents far more than mere "capital": "it is a uniquely potent bundle of capital, contacts, and managerial and technological knowledge. It is the cutting edge of globalization."[6] And yet most business activity by MNEs does not take place evenly within the framework of a seamless global market, but unevenly and predominantly within the core Triad economic regions of North America, Europe and Asia.

During the past decade each of these regions has opened its markets and extended its scope. The North American market now encompasses Mexico and Canada under NAFTA and may some day extend to a Free Trade Area of the Americas, encompassing the entire western hemisphere. The European Union now anchors a single continental market approaching half a billion people in 25 countries, with more to come. The economic ties binding Japan and China are expanding, helping to promote a broad Asia-Pacific market across the region that includes ASEAN partners and is extending to India.

Falling barriers within each of these regions over the past decade have driven considerable international economic activity. And yet most manufacturing and services companies remain bound to operations in their "home base" region. In fact, virtually all of the world's largest 500 MNEs derive the bulk of their overall revenues from their home base region. Of the world's largest MNEs, the vast majority on average register 80% of total sales in their home region of the Triad.[7] Many have extended their presence internationally, but most of these have essentially become "bi-regional," with a strong presence in two of the Triad markets—mainly North America and Europe.

Few are truly "global" in the sense of having balanced revenues and operations in all areas of the Triad, much less all areas of the world. Among the largest 500 companies, only about 10 match the description of being truly "global," with a significant footprint on every continent.[8] Only a limited number of firms have succeeded in becoming what Kenichi Ohmae calls a "triad power," a company that has become an "insider" through "(1) equal penetration and exploitation capabilities, and (2) no blind spots, in each of the triad regions."[9] As Alan Rugman has commented, the view that a global company "has the capability to

---

[5] For an extended analysis, see Joseph P. Quinlan, *Global Engagement: How American Companies Really Compete in the Global Economy* (New York: McGraw Hill, 2000)

[6] "The cutting edge," *The Economist*, February 24, 2001, p. 80

[7] Almost half of European inward and outward FDI is intra-regional. The U.S. accounts for the largest share of extra-regional European FDI. See Giorgio Barba Navaretti, Jan I. Haaland and Anthony Venables, "Multinational Corporations and Global Production Networks: The Implications for Trade Policy," Centre for Economic Policy Research, London, available at http://www.cepr.org/pubs/fdi_report.pdf See also two manuscripts by Alan M. Rugman and Alain Verbeke, "Regional and Global Strategies of Multinational Enterprises" and "Regional Multinationals and Triad Strategy," available at http://www.aueb.gr/deos/EIBA2002.files/PAPERS/C164.pdf

[8] Rugman and Verbeke, "Regional and Global Strategies of Multinational Enterprises;" and Alan Rugman and Karl Moore, "The Myths of Globalization," *Ivey Business Journal*, September/October 2001, Vol. 66, No. 1.

[9] K. Ohmae, *Triad Power: The Coming Shape of Global Competition* (New York: The Free Press, 1985), p. 165; Rugman and Verbeke, "Regional and Global Strategies of Multinational Enterprises."

go anywhere, deploy any assets, and access any resources, and it maximizes profits on a global basis" may be a useful image, but one that applies to few MNEs in practice.[10] Those companies that do have major international operations have in fact concentrated those activities primarily within the Triad, and usually with particular weight only on two continents, mainly Europe and America.

Why is this so? Is this a legacy of the past, or does it tell us something of the future?

MNEs decide to engage abroad for a variety of reasons. Two very different motivations are driving the acceleration and direction of such activity today. The first is the dramatic growth of the relatively traditional model of "asset-exploiting" FDI, particularly in some key emerging markets as China and India. This type of investment is prompted by the desire to take advantage of lower real labor costs, in the case of China primarily in the manufacturing sector and in the case of India primarily in the services sector.[11] Its dynamic has been bolstered by the sheer demographic size of these markets coupled with their liberalization in recent years.

A second and perhaps more significant change in the motives for FDI over the past two decades, however, has been the explo-sive growth in "asset-augmenting" investments, primarily across the Atlantic. This type of FDI is driven by the emergence of intellectual capital as the key wealth-creating asset in most industrial economies. The basis of global competition has changed from tangible assets such as energy, cheap labor and natural resources to intangible assets such as financial and intellectual capital—knowledge and information of all kinds. The knowledge component of the output of manufacturing goods is estimated to have risen from 20 percent in the 1950s to more than 75 per cent today.[12]

The growing importance of intangible assets, especially knowledge-building skills, in the wealth-creating process, requires companies to harness these assets from a variety of locations. But assets such as technical knowledge, learning experiences, innovative production networks or distribution chains, management expertise and organizational competence tend to be concentrated in the advanced industrialized countries. And as asset-augmenting investment has become more important, the locational needs of corporations have shifted from those having to do with access to markets or natural resources, to those having to do with access to knowledge-intensive assets and learning experiences. The growing importance of created assets is the single most important shift among the economic determinants of FDI location in a

[10] Alan M. Rugman and Alain Verbeke, "Regional Multinationals and Triad Strategy," comment on assertions made by George Yip in *Total Global Strategy II* (Englewood Cliffs: Prentice Hall, 2003). For other views on the importance of geography in globalization, see J. Dunning and J. Mucchielli, *Multinational Firms: The Global-Local Dilemma* (London: Routledge, 2002) and A. Morrison, D. Ricks and K. Roth, "Globalization versus regionalization: Which way for the multinational?" in *Organizational Dynamics* 19/3, pp. 17-29.

[11] John Dunning, "Location and the Multinational Enterprise: A Neglected Factor?" in *Journal of International Business Studies*, 29, 1 (1998), p. 54; Peter J. Buckley, Jeremy Clegg, Nicholas Forsans, and Kevein T. Reilly, "Increasing the Size of the "Country": Regional Economic Integration and Foreign Direct Investment in a Globalised World Economy," *Management International Review*, 41, 3 (2001), p. 261; and Dunning, *Regions*, op. cit., p. 14.

[12] Thomas A. Stewart, *Intellectual Capital* (New York: Doubleday/Currency Publishers, 1997); Authors' own estimates.

[13] Quinlan, *Global Engagement*, op. cit.; Dunning, *Regions*, p. 9; Dunning, *Location*, pp. 50-54; Rugman, *The End of Globalization*, op. cit.

globalizing economy.[13] The growth of strategic asset–augmenting FDI powered the tidal wave of mutual investment flowing across the Atlantic over the past decade.

These asset-augmenting strategies of MNEs are reinforcing another phenomenon, which serves to further enhance the transatlantic dimension of international economic activity, and that is what some have termed "coopetition" or "alliance capitalism." A particularly important development since the end of the Cold War has been the rise of strategic alliances or partnerships, which have become nearly as prominent, if not more so in some industries, as global mergers and acquisitions. Since the intellectual capital needed to augment assets is complex and rarely the property of only one firm, to deploy such knowledge a firm may have to enhance its capabilities by forging cooperative arrangements with other firms. The growth of "knowledge capitalism" has led to a proliferation of business networks and "coopetitive" alliances between companies that may be competitors one day and partners the next. Data on mergers and acquisitions and collaborative non-equity coalitions suggest that, whether by FDI or by cross-border licensing, franchising and other agreements, alliances have been most pronounced, and increased the most, in knowledge-intensive sectors, and have been predominantly concluded between MNEs in advanced industrial economies, primarily between Europe and the United States.[14]

Dunning has captured the differentiated impact of these strategies on the geography of the global economy:

Strategies of asset-augmenting and "alliance capitalism" are designed less to advance the static efficiency of the MNE and more to enhance its future wealth-creating capabilities in a cost-learning effective way. The geography of this kind of labor is mainly confined to the advanced industrial countries, and geared to either promoting the efficiency of the MNE's global R&D capabilities, or gaining access to foreign-created assets which will best protect or enhance its competitive advantages. It is this kind of specialization which is being increasingly fashioned by the imperative of the knowledge-based global economy, and by the need of firms located in one country to complement their core competencies with those of firms located in another country.[15]

In practice, a large percentage of these partnerships do not develop as envisioned. But many do, and U.S. firms still form many more strategic alliances with Europeans than with Asian firms, reinforcing the premise that the motivations driving FDI across the Atlantic and those driving FDI with countries such as China or India are very different. Most empirical work indicates that market-seeking FDI matters more than FDI motivated by wage differentials.[16] Semiskilled labor and natural resources are secondary to the strategic asset seeker.

These distinctions are important for the perennial Europe vs. Asia debate in the United States and other countries, i.e. whether the Old World is passé and the

---

[14] This section draws on work done by Dunning, *Regions*, p. 10-19, and Quinlan, *Global Engagement*, op. cit.

[15] Dunning, *Regions*, pp. 17-18.

[16] See Matthew Slaughter, "Host-Country Determinants of U.S. Foreign Direct Investment into Europe," available at http://www.dartmouth.edu/~mjs/Papers/Kap01_Slaughter.pdf

future is in the Pacific, as well as politically-charged discussions of "outsourcing" jobs. Such debates usually shed more heat than light, but a particularly glaring omission is the failure to distinguish between the differing motivations driving corporate FDI strategies.

The global forces driving the proliferation of strategic alliances are similar to the ones behind the surge in cross-border mergers and acquisitions: market liberalization, intensifying competition, and above all else, soaring costs of research and development, juxtaposed against shortened product life cycles and rapid technological obsolescence in a number of advanced industries. Many companies have concluded that going solo is just too expensive and time-consuming. It is more advantageous perhaps to find a partner or partners to spread the costs and risks of developing new products, entering new markets, gaining access to critical technologies and leveraging existing distribution channels.[17]

The competitive need for "asset-augmenting strategies" and strategic alliances in the global knowledge economy underscores the importance of strategic positioning within the Triad. Executives realize that a strong strategic position requires a foothold in both the U.S. and Europe. The drive to develop new business models capturing the value of new information and communication technologies accentuates this strategic positioning: European and American companies not only want the link to each other's business, consumer and financial markets, but they also need to stay abreast of the other's adaptation to new technologies. Particularly in Europe, companies that aspire to compete globally need to benchmark against U.S. business in the U.S. market.[18]

"Sticky Places in Slippery Space:" Globalization and Regionalization in the Transatlantic Economy

This leads to a third key element to understanding "uneven globalization," and that is how globalization interacts with localization, or how such microregions as the U.S. states and the German *Länder*, or such city-regions as Greater London, Barcelona-Catalonia or Charlotte-Spartanburg can remain competitive in the global economy.

The phenomena of "asset-augmenting" strategies and "alliance capitalism," described in the last section, underscore not only the importance of transatlantic economic networks, but also the importance of microregions to continued European and American prosperity. Most knowledge-intensive, asset-augmenting activities remain heavily concentrated in microregions within the advanced industrialized countries, particularly in Europe and the United States.[19]

Microregions are increasingly becoming key drivers of economic growth and gateways to the global market place.[20] As the world's economy becomes more networked and "global," the "local" becomes more

---

[17] Dunning, *Regions*, op. cit; Quinlan, op. cit.

[18] See the remarks by Robert B. Zoellick to the Transatlantic Policy Network, December 1, 2000, available at www.tpnonline.org/zoellick.html

[19] Vincenzo Spiezia, "Measuring Regional Economies," OECD *Statistics Brief*, October 2003, No. 6; Dunning, *Regions*, pp. 12-13.

[20] See Alan J. Scott, *Regions and the World Economy: The Coming Shape of Global Production, Competition, and Political Order* (Oxford: Oxford University Press, 1998); Ohmae, Spiezia, op. cit.

important. Globalization is simultaneously a tremendous force of geographic dispersion, because it can accelerate the diffusion of location and ownership of production across and among continents, and a powerful force of geographic concentration, because it can reward highly productive firms and workers who can capitalize on the knowledge, relationships and specialities that are often bunched spatially in key microregions or clusters. Ann Markusen has called this the paradox of "sticky places within slippery space."[21] If a microregion wants to sustain its competitiveness, its key goal must be to become a sticky place in the slippery space of the global economy.

The slippery space of the global knowledge economy both facilitates and channels greater FDI flows to specific locations where firms engaged in related activities may be bunched so as to take advantage of each other's presence and to access localized support facilities, specialized factor inputs, customized demand patterns, or shared service centers.[22] As core operations of companies become both more mobile and more knowledge-intensive, the competitive position of a microregion will depend increasingly on its ability to convince corporations that it offers the full range of capabilities that best enable them to exploit their assets and partnerships.

While foreign direct investment may play a minor role in the overall economy of a nation, it can be critical for a particular region or a particular industry. The extra "knowledge edge" may come as easily from across the ocean as from across town or across the nation. "Insourced" knowledge—and the competitive networks and jobs it creates—may be as significant for any particular region as domestically-sourced investments.

This means that a microregion's competitiveness in the new transatlantic global economy is likely to have as much, if not more, to do with *location competence* as *location cost*. In the slippery space of the global knowledge economy, asset-augmenting environments are more likely to remain competitive motors of economic growth than those tied to asset-exploitation alone. Increasingly, the most critical question a potential investor is likely to ask is not "How cheap are you?" but rather "How connected are you?" Dynamic "learning regions" attuned to knowledge-driven best practice and based on interrelated business networks are more likely to attract footloose firms.

In the case of the biotechnology industry, for example, where cross-border alliances are the primary mode of globalization, innovation and production, a microregion is more likely to attract an R&D center or manufacturing plant if it focuses on developing an environment conducive to cross-border alliances and providing the support services to facilitate such alliances. Moreover, the most relevant of these alliances may not necessarily be those forged between firms, but rather between firms, investors and universities.[23]

Asset-augmenting activities of firms benefit from being part of a knowledge-creating milieu—in which private firms, universities,

---

[21] Ann Markusen, "Sticky places in slippery space: A typology of industrial districts," *Economic Geography*, 72, 3 (1996); Rugman and Moore, op. cit.

[22] D. Rees and T. McLean, "Trends in Location Choice," in A. Jolly, ed., *European Business Handbook 1997* (London: Kogan Page and Confederation of British Industry, 1997); Dunning, *Location*, op. cit.

[23] See Oxford Intelligence, *The MedTech Report—Investment Strategies & European Benchmarking Survey*, available at www.oxint.com

technical colleges, and government research institutions are all involved. For the most part, such clusters tend to be concentrated in the Triad region, and as intellectual capital becomes more geographically diffused and cross-border innovatory competition becomes more intense, firms from one part of the Triad are finding it increasingly desirable to establish an R&D presence, and/or conclude technology-enhancing alliances with firms in another part. And as firms increasingly scan the globe for knowledge capital, they are engaging in FDI specifically to tap into, and harness, country- and firm-specific resources, capabilities and learning experiences.[24]

This means that the main competitors to some microregions in attracting and retaining mobile investment may not be other microregions in the same country, but microregions in other countries.[25] At the same time, microregions engaged in such knowledge-intensive industries as biotechnology may also gain competitive advantage by forging selective alliances with microregions across the Atlantic or around the world rather than across the nation. Just as firms in the global knowledge economy are engaging in "coopetition" and strategic alliances, so too must microregions. Microregion clusters that can capitalize on MNE interest in asset-augmenting and strategic alliance with their own region-to-region asset-augmenting and alliance strategies stand a better chance of becoming—and remaining—leading motors of change and economic growth.

MNEs provide critical channels for organizing cross-border asset-seeking and asset-exploiting activities not only between nations but also between microregions across continents. The economic linkages forged between Silicon Valley in California and Silicon Glen in mid-Scotland, between the Charlotte Regional Partnership and the Rhine river "elbow" region of Baden-Wurttemberg, Alsace-Lorrraine, Basel and Zurich, or between the New York and London financial districts, are at least as significant as the overall state of economic relations between the UK and the U.S. or the U.S. and Germany in determining the international location of economic activity or patterns of cross-border trade. In short, MNEs are being increasingly drawn to a network of "sticky" places for their wealth-creating activities.[26] In this volume, we have begun to "map" these places to highlight their role in the transatlantic economy.

Some writers, such as Ohmae, go so far as to suggest that microregions are replacing the nation state as the most relevant unit of governance. Others, such as Allen Scott or Michael Porter, are less extravagant, but do argue that such regions will become increasingly important for competitive-enhancing activities of mobile investors, and as engines of national growth. A core body of research is developing on this subject, building on work by John Dunning and Alan Rugman, as well as Paul Krugman's influential work on the determinants of the geographical concentration of economic activity, and the extension of Michael Porter's studies on the competitive advantage of firms to embrace a spatial dimension.[27] But interest has been largely confined to economists, economic geographers, or local development agencies.

---

[24] Dunning, *Regions*, p. 20.

[25] Dunning, *Regions*, p. 16.

[26] Dunning, *Regions*, p.p. 21, 29-30.

[27] Dunning, *Regions*, p. 22-27.

Mapping the Transatlantic Economy

The current outsourcing debate in the United States underscores, however, that globalization does not mean the death of distance or the end of geography. It means there is an urgent need to understand the 21st century's uneven and rapidly changing economic landscape, and then to position oneself strategically to reap its benefits and avoid its dangers. The geography of uneven globalization raises a host of domestic and foreign policy issues ranging far beyond economics.

A new and very different global playing field has emerged since the end of the Cold War. We need some new mental maps. Of course, even the best maps can only approximate reality. But as David Turnbull has stated, "Ultimately maps…gain their power and usefulness from making connections and enabling unanticipated connections."[28] That is what we are attempting in this volume—to offer what we believe are some powerful mental maps of the changing transatlantic economy. Together, these maps underscore the reality of deep transatlantic integration and, in the context of today's debates about globalization and transatlantic drift,

offer some unanticipated or counterintuitive connections.

This volume seeks to provide these new images in the following way. The following chapter takes a snapshot of the current transatlantic economy, and tells how transatlantic economic relations fared as transatlantic political relations deteriorated during 2003. Chapter three provides a broader contextual frame to this story by quantifying the economic ties that bind Europe and the United States. Chapter four then takes the analysis deeper by mapping European investment, trade and employment linkages with each of the 50 U.S. states. Chapter five maps U.S. investment, trade and employment linkages with the nations of the European Union, plus Norway and Switzerland. Chapter six takes a deeper look at the impact of EU enlargement on transatlantic economic relations and tracks U.S. commercial relations with the ten new EU member states. Chapter seven zooms in on key future drivers of economic activity such as services and communications "connectivity." We conclude with some summary thoughts on what these trends mean for the future. In the appendix we offer some new "mental maps" of the transatlantic economy, and further data detailing transatlantic links.

---

[28] Quoted in Gregory C. Staple, "Notes on Mapping the Net," TeleGeography 1995, October 1995, available at www.telegeography.com/ee/free_resources/essay-10.php

Chapter 2

Mars, Venus—or Mercury?
Commerce Trumps Diplomacy in a Year of War

These days, political pundits are fond of quoting Robert Kagan's quip that Americans are from Mars and Europeans are from Venus. Those images were reinforced by transatlantic disputes over Iraq in 2003. But the related tale of 2003 is that both Mars and Venus should take greater heed of Mercury, the god of commerce.

For transatlantic relations, 2003 was a year of political bust and economic boom. Even as transatlantic bickering engendered by America's war with Iraq plunged transatlantic political relations to one of their lowest points in six decades, the economic ties that bind the United States and Europe together only grew stronger in 2003.

2003 was a banner year for the transatlantic economy (see Table 1). Transatlantic trade, foreign direct investment, portfolio flows and profits all rebounded robustly from the cyclical economic downturn of 2001-02. Economic integration strengthened in a year of political disintegration. What is perhaps most striking is that during the first six months of the year—the months of greatest transatlantic political tension—economic engagement deepened considerably between the United States and those two bad "old" boys of Europe, France and Germany.[1]

Despite Washington's war-related frustrations with Europe, corporate America pumped over $87 billion in foreign direct investment (FDI) into Europe in 2003.

That represents a jump of 30.5% over 2002 and was more than double the rate of growth of total U.S. investment outflows for the year. As is customary, U.S. investment flows to the United Kingdom dominated total EU investment, with U.S. firms sinking nearly $25.4 billion in the UK in 2003, roughly 30% of the EU total. Yet even after adjusting for massive flows to the United Kingdom, U.S. foreign investment to Europe approached $62 billion in 2003, a staggering rise of 29% from a year earlier.

Germany was one favored destination of U.S. firms in 2003, notwithstanding the fact that U.S.-German relations ebbed to one of the lowest levels since World War II. American firms sank $7 billion in Germany in 2003, a sharp reversal from the corresponding period in 2002, when U.S. firms pulled some $5 billion out of Germany. One of the largest deals involved Procter & Gamble's $5.7 billion acquisition of Wella.

Transatlantic commerce with other European countries flourished. U.S. investment in Ireland ($4.7 billion) was more than two-and-a-half times greater than U.S. investment to China ($1.7 billion). The $19.2 billion of U.S. investment in the Netherlands was not far behind total U.S. investment in all of Asia ($22.4 billion). And despite intense diplomatic tensions between the U.S. and France in 2003, U.S. investment flows to France rose by more than 10% to $2.3 billion.

---

[1] U.S. Defense Secretary Donald Rumsfeld described France and Germany as part of "old Europe" and countries such as Spain, Britain, Poland and other central European nations as part of "new Europe" when asked why some European countries were supporting the U.S. effort against Iraq while others were opposed.

2003: A Record-Setting Year for the Transatlantic Economy

The following all-time highs were recorded in 2003:

Transatlantic Investment
European net purchases of U.S. corporate bonds: $169 billion

Transatlantic Trade
Total transatlantic trade in goods: $395 billion

U.S. trade deficit with European Union: $94.3 billion
U.S. current account deficit with the European Union: $94 billion
U.S. imports from the European Union: $244.8 billion

U.S. imports from Germany: $68.1 billion
U.S. trade deficit with Germany: $39.2 billion

U.S. imports from Italy: $25.4 billion
U.S. trade deficit with Italy: $14.9 billion

U.S. imports from Ireland: $18.1 billion
U.S. trade deficit with Ireland: $25.8 billion

U.S. imports from Spain: $6.7 billion

U.S. trade deficit with France: $12.2 billion

U.S. trade deficit with the Netherlands: $9.7 billion

Transatlantic Profits (affiliate income)
U.S. profits in Europe: $77.1 billion

U.S. profits in the Netherlands: $17.9 billion
U.S. profits in Switzerland: $10.7 billion
U.S. profits in Ireland: $6.8 billion
U.S. profits in France: $4.3 billion
U.S. profits in Italy: $3.1 billion
U.S. profits in Spain: $2.5 billion
U.S. profits in Belgium: $2.0 billion
U.S. profits in Denmark: $1.4 billion
U.S. profits in Sweden: $1.2 billion
U.S. profits in Austria: $578 million
U.S. profits in Poland: $466 million
U.S. profits in Czech Republic: $182 million

European profits in the U.S.: $46.4 billion

U.K. profits in the U.S.: $16.5 billion
Netherlands profits in the U.S.: $8.9 billion
Switzerland profits in the U.S.: $6.4 billion
Sweden profits in the U.S.: $2.1 billion

Source: U.S. Department of Commerce

In short, while the U.S. House of Representatives spent its time changing French fries to "freedom fries," U.S. firms in France and other parts of Europe were busy seeking out strategic acquisitions, further deepening transatlantic ties. In a year when U.S.-European political relations had seldom been rockier, American firms remained confident and committed to Europe, with the region alone accounting for nearly 65% of total U.S. foreign direct investment in 2003.

Meanwhile, virulent anti-war sentiment across Europe did not prevent European firms from investing $36.9 billion in foreign direct investment in the U.S. in 2003. That represented a sharp rebound from the depressed levels of the prior year, when European FDI inflows to the United States totaled $26 billion. As is usually the case, British firms lead the investment foray into the U.S., yet even after excluding the UK, European investment flows to the U.S. totaled just over $10 billion in 2003, roughly on par with aggregate inflows in 2002. Ironically, French firms were among the largest European investors in the U.S. in 2003, with Corporate France sinking some $4.2 billion in the United States. German foreign investment in the U.S. declined again in 2003 (with disinvestments of $1.2 billion), although the contraction in investment was a fraction of the decline experienced in 2002 ($4.6 billion).

In addition to the nearly $37 billion in foreign direct investment the U.S. received from Europe in 2003, Euroland investors (excluding the United Kingdom) ploughed another $50 billion into U.S. dollar-denominated assets like U.S. Treasuries, government agency bonds, corporate bonds and U.S. equities. European investors (including UK flows) were particularly enamored with U.S. corporate bonds, purchasing a record $169 billion in corporate bonds in 2003—52% above the levels of the prior year. The UK accounted for the bulk of purchases of corporate bonds ($108 billion), but net corporate purchases from Euroland still totaled a record $29 billion in 2003, a rise of 82% from the previous year.

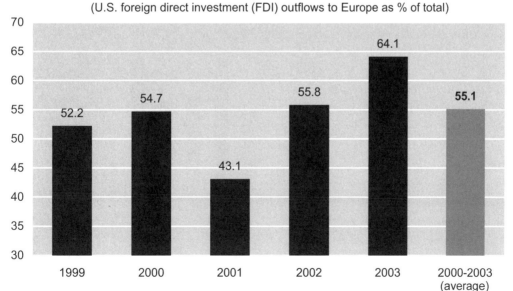

Corporate America's Bias Towards Europe
(U.S. foreign direct investment (FDI) outflows to Europe as % of total)

Source: Bureau of Economic Analysis

On a country basis, German portfolio managers snapped up nearly $10 billion in total U.S. securities in 2003, following net purchases of just $1.1 billion in 2002. French investors bought $4 billion in U.S. securities in 2003, down from $5.6 billion the prior year. Total net purchases from the United Kingdom totaled a staggering $164.4 billion in 2003. However, net buying from London, reflecting the city's role as a global financial hub, includes net purchasing from the Middle East, eastern Europe and other geographic areas.

All totaled, transatlantic capital flows—both foreign direct investment and portfolio flows—rose dramatically in 2003. Whenever and wherever strategic opportunities presented themselves, U.S. firms were unhesitant about acquiring European firms. General Electric, Procter & Gamble, United Technologies—a fairly representative body of Corporate America—all made European acquisitions in excess of $1 billion in 2003. In the United States, European firms like Henkel, Axa and Deutsche Post did the same, building out

their strategic U.S. presence amid all the threats of a transatlantic alliance in crisis. European portfolio managers, meanwhile, were busy adding high-grade U.S. corporate bonds to their portfolios.

2003 was also a record year for transatlantic trade flows. Total transatlantic trade in goods rose to $395 billion in 2003. U.S. imports from Europe hit a record $245 billion in 2003—despite the massive appreciation of the euro against the dollar. America's goods deficit with the EU widened to a record $94.3 billion in 2003. Meanwhile, the U.S. current account deficit with Europe reached a record $94 billion, up 9% from the prior year.

The rise in the euro against the dollar has spawned a great deal of angst across Europe. However, the strong euro/weak dollar did not have much effect on U.S. imports from Europe in 2003. In fact, U.S. imports from Germany, Italy, Ireland, and Spain all reached record levels in 2003, with strong U.S. demand offsetting the negative effect from the strong euro. Not surpris-

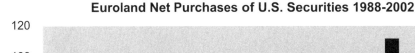

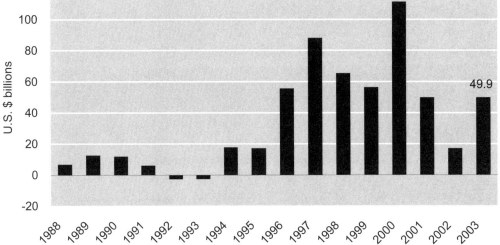

Euroland Net Purchases of U.S. Securities 1988-2002

Excludes purchases from the United Kingdom
Source: U.S. Treasury Department

ingly, surging imports from Europe produced record U.S. trade deficits with Germany, Italy, Ireland, France and the Netherlands.

Finally, despite all the talk of a transatlantic boycott or a consumer backlash on both sides of the ocean, 2003 was a banner year for transatlantic profits as measured by foreign affiliate income. U.S. foreign affiliates in Europe reaped a profits windfall from the declining U.S. dollar against the euro, with the dollar sliding 30% against the euro from the end of 2001 to the end of 2003. The effect was to greatly inflate the dollar-based earnings of U.S. affiliates in Europe. Indeed, U.S. foreign affiliate income from Europe surged to a record $77.1 billion last year, a 30% jump from the prior year. Over the same period, U.S. affiliate profits in France more than doubled, to $4.3 billion, while profits earned in Ireland surged by 45%, in Italy by 40%, and in the Netherlands by 24.5%. In all, U.S. affiliate earnings in some twelve European markets (France, the Netherlands, Switzerland, Italy, Ireland, Spain, Belgium, Denmark,

Sweden, Austria, Czech Republic and Poland) reached record highs in 2003. This broadly-based profits bonanza helped boost total U.S. pretax corporate profits by 18% last year, one of the strongest annual rises in decades.

2003 was also a record year for profits of European affiliates operating in the United States. Notwithstanding the strength of the euro against the U.S. dollar—a significant headwind to earnings—European affiliate earnings of $46.4 billion in 2003 easily surpassed earnings of 2002 ($32.23 billion) and 2001 ($17.4 billion), and the previous peak in earnings of $38.8 billion in 2000. The earnings boost was driven by robust U.S. demand, which greatly offset the negative effect of the appreciation of the euro and the British pound, as well as weak European growth again in 2003. British, Dutch, Swiss and Swedish foreign affiliates all enjoyed record U.S. profits in 2003.

At first glance, the news is good: transatlantic commerce, fueled by mutual investment, remains robust and seems more

A Banner Year for Transatlantic Profits*

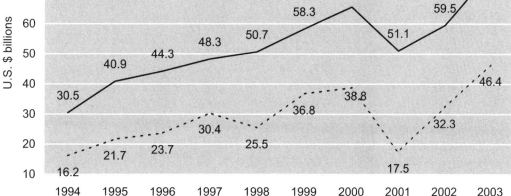

* Income of affiliates
Source: Bureau of Economic Analysis

attuned to good economics than bad diplomacy. But the underlying reality is that the relationship between the transatlantic strategic and economic agendas has reversed. During the Cold War, leaders strove to keep transatlantic economic conflicts from spilling over to the core political alliance. Now the challenge is to keep transatlantic political disputes from damaging the core economic relationship.

Pouring French wine down the drain or vandalizing McDonald's may make for splashy headlines, but the more significant development is the accelerating integration of the European and U.S. economies.

Case Study:

Why Exchange Rates Matter Less Than We Think— The Story of Related Party Trade

How Related Party Trade Influences Transatlantic Trade Flows

Transatlantic trade rebounded in 2003 following a two-year slump, which saw total trade between the U.S. and European Union fall 4% between 2000 and 2002. In 2003, total transatlantic trade in goods rose to $395 billion, a 7% increase from the prior period.

Not unexpectedly, U.S. exports, supported by the weaker U.S. dollar, recovered from the two-year downturn in trade with Europe, rising to $150.6 billion in 2003. That represented a healthy 4.8% annual increase—yet U.S. export growth pales in comparison to U.S. import growth from Europe in 2003. In fact, U.S. imports from Europe jumped 8.5% in 2003, rising to a record $245 billion in a year when the euro appreciated by 20% against the dollar between year-end 2002 and year-end 2003.

Following such a large shift in prices or exchange rates, Economics 101 would have predicted a rebalancing of bilateral trade. Theory would have expected U.S. export growth to outstrip U.S. import growth, leading to an improvement in the overall trade balance. In fact, the opposite occurred: America's trade deficit with Europe actually widened by nearly 15% in 2003, with the deficit jumping to a record $94.3 billion.

Seemingly impervious to the strength of the euro, U.S. imports from Germany rose by nearly 9% in 2003. U.S. exports to Germany actually declined, dropping by over 11%, leaving a record trade deficit of $39.2 billion with Europe's largest economy. Elsewhere, U.S. imports from the Netherlands rose by 11.2% in 2003, while imports from Spain jumped by nearly 10%. U.S. imports from France did fall in 2003, by 6.6%, but so did U.S. exports to France, leaving a record U.S. trade deficit of just over $12 billion.

The fact that transatlantic trade flows have yet to adjust to the massive revaluation of the euro against the U.S. dollar have confounded many on both sides of the Atlantic. Two years after the euro's stunning rise against the dollar, America's trade deficit with Europe should have begun to narrow, with U.S. exports growing at a faster pace than imports. That is conventional wisdom, which has not panned out.

Missing from the debate over trade and missing from conventional analysis is this: an unusually large percentage of U.S. imports from Europe is considered related party trade, or trade that takes place between a parent cooperation, such as Siemens of Germany, and its foreign affiliate in the United States.

Parent-affiliate trade is less responsive to shifts in prices or exchange rates and more attuned to domestic demand. Accordingly, while a strong euro, in theory at least, would be associated with a decline in European competitiveness in the United States, the fact that many European multinationals produce, market and distribute goods on both sides of the ocean gives firms a high degree of immunity to a dramatic shift in exchange rates. Roughly 57% of total U.S. imports from Europe are considered related party trade, which means more than half of U.S. imports from Europe are not affected by exchange rates in the traditional sense. That is well above the global average for the U.S., with some 48% of all U.S. imports considered related party trade.

Related Party Trade 2002

	U.S. Imports: "Related Party Trade," as % of Total	U.S. Exports: "Related Party Trade," as % of Total
European Union	56.8	31.0
France	42.6	27.9
Germany	67.2	33.6
Netherlands	58.9	42.6
United Kingdom	53.3	28.1
Other European Union	55.1	28.1

Source: U.S. Census Bureau

Under this structure, trade flows are driven more by demand in the host nation. As such, when the U.S. economy exhibits strong growth, as in 2003, European affiliates in the United States produce and sell more products, which in turn, generates more demand (imports) from the parent company for parts and components irrespective of exchange rate movements.

Related party trade can have a significant impact on bilateral trade between individual nations. Only after recognizing that roughly two-thirds of U.S. imports from Germany are considered related party trade, for example, can one begin to understand and explain why U.S. imports from Germany remained so strong in a year when the dollar plummeted against the euro (U.S. imports from Germany rose 8.8% in 2003 from the prior year). Roughly 59% of U.S. imports from the Netherlands are considered related party trade; around 54% of U.S. imports from the United Kingdom are classified as related party trade as well.

Around one-third of U.S. exports to Europe are classified as related party trade, lower than U.S. imports from Europe. This, in part, reflects the fact that U.S. affiliates in Europe source more goods from local sources, thus reducing trade, than European affiliates in the United States.

Chapter 3

The Ties That Bind: Quantifying the Primacy of the Transatlantic Economy

Many feared the United States and Europe were drifting apart in 2003 and that a seismic geopolitical shift was in the making. The reality, however, is that while the "Iraq" effect did place a great deal of stress on one of the world's most important bilateral relationships, one reason why the transatlantic alliance held together in 2003 is that it is firmly anchored by deep and far-reaching commercial ties.

Loose talk about an alliance without common bonds, or a partnership devoid of relevance, ignores the simple yet powerful fact that transatlantic commercial ties are the largest and deepest in the world—bar none. The transatlantic economy is bound together by foreign direct investment (a deep form of integration) as opposed to trade (a shallow form of integration). Foreign affiliate sales, not exports, are the primary means by which U.S. firms deliver goods and services to customers in Europe. The same holds true for European firms delivering products in the United States— trade flows are secondary to foreign affiliate sales. This has been the transatlantic norm for decades, not years. While exports and imports are the most common measures used in the media or by political pundits to evaluate cross-border activity between two parties, foreign direct investment and the activities of foreign affiliates are the backbone of transatlantic commercial activity.

Lost in the transatlantic debate is the fact that the U.S. and European companies invest more in each other's economies than they do in the entire rest of the world.

Transatlantic commercial ties are the largest in the world, with total commerce amounting to roughly $2.5 trillion in 2001. That figure includes total two-way trade between the U.S. and Europe, plus total foreign affiliate sales, adjusted for potential double counting of affiliate sales and exports/imports. This relationship employs directly or indirectly over 12 million people on both sides of the Atlantic who enjoy higher wages, higher labor and environmental standards, and open, largely non-discriminatory access to each other's markets.

Despite rhetorical flourishes one hears about shifting American priorities due to Nafta or the "Asian Century," over the past decade American investment in the Netherlands alone was more than twice what it was in Mexico and nearly ten times what it was in China. Europe, not Asia or Latin America, is the most important source of global earnings for American companies. Similarly, for many leading European firms, the United States remains the most important market in the world.

Total transatlantic sales of foreign affiliates topped $2.8 trillion in 2001, the last year of available data. That is some five times greater than total transatlantic trade of goods and services. Foreign affiliate sales not only dwarf transatlantic trade flows but also every other cross-border commercial artery linking the United States with the rest of the world. For instance, total foreign affiliate sales between the United States and Europe were more than double the comparable figures for total U.S.-transpacific foreign affiliates sales in 2001 and more than three times larger than total transpacific trade flows. They were also four times larger than foreign affiliate sales between the United States and its Nafta partners, Mexico and Canada.

Seven Key Indices of Transatlantic Commercial Activity

The primacy of foreign affiliate sales in driving transatlantic commerce reflects the underlying commercial infrastructure that links the United States with Europe. This infrastructure has been in the making for over a century, yet remains largely invisible to policy makers on both sides of the Atlantic. After examining the following seven variables, however, a clearer picture of the transatlantic economy emerges.

1. Gross Product of Foreign Affiliates. In various European countries, the presence of U.S. affiliates remains striking. In Ireland, for instance, U.S. affiliates accounted for 16% of the nation's total output in 2001. U.S. affiliates accounted for 7.2% of the UK's aggregate output in the same year and 6.2% of the Netherlands'. In the United States, the total output of British affiliates topped $100 billion in 2001; the economic output of German, Dutch and French foreign affiliates totaled $50 billion, $44 billion and $40 billion, respectively.[1]

The 2001-2002 cyclical recession dampened transatlantic affiliate output. Total output of U.S. foreign affiliates in Europe and of European affiliates in the United States declined in 2001 on account of weak economic growth on both sides of the Atlantic. Output of U.S. foreign affiliates in Europe dropped 3% in 2001 from the prior year, yet

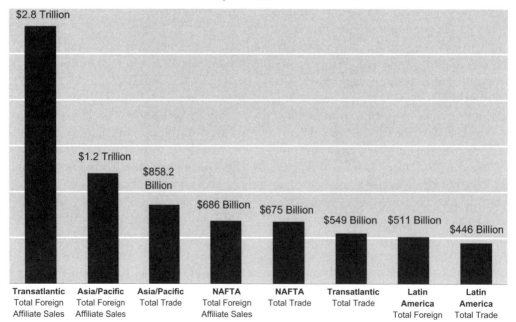

America's Major Commercial Arteries

Foreign Affiliate Sales: Data for 2001; Total Trade: Data in goods & services, for 2002. Source: U.S. Department of Commerce

---

[1] An affiliate is defined as a business enterprise whereby a U.S. or foreign firm owns or controls 10% or more of the voting securities of the incorporated firm. Gross product of affiliates is for majority-owned affiliates.

still totaled some $318 billion for the year. European affiliates in the United States produced some $308 billion in output in 2001, down sharply from the $345 billion in total output in 2000. Since the U.S. economy was the weakest link of the transatlantic economy in 2001, with the U.S. experiencing a three-quarter economic recession, European affiliates in the U.S. bore the largest brunt of the transatlantic downturn of 2001. However, with foreign affiliate output on both sides of the Atlantic in excess of $300 billion, U.S.

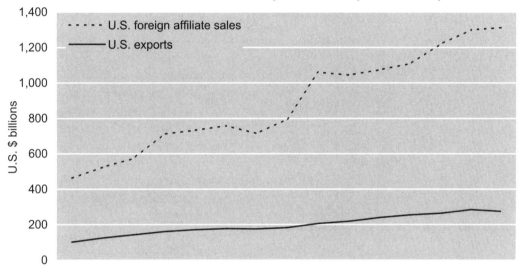

Sales of U.S. Affiliates in Europe vs. U.S. Exports to Europe

Source: Bureau of Economic Analysis

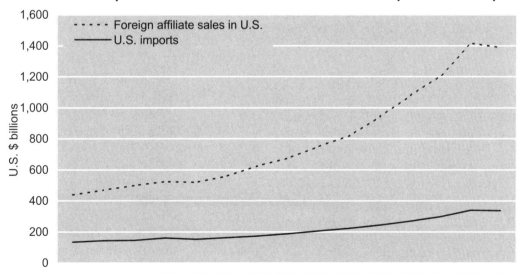

Sales of European Affiliates in the United States vs. U.S. Imports from Europe

Source: Bureau of Economic Analysis

and European affiliates—even in a bad year—generate more economic output every twelve months than most countries. On a global basis, the gross product of U.S. affiliates slumped to $583 billion in 2001, down from $606 billion in 2000. Europe accounted for roughly 55% of the total.

2. Overseas Assets of Foreign Affiliates. Corporate America's overseas commercial presence as measured by foreign assets totaled $5.8 trillion in 2001, with the bulk of these assets located in Europe. Total U.S. assets in Europe exceeded $3.3 trillion, representing roughly 60% of the global total. The largest share of U.S. assets are in the United Kingdom, America's long-standing favorite destination in terms of foreign investment. U.S. assets in the United Kingdom—roughly $1.4 trillion in 2001—were more than 50% larger than the entire U.S. asset base in Asia. In Germany, U.S. assets of $320 billion were greater than total U.S. assets in South America. As for foreign assets held in the United States, European firms held some $3.7 trillion in U.S. assets in 2001, nearly 70% of the total. The geographic reach of Europe's investment in the United States is quite diverse. In fact, European companies are the top foreign investor in 45 states, and ranked second in the remaining five states in 2001.

3. Affiliate Employment. The transatlantic workforce deployed directly by U.S. and European foreign affiliates is massive, totaling over 8.4 million workers in 2001. That is three times the number of total workers employed by U.S. affiliates in Nafta partners Canada and Mexico (2.8 million). It is also well above total foreign employment of U.S. foreign affiliates in Asia and Asian foreign affiliates in the United States (2.3 million).

On a global basis, U.S. foreign affiliates directly employed nearly 9.8 million work-

ers in 2001, with roughly 43% in Europe. U.S. majority-owned affiliates employed some 3.8 million workers in Europe in 2001, with the workforce evenly split between manufacturing employment and services. While the number of manufacturing workers in Europe as a percentage of the global total of U.S. affiliates has leveled off in recent years, U.S. firms still employed 1.9 million manufacturing workers in Europe in 2001. That is more than double the number of manufacturing workers employed by U.S. affiliates in Asia. The transportation equipment sector was the largest source of manufacturing employment in Europe; wholesale employment was among the largest sources of service-related employment, and includes employment in such areas as logistics, trade, insurance and other service-enhancing activities.

European affiliates employed roughly 4.3 million American workers in 2001, slightly more than U.S. affiliate employment in Europe. The top five employers in the U.S. were from the United Kingdom (1.1 million), Germany (734,000), France (578,000), the Netherlands (571,000) and Switzerland (546,000). Out of the 6.4 million U.S. workers on the payrolls of foreign affiliates in 2001, European firms accounted for roughly two-thirds of total employment. As a footnote, the figures cited above understate the employment effects of investment in that the numbers are for direct employment only, and do not include indirect employment related to nonequity arrangements like strategic alliances, joint ventures and other deals. Moreover, affiliate employment figures do not include jobs supported by trade with Europe. Trade-related employment is substantial in many states. In total, and adding in indirect employment, we estimate that the transatlantic work force numbers some 12-14 million workers.

4. Research & Development (R&D) of Foreign Affiliates. Foreign affiliate R&D has become more prominent over the past decade as firms on both sides of the Atlantic seek to share the costs of development, spread the risks and tap into the intellectual talent of other nations. Alliances, cross-licensing of intellectual property, mergers and acquisitions and other forms of cooperation have become more prevalent in the transatlantic economy over the past decade. Indeed, the advent and spread of the internet on both sides of the Atlantic has been key in bolstering greater R&D collaboration: interregional internet bandwidth between the North America and Europe is 3½ times greater than bandwidth between North America and Asia (See Chapter 7).

As discussed in chapter 1, asset-augmenting strategies of firms point to greater transatlantic economic activity in knowledge-based sectors of the economy. The R&D demands of both U.S. and European firms dictate that companies tap into innovative talent on both sides of the ocean. The cyclical recession of 2001 took a toll as global R&D expenditures of U.S. foreign affiliates declined to $19.4 billion from $20.4 billion in 2000, an expected outcome given the weak profit performance of many firms. In Europe, U.S. foreign affiliate R&D totaled $11.7 billion, down from $12.9 billion, although Europe still accounted for roughly 60% of the global total. The United Kingdom, Germany and France, in that order, were the top three markets for R&D expenditures by U.S. foreign affiliates. No comparable figures for Europe's R&D investment in the U.S. are available. However, given America's highly skilled labor force and the research intensity of many European sectors (chemicals, telecoms, automobiles), European R&D expenditures in the U.S. are substantial and dwarf expenditures spent by Asian counterparts, namely Japan.

As a recent example of expanding European R&D expenditures in the United States, Novartis, the Swiss pharmaceutical giant, recently opened a research and development center in Boston, a strategic move designed to tap the intellectual capital of the greater Boston area. The move will bolster the innovative capacity of the firm, while providing high-paying jobs for American workers.

5. Intra-firm Trade of Foreign Affiliates. Foreign affiliate sales are the primary means by which transatlantic commerce is conducted. Cross border trade is a secondary means of delivery, although the modes of delivery—affiliate sales and trade—should not be viewed independently of each other. They are more complements than substitutes, since foreign investment and foreign affiliate sales increasingly drive and determine trade flows. A substantial share of transatlantic trade is classified as intra-firm trade or related party trade, which is cross border trade that stays within the ambit of the company—for instance when Siemens of Germany sends parts and components to Siemens North Carolina, or when a Dupont affiliate in Delaware exports a specialty chemical to an affiliate in the Netherlands. This type of trade is evident among countries or regions with deep, investment-led linkages, which defines the transatlantic economy. Accordingly, roughly 55% of U.S. imports from the European Union consisted of related party trade in 2002. In the case of Germany, the percentage (66%) was even higher. Meanwhile, roughly one-third of U.S. exports to Europe in 2002 represented related party trade. Related party trade played a key role in shaping transatlantic trade flows in 2003, a topic explored in greater detail in a case study in Chapter 2.

6. Foreign Affiliate Sales. With over 20,000 foreign affiliates dispersed around the world, U.S. firms easily derive more sales from foreign affiliates than exports. That is notably the case with Europe, with U.S. foreign affiliates in Europe achieving sales of $1.5 trillion in 2001 versus U.S. exports of $276 million to Europe in the same year. Of global foreign affiliate sales in 2001 (a record $2.9 trillion), Europe accounted for just over 51% of the total. On a comparative basis, affiliate sales in Europe were more than double affiliate sales in the entire Asia/Pacific region in 2001. Affiliate sales in the United Kingdom alone ($428 billion) exceeded aggregate sales in Latin America. While sales in China soared over the 1990s on account of surging U.S. foreign direct investment, sales of only $36 billion in China in 2001 were on par with total sales in Sweden ($33 billion) and well below sales in both Germany ($240 billion) and France ($135 billion).

Affiliate sales are also the primary means by which European firms deliver goods and services to U.S. consumers. In 2001, for instance, European affiliate sales in the U.S. ($1.4 billion) were over four times larger than U.S. imports from Europe. In the case of the United Kingdom, the gap between affiliate sales and imports was even wider, with UK affiliate sales in the U.S. more than five times the amount of U.S. imports from the UK. German affiliate sales in the U.S. were more than four times greater than U.S. imports from Germany—a striking statistic for Germany, a country commonly thought to be a classic "trading" nation.

7. Foreign Affiliate Profits. In terms of profits, Europe remains by a wide margin the most important region in the world for corporate America. Indeed, U.S. corporate profits soared to record highs in 2003 due in large part to U.S. dollar weakness, which helped inflate the bottom line of many U.S. multinationals and drive the major U.S. financial indices to robust levels. It was the U.S. dollar's weakness against the euro— with the greenback depreciating by over 20% against the euro in 2003—that provided the most bang for the buck to U.S. firms, since Europe typically accounts for half of U.S. global earnings (earnings out-

The U.S. Earnings Boost From Europe
(U.S. foreign affiliate income from Europe)

Source: Bureau of Economic Analysis

side the U.S.). For all of 2003, U.S. foreign affiliate income from Europe, a proxy for global earnings, topped a record $77 billion, up nearly 30% from the prior year. In the United Kingdom, the sharp slide of the U.S. dollar against the British pound helped boost affiliate earnings by 18.4% in 2003. In all, U.S. affiliate earnings in some twelve European markets (France, the Netherlands, Switzerland, Italy, Ireland, Spain, Belgium, Denmark, Sweden, Austria, Czech Republic, and Poland) reached record highs in 2003.

Similarly, the United States remains the most important market in the world in terms of earnings for many European multinationals. Profits of European foreign affiliates in the United States also reached new highs in 2003 and sparked solid gains across various Europe stock markets. European affiliate profits totaled just over $46 billion in 2003, with the earnings boost driven by strong U.S. demand, which offset the adverse price effect from the strength of the euro and pound. British, Dutch, Swedish and Swiss foreign affiliates all enjoyed record U.S. profits in 2003. Contrary to most assessments of transatlantic drift since the end of the Cold War, Europe's investment stake in the U.S. has deepened dramatically since the fall of the Berlin Wall: U.S. affiliate income in Europe European affiliates rose more than ten-fold between 1990 and 2003, or from $4.4 billion to $46 billion. European sectors most exposed to the U.S. market include automobiles, media, financial services and pharmaceuticals. In the pharmaceuticals sector, revenues from the North American market, namely the United States, accounted for 52.2% of total global revenues in 2002, according to figures from Morgan Stanley. In the same year, Europe's media sector derived some 38% of total revenue from North America; Europe's financial service sector, meanwhile, relied on North America for 36% of total revenue in 2002, while

U.S. Foreign Affiliate Income Breakdown, 2003

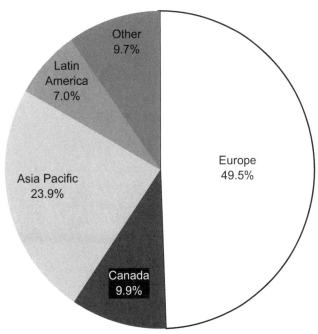

Source: Bureau of Economic Analysis

European automobile manufacturers generated nearly 30% of total revenues from North America.

In terms of individual European countries, the Netherlands is the most exposed to the North American market, according to survey results from Morgan Stanley, deriving some 41.8% of total revenue from North America in 2002. Ireland (32.5%), Switzerland (31.9%), the United Kingdom (22.7%), Germany (21.6%), and Belgium (21.3%) were also significantly exposed to the North American market.

In sum, these seven indices convey a more complete and complex picture of international economic flows than simple tallies of exports and imports. Foreign direct investment represents the backbone of the transatlantic economy, with other variables such as overseas assets, affiliate employment and sales, and R&D all derived from the level and depth of investment linkages. No other commercial artery in the world is as integrated and fused together by foreign investment, a fact lost on many pundits, parliamentarians and policy makers on both sides of the Atlantic.

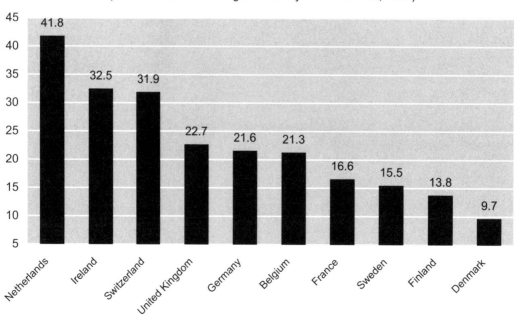

Europe's Exposure to North America
(share of total revenues generated by North America, 2002)

Source: Morgan Stanley

Chapter 4

European Commerce and the 50 States—
A State-by-State Comparison

European firms have never been more embedded in the U.S. economy, a fact largely overlooked and unrecognized by many in the United States. Most U.S. consumers, for instance, are unaware that when purchasing Dove soap, Lipton Tea or Skippy peanut butter at a grocery chain like Stop & Shop or Giant Foods, they are really purchasing products from the European consumer products giant, Unilever, in a Dutch-owned grocery firm called Ahold. When buying a BMW automobile, many Americans do not realize that the vehicle may have been manufactured by American workers in Spartanburg, South Carolina, rather than in Germany.

Similarly, it is unrecognizable to many consumers that one of their favorite ice cream outlets, Ben & Jerry's, is owned by Unilever, and another, Baskin Robbins, is owned by the British firm Allied Domecq; that their local financial advisor could be employed by a European financial giant like Axa or UBS; that the popular bottled water brand, Dannon, is owned by Groupe Danone, the French food group; or that such a quintessentially "local" beer as Rolling Rock is brewed by Belgian giant Interbrew. Other examples abound—the key point is this: what is all too familiar to U.S. consumers is in many cases foreign, or in these cases, European.

These examples reflect Corporate Europe's longstanding commitment to be an "insider" in the American marketplace. Quantifying this point, Europe's investment stakes in the United States on a historic cost basis exceeded $1 trillion in 2002, the last year of available data. That is nearly double the level of 1998 ($518 billion), highlighting the surge in European investment in the U.S. in the late 1990s.

No other region of the world has made such a large capital commitment to the United States, with Europe accounting for nearly three-fourths of all foreign investment in the U.S. Because of this outsized capital stake, hundreds of European firms are intertwined in the daily lives of U.S. consumers—whether U.S. consumers know it or not. European firms are not only major providers of goods and services to U.S. households but also critical sources of employment for U.S. workers. The latter has been all but ignored in the raging debate in the United States about outsourcing and the migration of U.S. jobs overseas.

Insourcing vs. Outsourcing: European Multinationals and U.S. Workers

Nothing of late has produced more angst and anxiety in the U.S. than America's so-called "jobless recovery." While the U.S. economy has recovered from the 2001-2002 recession and exhibited extraordinary strength in 2003 and 2004, the job creation that typically follows a cyclical rebound has been largely absent. In fact, roughly 2 million U.S. jobs have been lost since 2001. And despite robust economic activity over the second half of 2003, when the economy expanded by 6% in real terms, employment growth remained quite weak and well below previous cyclical levels.

Various reasons have been offered for America's dismal job performance, but outsourcing—or the shift of U.S. jobs to such low-cost places as China and India—has been front and center as a key culprit. Outsourcing, in fact, has become a lightning rod in the 2004 Presidential elections. Missing from the heated media debate, however, is this: the migration of U.S. jobs overseas is not a zero-sum game—particularly not for the United States. Just as millions of foreign workers are on the payrolls of U.S. firms, millions of U.S. workers depend on foreign firms for their livelihoods. The U.S. ranks as one of the most desirable destinations for foreign investment in the world—and the vast majority of those investors are European.

European firms are critical sources of employment for U.S. workers. U.S. affiliates of European multinationals directly employed over 4 million American workers in 2001, the last year of available data. This total represents two-thirds of all U.S. workers employed by U.S. affiliates of foreign multinationals.

On a global basis, U.S. firms employ more workers overseas than foreign firms employ in the United States. U.S. foreign affiliates, for instance, had roughly 9.8 million foreign workers on their payrolls in 2001 versus 6.4 million workers at U.S. affiliates of foreign companies in the same year. On a net basis, then, the U.S. outsources more jobs than it insources. The global norm, however, does not apply to the United States and Europe. To the contrary, the U.S. enjoys an employment surplus with Europe, or the U.S. insources more jobs from Europe than it outsources across the Atlantic.

America's Million Worker Surplus

The U.S.-European employment balance is tilted by a wide margin towards the United States. European affiliates of U.S. firms directly employed roughly 3.2 million workers in 2001, but U.S. affiliates of European firms directly employed one million more—just over 4.2 million U.S. workers. In all probability, this figure was trimmed in 2003 on account of weak U.S. economic growth during 2001-02 and the cyclical downturn of European investment in the U.S. over the same period. Yet even after taking into account some cyclical weakness, and given the large spread between Europe-U.S. foreign affiliate employment levels, America still insources more jobs from Europe than it outsources.

The U.S.–European Employment Balance
Thousands of employees, 2001

Country	European Affiliates of U.S. Companies	U.S. Affiliates of European Companies	Employment Balance
Belgium	113.5	145.6	+32.1
France	540.5	578.6	+38.1
Germany	601.0	735.0	+134.0
Ireland	86.8	66.9	(19.9)
Italy	211.3	101.3	(110.0)
Netherlands	175.8	572.0	+396.2
Spain	184.3	14.8	(169.5)
Switzerland	58.3	248.8	+190.5
United Kingdom	1,204.8	1,121.0	(83.8)
Total	3,180.0	4,251.0	+1,071.0

"Note: Employment balance "+" favors the U.S.
Source: Bureau of Economic Analysis

By country, the U.S. insourced more jobs from Belgium, France, Germany, the Netherlands and Switzerland than it outsourced in 2001. In the same year, U.S. firms employed slightly more workers in the United Kingdom than British firms in the United States.

The bottom line is that while outsourcing has become a pejorative term in the United States, European firms provide more employment to U.S. workers than U.S. firms to European laborers. This fact is lost on some legislators who continue to think the migration of U.S. jobs overseas is a one-way street. It is not, thanks in large part to European multinationals and their U.S. affiliates. Foreign investment, in fact, is an important source of new jobs, exports and production. In the end, if anyone should be lamenting the outsourcing phenomenon, it is Europe, whose firms continue to outsource jobs to both the United States and the developing nations.

European Investors in the U.S.: Regional, Industry and State Preferences

European affiliates operate in all fifty United States, although on a geographic basis, no other region of the U.S. has benefited more from Europe's large investment position in America than the Southeast. Of total European investment in the U.S. in 2001 (measured as the stock of gross property, plant and equipment held by European affiliates in the U.S.), the Southeast accounted for nearly 23% of the aggregate. The Southeast ranked as the top U.S. investment site for British, French, Dutch, Swedish and Belgian firms in 2001. The sector focus of European multinationals runs the gamut, from automotives to pulp and paper to various service activities like banking, insurance and hotels.

The following charts outline the importance of European foreign direct investment for specific geographic regions of the United States. In the map section of the appendix, we have also constructed new "maps" of the 50 United States geared to European-sourced American jobs, investment and trade.

Many localized variables account for the attraction of the Southeast, including the region's largely non-unionized labor force, relatively low real estate costs, and superb infrastructure, including various container ports that facilitate the efficient movement of goods between European parents and their U.S. affiliates. Local tax incentives have also played a large part in attracting European investment, underscoring the

European Foreign Investment in the U.S.
By geographic region

Region	U.S. $ Billions	% of Total European Investment
Southeast	136.0	22.8
Great Lakes	110.6	18.6
Mid-Atlantic	104.2	17.5
Southwest	79.7	13.4
West	76.7	12.9
New England	36.8	6.2
Rocky Mountains	28.9	4.6
Plains	25.0	4.0

Source: Bureau of Economic Analysis

point that it is not only countries that compete for investment, but also states, with many in the Southeast notably successful in the past decade. All of the above has made the Southeast the main focal point of European investment. This capital injection from Europe, in turn, has contributed to the region's economic revival and vigor of the past few decades.

Among southeastern states, Georgia is the preferred location of European investors, accounting for 13.2% of the region's total European investment position. Florida was a close second (12.1%), followed by South Carolina (11.6%). In both South Carolina and Georgia, European investment accounted for more than half of all total foreign investment

Gross Property, Plant, and Equipment of French Affiliates in U.S. Regions, 2001
(millions of dollars)

Southeast	20,119
Mideast	18,960
Southwest	15,362
Great Lakes	9,491
Far West	9,120
New England	5,251
Plains	4,316
Rocky Mountains	1,296
Total	**84,818**

Source: Bureau of Economic Analysis

Gross Property, Plant, and Equipment of German Affiliates in U.S. Regions, 2001
(millions of dollars)

Great Lakes	54,041
Southeast	34,162
Mideast	25,183
Southwest	15,141
Far West	12,688
Plains	7,062
New England	6,110
Rocky Mountains	1,504
Total	**180,205**

Source: Bureau of Economic Analysis

Overall Direct Employment of French Affiliates in U.S. Regions
(thousands of employees)

Southeast	141.5
Mideast	119.1
Great Lakes	94.6
Far West	79.9
Southwest	65.1
New England	35.0
Plains	30.7
Rocky Mountains	11.0
Total	**578.6**

Source: Bureau of Economic Analysis

Overall Direct Employment of German Affiliates in U.S. Regions
(thousands of employees)

Great Lakes	208.7
Southeast	168.9
Mideast	147.5
Far West	79.9
New England	40.8
Plains	40.5
Southwest	36.2
Rocky Mountains	9.7
Total	**734.8**

Source: Bureau of Economic Analysis

Manufacturing Employment of French Affiliates in U.S. Regions
(thousands of employees)

Southeast	71.9
Mideast	40.6
Great Lakes	36.4
Southwest	23.6
Far West	21.1
Plains	13.0
New England	11.6
Rocky Mountains	2.1
Total	**220.5**

Source: Bureau of Economic Analysis

Manufacturing Employment of German Affiliates in U.S. Regions
(thousands of employees)

Great Lakes	129.4
Southeast	92.9
Mideast	36.6
Plains	23.0
New England	19.4
Far West	18.4
Southwest	13.4
Rocky Mountains	2.2
Total	**338.7**

Source: Bureau of Economic Analysis

in 2001. In Florida, European firms accounted for 46% of total foreign direct investment (for more state detail, see the accompanying state profiles at the end of this chapter).

The geographic bias of German firms is toward the Great Lakes region, which ranked second to the southeast in overall

Gross Property, Plant, and Equipment of British Affiliates in U.S. Regions, 2001
(millions of dollars)

Southeast	41,484
Mideast	31,568
Great Lakes	29,653
Far West	28,768
Southwest	26,498
Rocky Mountains	22,165
New England	17,412
Plains	6,906
Total	**249,271**

Source: Bureau of Economic Analysis

Overall Direct Employment of British Affiliates in U.S. Regions
(thousands of employees)

Southeast	267.7
Mideast	221.1
Great Lakes	177.1
Far West	154.4
Southwest	102.5
New England	99.9
Plains	56.6
Rocky Mountains	36.2
Total	**1120.7**

Source: Bureau of Economic Analysis

Manufacturing Employment of British Affiliates in U.S. Regions
(thousands of employees)

Southeast	77.9
Great Lakes	77.7
Mideast	58.1
Far West	40.6
Southwest	29.9
New England	22.1
Plains	19.3
Rocky Mountains	5.9
Total	**333.1**

Source: Bureau of Economic Analysis

investment attractiveness. Germany's tilt towards the region reflects the large automobile presence of leading German manufacturers in Michigan, which has resulted in a clustering of automotive investment in and around the state. On account of this effect, Germany's investment position in Michigan totaled just over $31 billion in 2001, accounting for nearly 80% of total European investment in the state.

Swiss investment in the U.S. is clustered around the Midatlantic states, or more precisely, New Jersey and New York. This reflects the large capital position of Swiss pharmaceutical firms in New Jersey and the extensive presence of Swiss financial service firms in New York. The Midatlantic region ranked third among U.S. geographic regions, accounting for 17.5% of total European investment in 2001. At the other end of the spectrum—or the least favored regions for investment among European multinationals—are the Plains states and the Rocky mountain region.

Texas and California are the two most attractive states for European investors and are independent of or outside the regional favorites—almost regions on their own. Based on 2001 investment figures, Texas ranked as the top U.S. state for European investment as a whole and for French investment in particular, a rather ironic fact given bitter Franco-American tensions over Iraq and ongoing diplomatic tensions between the European Union and the Bush Administration from nearly day one of the Bush presidency. Europe's investment stake in Texas—reflecting capital outlays in the state's energy sector—topped $68 billion in 2001, a level greater than European investment levels in most countries. European affiliates employed over 252,000 workers in Texas in 2001.

Case Study I:

Charlotte, North Carolina and the European "Elbow"

The Southeast region of the United States has been among the most successful regions in the U.S. when it comes to securing foreign direct investment. The attractiveness of the region pivots on many variables, ranging from a large non-unionized labor force, to a first-class infrastructure, and to relative low real estate costs. These variables are particularly prized by multinationals. Yet these same factors must nevertheless be packaged, promoted and properly marketed by local and state officials in order to attract the attention and hopefully, the capital, of foreign companies looking to invest in the United States.

Competition among state and local officials for the capital of foreign multinationals is intense, with success increasingly dependent on a strategic and well-coordinated effort at the local level. In other words, while U.S. trade policy is set in Washington, America's policies towards foreign direct investment are more localized and dictated and influenced by such organizations as the Charlotte Regional Partnership (CRP).

The CRP is a marketing and economic development organization seeking to attract international business to the greater Charlotte area, which encompasses 16 counties straddling the border of South and North Carolina.

In the late 1980s, the Carolinas witnessed a shift from traditional textile manufacturing along the Interstate 85 *Autobahn* to foreign-made textile machinery, thereby changing the marketplace for new business. The CRP took note of this retooling process and devised a strategy around it. Under the resulting "Elbow Strategy," the region focused less on attracting a specific type of industry and more on the size and geographic location of foreign companies to be courted. Recruitment focused mainly on *Mittelstand*, or middle market companies that supply larger OEMs, that tend to be located along the "elbow" of the Rhine river in Germany's Baden-Wuerttemberg and France's Alsace-Lorraine, extending eastward through the northern Swiss cantons of Basel and Zurich and into Austria.

The results are impressive. One-third of all foreign-owned companies in the two Carolinas are located in the 16-county Charlotte region. 250 of the Charlotte region's 617 foreign firms are from "Elbow strategy" countries. Similar companies from outside the "elbow," including the UK, Sweden, Italy and Japan, have followed suit.

More than 1,800 foreign-owned companies employ more than 350,000 people in the Carolinas, and more than 1/3 of these are located in the Charlotte region. More than 500 of the 600 foreign companies in the Charlotte region are European, including more than 165 German-owned companies – the single largest cluster of German industrial investment in the United States, mostly *Mittelstand* enterprises rather than large corporations.

The Charlotte region has emerged as the second biggest banking and financial center in the United States, second only to New York City. But for every financial services worker in Charlotte, five others go to work each day in manufacturing plants scattered throughout the region.

The organization has been notably successful in highlighting and promoting the region's excellent transportation system, a regional strength given the close linkages that exist between the operations of a parent company and its foreign affiliates. Foreign affiliates rarely operate in isolation and are constantly receiving parts and components from the parent firm or related affiliates. The cross-border flow of goods and people is intense between parent and affiliates, making it all the more important that local infrastructure be supportive of parent-affiliate cross border linkages. And on this score, as the Charlotte partnership has effectively highlighted and sold to foreign multinationals, the greater Charlotte region stands out. The region not only boasts a world-class international airport, but is also endowed with an integrated interstate highway system, deep sea container ports in Wilmington, Charlestown and Savannah, and intermodal rail facilities that allows foreign affiliates to effectively bring goods into the United States and distribute and reach the broader U.S. market.

Because of its strategic foresight and success in attracting foreign direct investment, the Charlotte Regional Partnership has helped "globalize" the greater Charlotte area, integrating a large swath of the southeast into the global economy. The upshot is that the Charlotte region in particular, and North and South Carolina in general, are increasingly linked to the global business cycle. The economic future of both states is increasingly bound to the ebb and flow of the global economy, meaning the more the U.S. and Europe work together to promote greater global cooperation in the realms of trade, investment and other market-liberalizing efforts, the greater the rewards for such global-linked regions of the United States as the greater Charlotte area.

Conversely, the future performance of more and more foreign multinationals is increasingly tied to the success of their foreign affiliates operating in the greater Charlotte region. How well these affiliates leverage the assets of the greater Charlotte area—its skilled labor pool, technological capabilities and world class infrastructure—increasingly dictates the success of the company's overall performance.

The allure of California is its large and wealthy consumer market, as well as its technological endowments, educational facilities and agricultural capabilities. These factors are among the key variables behind the $60 billion in European investment in California. Like Texas, total European investment in California is greater than total European investment in most nations. This is not surprising given that California's $1.3 trillion economy is the sixth largest in the world, just behind France and Britain. European affiliates are significant employers in the state, supporting nearly 400,000 jobs in 2001, with roughly one-quarter of these jobs in manufacturing activities.

Ranking of U.S. States Benefiting from European Investment

Ranking of States for European Direct Investment		Ranking of States for Jobs Supported Directly by European Investment	
U.S. State	Foreign Direct Investment[1] (FDI) from Europe	U.S. State	Number of Jobs[2]
Texas	68.3	California	396.5
California	60.3	New York	337.1
Michigan	39.2	Texas	252.2
New York	39.0	Illinois	194.7
Illinois	27.1	New Jersey	194.4
New Jersey	25.2	Pennsylvania	191.2
Pennsylvania	24.6	Florida	179.9
Ohio	19.4	Michigan	171.8
Louisiana	18.5	Georgia	160.6
Indiana	18.3	Massachusetts	154.7
Massachusetts	18.3	Ohio	148.8
Georgia	18.0	North Carolina	148.1
Florida	16.4	South Carolina	104.3
South Carolina	15.8	Virginia	103.7
North Carolina	14.6	Indiana	100.5
Virginia	12.8	Maryland	87.9
Alabama	11.8	Connecticut	85.8
Utah	11.1	Tennessee	82.5
Missouri	10.1	Missouri	74.6
Kentucky	9.3	Wisconsin	64.0
Connecticut	9.2	Minnesota	58.6
Tennessee	8.8	Alabama	57.6
Maryland	8.7	Washington	56.8
Colorado	8.2	Colorado	51.7
Wyoming	7.6	Kentucky	45.5
Washington	7.5	Arizona	45.0
Wisconsin	6.5	Louisiana	33.8
Oregon	5.7	Oregon	30.9
Minnesota	5.4	Iowa	28.2
West Virginia	5.4	New Hampshire	27.2
Oklahoma	5.2	Kansas	27.2
Delaware	5.0	Arkansas	25.0
Arizona	4.8	Oklahoma	24.9
Kansas	3.8	Utah	23.9
New Hampshire	3.8	West Virginia	19.6
Iowa	3.7	Delaware	18.7
Arkansas	2.3	Nevada	17.4
Mississippi	2.3	Rhode Island	16.4
Rhode Island	2.3	Mississippi	14.9
Nevada	2.1	Nebraska	12.5
Vermont	2.1	District of Columbia	12.0
District of Columbia	1.7	Maine	11.6
New Mexico	1.4	New Mexico	8.3
Idaho	1.4	Hawaii	8.1
Maine	1.2	Vermont	6.6
Nebraska	1.1	Idaho	6.6
Hawaii	1.0	Wyoming	5.4
Montana	0.7	Alaska	5.4
North Dakota	0.5	Montana	4.7
South Dakota	0.3	North Dakota	4.2
Alaska	0.1	South Dakota	3.2

Notes: [1]U.S. $ billions, 2001. [2]Thousands of jobs, 2001.
Source: Bureau of Economic Analysis

Trade Linkages: European Multinationals and American States

Virtually every U.S. state benefits from European foreign direct investment, with European foreign affiliates across America acting not only as key providers of goods and services to U.S. consumers but also as critical sources of U.S. employment. In addition, Europe is also a key export market for many U.S. states, a role that bestows even more income growth, revenue generation and employment benefits to states.

California alone exported some $20.4 billion in goods to Europe in 2003, an amount greater than total U.S. exports to OPEC. Europe represents one of the largest markets in the world for information technology, and technology firms in California have seen exports of computers and related parts to Europe expand sharply over the past few years. Greater IT spending in Europe, along with a weaker dollar against the euro and British pound, were behind the rise in IT exports.

New York and Texas are also sizable exporters to Europe. New York's exports to Europe topped $13 billion in 2003; Texas' exports to Europe exceeded $11 billion. The composition of exports ran the gamut—from machinery to chemicals—with the United Kingdom the top export market for both states. The United Kingdom was also the top export market for California and for many other states. In fact, the United Kingdom ranked as the number one export market for 25 states last year. Germany was a distant second, the top export market for 10 U.S. states in 2003.

The map section of the appendix contains a new map of the 50 United States that charts their export relationship with Europe.

The Micro View: What Does It All Mean?

In many U.S. states and across many U.S. sectors, European firms have seamlessly inserted themselves into the mainstream of the U.S. economy and the daily lives of U.S. consumers. Hundreds of European affiliates in the United States have become so "local" that American consumers, along with various local and state officials cannot tell or do not care whether the local grocery store, bank or automobile dealer is either American or foreign.

Consumers and legislators, though, do care about access to competitively priced goods and services, job creation, and the overall health of the local economy. And on all three counts, European firms have made and continue to make significant contributions to all regions of the United States. That said, many of these underlying contributions have gone largely unnoticed in the United States.

Europe's micro contribution in the U.S. comes in various forms:

A catalyst for economic growth in the Southeast. The southeast region of the U.S. continues to be a leading area of growth, and the expanding regional presence of European investment has been a major contributor to this trend. In particular, European automobile manufacturers, along with Japanese multinationals, have been instrumental in creating new and high-paying manufacturing jobs in such states as South Carolina and Alabama. Both states have seen their terms of trade improve on account of expanding automotive trade between European parents and their U.S. foreign affiliates. Reflecting this dynamic, Alabama's exports of transportation-related goods to Europe rose by more than 110% between 1999 and 2003. South Carolina's export growth was even more impressive—transportation-related exports rose from just $532 million in 1999 to roughly $3 billion in 2003, nearly a six-fold increase. Greater transatlantic trade flows in general have fueled growth among the region's container ports. The volume of both sea-borne and air-borne trade has increased over the past decade as more European firms assemble, manufacture, market and distribute from the region, creating, directly and indirectly, thousands of jobs across various sectors of the economy.

A counterbalance to Chinese competition. As states such as North Carolina and South Carolina confront the harsh winds of Chinese competition in textile trade, expanding transatlantic ties have been a key factor offsetting the competitive challenge posed by the mainland. In light of China's rapid emergence, the question is where would the southeastern states—many dependent on textile trade—be today without the foreign direct investment of European multinationals? The answer: they would be further behind, more economically challenged and in even greater danger of being overwhelmed by Chinese competition.

A bright spot in an otherwise discouraging Michigan economy. A similar question can be posed regarding Michigan: how many more manufacturing jobs would the state have lost over the past few years absent Europe's large investment stake in the state's automotive sector? The state's economic future has become increasingly intertwined with the economic success and prosperity of Europe's leading automobile manufacturers.

A stabilizing force on Wall Street. Similarly, Wall Street's future is more than ever linked to the profits and performance of many leading European financial giants, now major employers in New York, Connecticut and New Jersey. As the U.S. financial sector continues to downsize and consolidate, the commitment, growth and expansion of European service firms in the U.S. has become even more important.

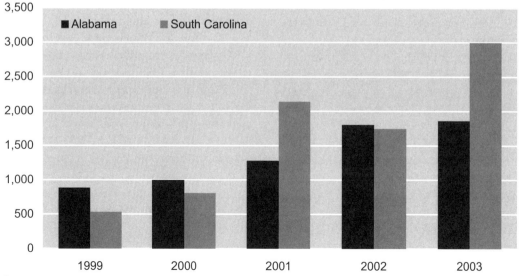

Transportation-related Exports from Alabama and South Carolina to Europe (U.S. $ millions)

Source: U.S. Department of Commerce

A critical source of demand for information technology. While employment in America's information technology sector is under threat from low-cost labor in China and India, America's IT outlook would be even more dire absent Europe's demand for U.S. IT goods and services.

The bottom line is that Europe's investment presence in the U.S. is pronounced and substantial, yet largely invisible and indiscernible at the local or micro level. The most successful European affiliates in the United States have localized themselves to the point where U.S. consumers cannot tell the difference between an American firm and European entity. Nothing, perhaps, better illustrates the deep integration of the transatlantic economy.

Case Study II:

Nafta: How Much of an Impact on the Transatlantic Economy?

The North American Free Trade Agreement (Nafta) has spurred economic ties and development among the U.S., Canada and Mexico with only a nominal impact on the transatlantic economy.

Quantifying the level of trade and investment diversion on account of Nafta is a difficult task and one beyond the scope of this report. However, after examining various metrics—ranging from trade flows to employment growth among affiliates—it is hard to make the case that Nafta has had an adverse effect on the development and integration of the transatlantic economy.

Based on foreign direct investment flows, U.S. investment to Mexico and Canada did rise over the balance of the 1990s, climbing from $10.5 billion in 1994, the first year Nafta was in effect, to $31 billion in 1999. Over the balance of the 1990s, U.S. investment levels ebbed and flowed, but generally trended higher. U.S. investment flows to Nafta peaked at $30.8 billion in 2001, well above the $17.7 billion annual average over the 1994-03 period. On a comparable basis, U.S. investment outflows to Europe averaged over $57 billion annually over the 1994-03, more than three times larger than annual average flows to its Nafta partners.

In terms of U.S. investment inflows, the EU provided the bulk of FDI to the United States in the 1990s, accounting, in fact, for nearly three quarters of all foreign direct investment received in the last decade. Canadian multinationals did increase their investments in the United States over the 1990s, notably in the energy sector. Yet Canadian inflows to the United States ($118 billion over the 1994-03 period) were a fraction of FDI inflows from the European Union over the same period ($900 billion).

As the lowest cost producer in Nafta, Mexico has experienced a rise in foreign investment from the U.S., Europe and Canada over the past decade. Yet investment inflows to Mexico have not been as large as many expected given that global FDI flows are typically channeled to economies that are more similar in terms of wealth, infrastructure and regulations. Accordingly, global inflows and outflows are predominantly between the developed nations, with the United States and Europe being the strongest examples.

The greater barriers to investment flows to Mexico are the nation's underdeveloped economy and its lagging education and infrastructure relative to the United States and Europe. Mexico's substandard institutional quality, weak technological capabilities and small pool of skilled labor have also worked against it. The bottom line is that multinationals invest in overseas markets that are similar to their home market, a dynamic that has long underpinned robust U.S.-European investment flows.

Even in terms of trade, the data show little in the way of diversion. Indeed, as a share of total U.S. imports, Europe's share actually increased from 18% in 1994 to 19.3% in 2002. Canada's share of U.S. imports decreased over the past decade, falling from a share of 19.1% in 1994 to 17.8% in 2002. In contrast, Mexico's share of U.S. imports rose over the past decade, climbing to 11.3% in 2002 from 7.3% in 1994. A great deal of Mexico's rising share of U.S. imports has come at the expense of Asia rather than Europe. In particular, Mexico has increased its share of automobile exports to the U.S. at the expense of the Japanese and claimed more U.S. market share in apparel and footwear from non-Japanese producers.

Viewed from the perspective of the EU, the EU's share of total exports to the United States expanded between 1994 and 2002, with the U.S. share rising from 7.4% to 9.3%. Canada's share of EU exports remained relatively constant at 0.9%. Mexico's share of EU exports, even with the conclusion of a EU-Mexican free trade agreement in 1997, rose very little, from 0.5% in 1994 to just 0.6% in 2002.

The bottom line is that Nafta has had only a nominal effect on the transatlantic economy. Any diversion in trade has been small; integration through foreign direct investment has not been impeded or diverted, evident by the record levels of transatlantic investment flows of the past decade.

Alabama and Europe
Employment, Investment, and Trade Linkages

Employment

European investment in Alabama supported 58,000 jobs in 2001; 45% of the jobs were in manufacturing.

Investment

Of the $17.4 billion invested in Alabama in 2001, 68%, or $11.8 billion came from Europe.

Trade

In 2003, Europe purchased $3.1 billion worth of goods from Alabama.

Nearly 60% of total exports represented transportation equipment, reflecting the state's linkages with European auto manufacturers.

Top Sources of FDI within Alabama, 2001

Country	FDI ($ Millions)
United Kingdom	3,601
Germany	3,368
France	2,271
Japan	1,855
Canada	1,528

Source: Bureau of Economic Analysis

Top European Export Markets, 2003

Country	Exports ($ Millions)
Germany	1,618
UK	443
Netherlands	253
France	221
Ireland	134

Source: Office of Trade and Economic Analysis

Top Ten Exports to Europe ($ Millions)

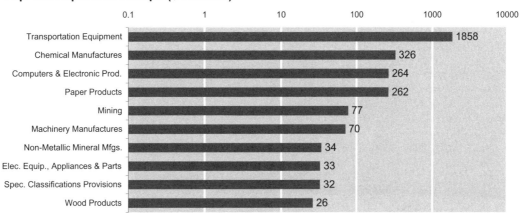

Source: Office of Trade and Economic Analysis

Alaska and Europe
Employment, Investment, and Trade Linkages

Employment

European investment in Alaska supported 5,000 jobs in 2001.

Investment

Of the $29.6 billion invested in Alaska in 2001, 0.3%, or $0.1 billion came from Europe.

Trade

In 2003, Europe purchased $500 million worth of goods from Alaska.

The bulk of exports consist of primary commodities.

Top Sources of FDI within Alaska, 2001

Country	FDI ($ Millions)
Japan	757
France	83
Mexico	33
Netherlands	19
Switzerland	10

Source: Bureau of Economic Analysis

Top European Export Markets, 2003

Country	Exports ($ Millions)
Germany	113
Netherlands	97
Switzerland	94
Belgium	51
Spain	38

Source: Office of Trade and Economic Analysis

Top Ten Exports to Europe ($ Millions)

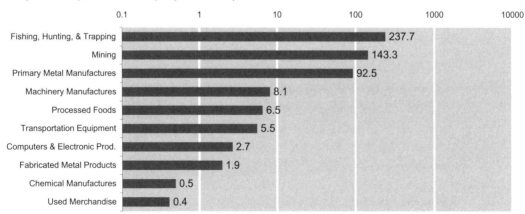

Source: Office of Trade and Economic Analysis

Arizona and Europe
Employment, Investment, and Trade Linkages

Employment

European investment in Arizona supported 45,000 jobs in 2001; nearly one-quarter were in manufacturing.

Investment

Of the $10.2 billion invested in Arizona in 2001, 47%, or $4.8 billion came from Europe.

Trade

In 2003, Europe purchased $2.7 billion worth of goods from Arizona.

Nearly half of the state's exports consist of transportation equipment.

Top Sources of FDI within Arizona, 2001

Country	FDI ($ Millions)
Japan	2,341
Netherlands	1,684
United Kingdom	1,211
Germany	948
Mexico	748

Source: Bureau of Economic Analysis

Top European Export Markets, 2003

Country	Exports ($ Millions)
UK	742
Germany	607
France	350
Switzerland	266
Ireland	160

Source: Office of Trade and Economic Analysis

Top Ten Exports to Europe ($ Millions)

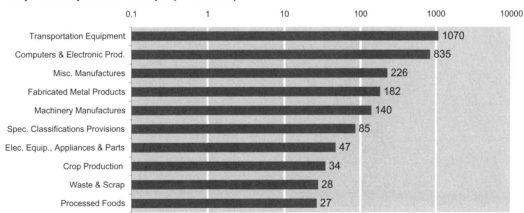

Source: Office of Trade and Economic Analysis

Arkansas and Europe
Employment, Investment, and Trade Linkages

Employment

European investment in Arkansas supported 25,000 jobs in 2001.

Investment

Of the $5.9 billion invested in Arkansas in 2001, 39%, or $2.3 billion came from Europe.

Trade

In 2003, Europe purchased $602 million worth of goods from Arkansas.

Transportation equipment was the top export to Europe.

Top Sources of FDI within Arkansas, 2001

Country	FDI ($ Millions)
Japan	1,066
United Kingdom	500
Germany	482
France	468
Australia	354

Source: Bureau of Economic Analysis

Top European Export Markets, 2003

Country	Exports ($ Millions)
UK	147
Netherlands	133
Italy	63
Belgium	62
Germany	59

Source: Office of Trade and Economic Analysis

Top Ten Exports to Europe ($ Millions)

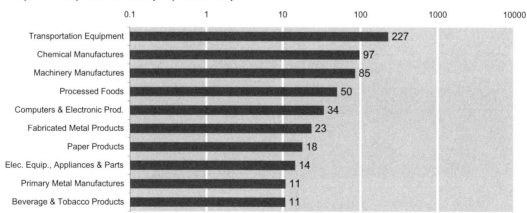

Source: Office of Trade and Economic Analysis

California and Europe
Employment, Investment, and Trade Linkages

Employment

European investment in California supported 397,000 jobs in 2001; roughly one-quarter of those jobs were in manufacturing activities.

Investment

Of the $120 billion invested in California in 2001, 50%, or $60.3 billion came from Europe.

Trade

In 2003, Europe purchased $20.4 billion worth of goods from California.

Over 40% of Californian exports to Europe consist of high-tech goods.

Top Sources of FDI within California, 2001

Country	FDI ($ Millions)
Japan	30,422
United Kingdom	20,139
Netherlands	15,148
Germany	9,936
Canada	7,327

Source: Bureau of Economic Analysis

Top European Export Markets, 2003

Country	Exports ($ Millions)
UK	4,360
Germany	3,560
Netherlands	3,412
France	1,915
Belgium	1,425

Source: Office of Trade and Economic Analysis

Top Ten Exports to Europe ($ Millions)

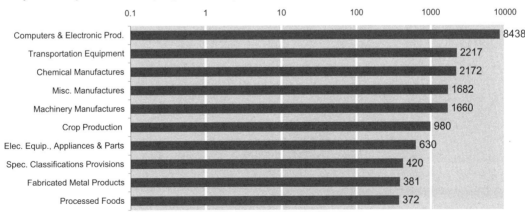

	$ Millions
Computers & Electronic Prod.	8438
Transportation Equipment	2217
Chemical Manufactures	2172
Misc. Manufactures	1682
Machinery Manufactures	1660
Crop Production	980
Elec. Equip., Appliances & Parts	630
Spec. Classifications Provisions	420
Fabricated Metal Products	381
Processed Foods	372

Source: Office of Trade and Economic Analysis

Colorado and Europe
Employment, Investment, and Trade Linkages

Employment

European investment in Colorado supported 52,000 jobs in 2001; more than 60% were in manufacturing.

Investment

Of the $12.9 billion invested in Colorado in 2001, 64%, or $8.2 billion came from Europe.

Trade

In 2003, Europe purchased $1.4 billion worth of goods from Colorado.

Over 60% of the state's exports consist of high-tech goods like computers and electronic products.

Top Sources of FDI within Colorado, 2001

Country	FDI ($ Millions)
United Kingdom	4,506
Canada	1,826
Japan	1,403
Netherlands	980
Switzerland	899

Source: Bureau of Economic Analysis

Top European Export Markets, 2003

Country	Exports ($ Millions)
Germany	282
France	267
Netherlands	246
UK	237
Switzerland	81

Source: Office of Trade and Economic Analysis

Top Ten Exports to Europe ($ Millions)

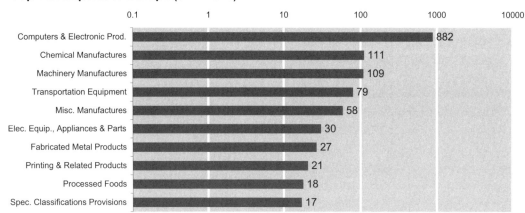

	$ Millions
Computers & Electronic Prod.	882
Chemical Manufactures	111
Machinery Manufactures	109
Transportation Equipment	79
Misc. Manufactures	58
Elec. Equip., Appliances & Parts	30
Fabricated Metal Products	27
Printing & Related Products	21
Processed Foods	18
Spec. Classifications Provisions	17

Source: Office of Trade and Economic Analysis

Connecticut and Europe
Employment, Investment, and Trade Linkages

Employment

European investment in Connecticut supported 86,000 jobs in 2001.

Investment

Of the $14.4 billion invested in Connecticut in 2001, 64%, or $9.2 billion came from Europe.

Trade

In 2003, Europe purchased $3.5 billion worth of goods from Connecticut.

Exports are heavily skewed towards transportation equipment.

Top Sources of FDI within Connecticut, 2001

Country	FDI ($ Millions)
Germany	2,916
United Kingdom	2,405
Netherlands	1,713
Canada	884
France	876

Source: Bureau of Economic Analysis

Top European Export Markets, 2003

Country	Exports ($ Millions)
France	1,096
Germany	760
UK	513
Netherlands	199
Belgium	163

Source: Office of Trade and Economic Analysis

Top Ten Exports to Europe ($ Millions)

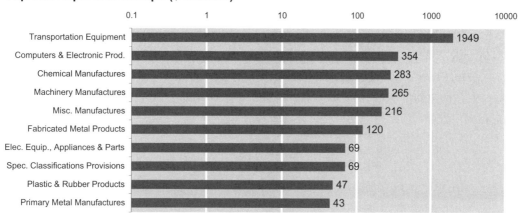

	$ Millions
Transportation Equipment	1949
Computers & Electronic Prod.	354
Chemical Manufactures	283
Machinery Manufactures	265
Misc. Manufactures	216
Fabricated Metal Products	120
Elec. Equip., Appliances & Parts	69
Spec. Classifications Provisions	69
Plastic & Rubber Products	47
Primary Metal Manufactures	43

Source: Office of Trade and Economic Analysis

Delaware and Europe
Employment, Investment, and Trade Linkages

Employment

European investment in Delaware supported 19,000 jobs in 2001; more than 60% of these were in manufacturing.

Investment

Of the $8.2 billion invested in Delaware in 2001, 61%, or $5 billion came from Europe.

Trade

In 2003, Europe purchased $524 million worth of goods from Delaware.

Chemical exports are the primary export to Europe.

Top Sources of FDI within Delaware, 2001

Country	FDI ($ Millions)
United Kingdom	2,712
Germany	1,018
France	623
Switzerland	336
Mexico	266

Source: Bureau of Economic Analysis

Top European Export Markets, 2003

Country	Exports ($ Millions)
Germany	149
UK	106
Netherlands	60
Belgium	58
Switzerland	47

Source: Office of Trade and Economic Analysis

Top Ten Exports to Europe ($ Millions)

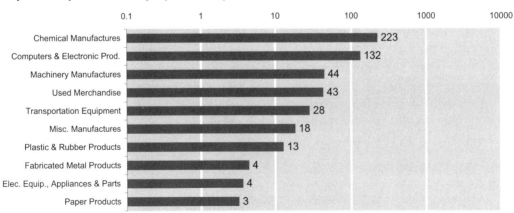

Source: Office of Trade and Economic Analysis

Florida and Europe
Employment, Investment, and Trade Linkages

Employment

European investment in Florida supported 180,000 jobs in 2001.

Investment

Of the $35.8 billion invested in Florida in 2001, 46%, or $16.4 billion came from Europe.

Trade

In 2003, Europe purchased $3.8 billion worth of goods from Florida.

The state exports a great deal of agricultural goods to the EU, although computers and transportation equipment account for over 50% of total exports.

Top Sources of FDI within Florida, 2001

Country	FDI ($ Millions)
Canada	5,488
United Kingdom	5,176
Netherlands	3,545
Germany	3,297
Japan	3,107

Source: Bureau of Economic Analysis

Top European Export Markets, 2003

Country	Exports ($ Millions)
UK	762
Spain	546
Germany	499
Netherlands	407
France	397

Source: Office of Trade and Economic Analysis

Top Ten Exports to Europe ($ Millions)

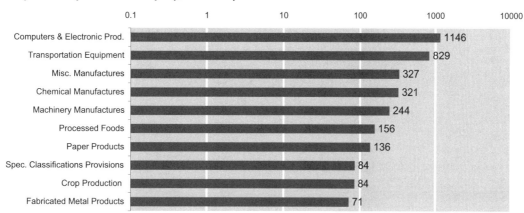

Source: Office of Trade and Economic Analysis

Georgia and Europe
Employment, Investment, and Trade Linkages

Employment

European investment in Georgia supported 161,000 jobs in 2001; just over one-quarter of these were in manufacturing.

Investment

Of the $31.1 billion invested in Georgia in 2001, 58%, or $18 billion came from Europe.

Trade

In 2003, Europe purchased $4.4 billion worth of goods from Georgia.

Exports are broadly diversified among such exports as chemicals, transportation equipment and computers.

Top Sources of FDI within Georgia, 2001

Country	FDI ($ Millions)
United Kingdom	6,590
Japan	5,373
Germany	3,739
France	2,821
Canada	2,661

Source: Bureau of Economic Analysis

Top European Export Markets, 2003

Country	Exports ($ Millions)
UK	1,036
Netherlands	893
Germany	609
France	358
Italy	316

Source: Office of Trade and Economic Analysis

Top Ten Exports to Europe ($ Millions)

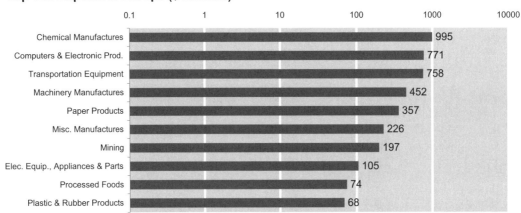

Source: Office of Trade and Economic Analysis

Hawaii and Europe
Employment, Investment, and Trade Linkages

Employment

European investment in Hawaii supported 8,000 jobs in 2001.

Investment

Of the $10 billion invested in Hawaii in 2001, 10%, or $1 billion came from Europe.

Trade

In 2003, Europe purchased $30 million worth of goods from Hawaii.

Exports reflect a range of goods, from transportation equipment to chemicals.

Top Sources of FDI within Hawaii, 2001

Country	FDI ($ Millions)
Japan	8,178
France	344
United Kingdom	292
Germany	251
Netherlands	67

Source: Bureau of Economic Analysis

Top European Export Markets, 2003

Country	Exports ($ Millions)
Germany	11
France	9
UK	5
Netherlands	2
Italy	1

Source: Office of Trade and Economic Analysis

Top Ten Exports to Europe ($ Millions)

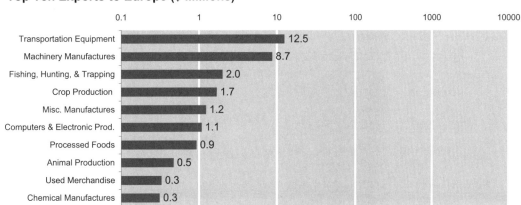

Source: Office of Trade and Economic Analysis

Idaho and Europe
Employment, Investment, and Trade Linkages

Employment

European investment in Idaho supported 7,000 jobs in 2001.

Investment

Of the $2.7 billion invested in Idaho in 2001, 52%, or $1.4 billion came from Europe.

Trade

In 2003, Europe purchased $484 million worth of goods from Idaho.

Exports are concentrated in computers and electronic products.

Top Sources of FDI within Idaho, 2001

Country	FDI ($ Millions)
United Kingdom	853
Canada	486
Japan	381
France	331
Mexico	141

Source: Bureau of Economic Analysis

Top European Export Markets, 2003

Country	Exports ($ Millions)
UK	350
Germany	30
Netherlands	28
Italy	27
France	14

Source: Office of Trade and Economic Analysis

Top Ten Exports to Europe ($ Millions)

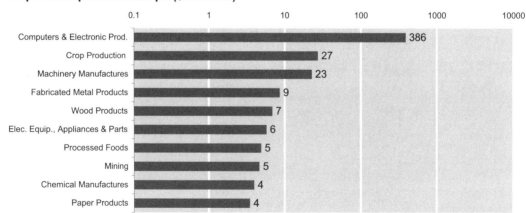

Source: Office of Trade and Economic Analysis

Indiana and Europe
Employment, Investment, and Trade Linkages

Employment

European investment in Indiana supported 101,000 jobs in 2001; roughly two-thirds of these were in manufacturing.

Investment

Of the $29.3 billion invested in Indiana in 2001, 63%, or $18.3 billion came from Europe.

Trade

In 2003, Europe purchased $4 billion worth of goods from Indiana.

Exports are heavily skewed toward chemicals.

Top Sources of FDI within Indiana, 2001

Country	FDI ($ Millions)
Japan	8,433
United Kingdom	7,697
Germany	7,182
France	1,666
Canada	991

Source: Bureau of Economic Analysis

Top European Export Markets, 2003

Country	Exports ($ Millions)
UK	1,209
France	922
Germany	552
Netherlands	289
Spain	188

Source: Office of Trade and Economic Analysis

Top Ten Exports to Europe ($ Millions)

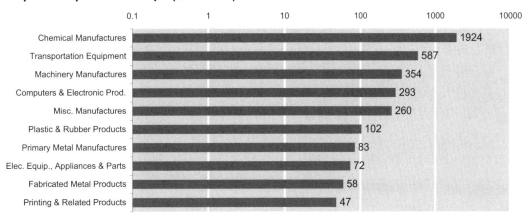

Source: Office of Trade and Economic Analysis

Illinois and Europe
Employment, Investment, and Trade Linkages

Employment

European investment in Illinois supported 195,000 jobs in 2001; 30% of the workforce was employed in manufacturing activities.

Investment

Of the $49.6 billion invested in Illinois in 2001, 55%, or $27.1 billion came from Europe.

Trade

In 2003, Europe purchased $6.3 billion worth of goods from Illinois.

Machinery is a key export, followed by computers and chemicals.

Top Sources of FDI within Illinois, 2001

Country	FDI ($ Millions)
United Kingdom	11,220
Japan	11,048
Germany	6,097
Canada	5,468
Netherlands	3,746

Source: Bureau of Economic Analysis

Top European Export Markets, 2003

Country	Exports ($ Millions)
UK	1,544
Germany	1,209
Belgium	825
Netherlands	786
France	679

Source: Office of Trade and Economic Analysis

Top Ten Exports to Europe ($ Millions)

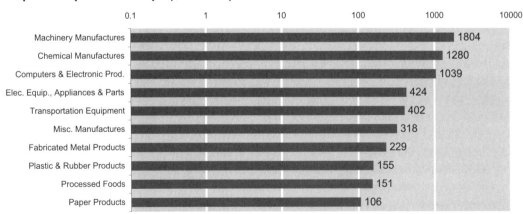

Source: Office of Trade and Economic Analysis

Iowa and Europe
Employment, Investment, and Trade Linkages

Employment

European investment in Iowa supported 28,000 jobs in 2001.

Investment

Of the $7.4 billion invested in Iowa in 2001, 50%, or $3.7 billion came from Europe.

Trade

In 2003, Europe purchased $1.1 billion worth of goods from Iowa.

The state's exports to the European Union are diverse, ranging from machinery to processed food.

Top Sources of FDI within Iowa, 2001

Country	FDI ($ Millions)
Canada	1,756
Japan	938
United Kingdom	879
France	874
Germany	639

Source: Bureau of Economic Analysis

Top European Export Markets, 2003

Country	Exports ($ Millions)
Germany	214
UK	211
France	204
Netherlands	90
Belgium	70

Source: Office of Trade and Economic Analysis

Top Ten Exports to Europe ($ Millions)

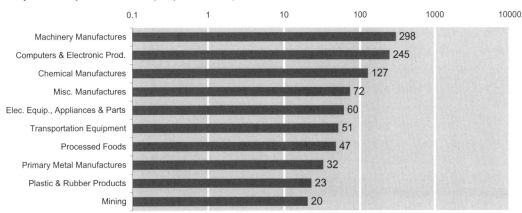

Machinery Manufactures	298
Computers & Electronic Prod.	245
Chemical Manufactures	127
Misc. Manufactures	72
Elec. Equip., Appliances & Parts	60
Transportation Equipment	51
Processed Foods	47
Primary Metal Manufactures	32
Plastic & Rubber Products	23
Mining	20

Source: Office of Trade and Economic Analysis

Kansas and Europe
Employment, Investment, and Trade Linkages

Employment

European investment in Kansas supported 27,000 jobs in 2001.

Investment

Of the $5.3 billion invested in Kansas in 2001, 72%, or $3.8 billion came from Europe.

Trade

In 2003, Europe purchased $878 million worth of goods from Kansas.

Roughly half of the state's exports consist of transportation equipment.

Top Sources of FDI within Kansas, 2001

Country	FDI ($ Millions)
United Kingdom	1,387
France	786
Germany	692
Canada	588
Netherlands	562

Source: Bureau of Economic Analysis

Top European Export Markets, 2003

Country	Exports ($ Millions)
UK	249
Germany	180
France	121
Italy	58
Belgium	44

Source: Office of Trade and Economic Analysis

Top Ten Exports to Europe ($ Millions)

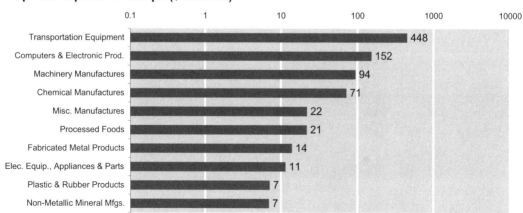

Source: Office of Trade and Economic Analysis

Kentucky and Europe
Employment, Investment, and Trade Linkages

Employment

European investment in Kentucky supported 46,000 jobs in 2001; nearly half in manufacturing.

Investment

Of the $22.9 billion invested in Kentucky in 2001, 41%, or $9.3 billion came from Europe.

Trade

In 2003, Europe purchased $3.3 billion worth of goods from Kentucky.

Reflecting the large presence of automobile manufacturers in the state, Kentucky's top export to the European Union is transportation equipment.

Top Sources of FDI within Kentucky, 2001

Country	FDI ($ Millions)
Japan	8,967
United Kingdom	4,943
Germany	2,275
Canada	2,058
France	792

Source: Bureau of Economic Analysis

Top European Export Markets, 2003

Country	Exports ($ Millions)
UK	850
France	740
Netherlands	396
Germany	355
Belgium	237

Source: Office of Trade and Economic Analysis

Top Ten Exports to Europe ($ Millions)

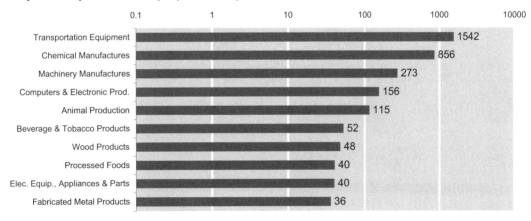

Source: Office of Trade and Economic Analysis

Louisiana and Europe
Employment, Investment, and Trade Linkages

Employment

European investment in Louisiana supported 34,000 jobs in 2001.

Investment

Of the $33 billion invested in Louisiana in 2001, 56%, or $18.5 billion came from Europe.

Trade

In 2003, Europe purchased $3.2 billion worth of goods from Louisiana.

The state's exports consist of a mix of manufacturing goods and agricultural products.

Top Sources of FDI within Louisiana, 2001

Country	FDI ($ Millions)
Netherlands	6,697
United Kingdom	5,040
Germany	2,834
France	2,823
Canada	1,745

Source: Bureau of Economic Analysis

Top European Export Markets, 2003

Country	Exports ($ Millions)
Netherlands	500
Spain	497
Belgium	451
Germany	346
UK	297

Source: Office of Trade and Economic Analysis

Top Ten Exports to Europe ($ Millions)

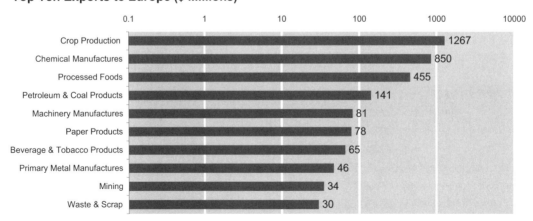

Source: Office of Trade and Economic Analysis

Maine and Europe
Employment, Investment, and Trade Linkages

Employment

European investment in Maine supported 12,000 jobs in 2001.

Investment

Of the $5.4 billion invested in Maine in 2001, 22%, or $1.2 billion came from Europe.

Trade

In 2003, Europe purchased $371 million worth of goods from Maine.

Paper and transportation equipment are the state's top exports to Europe.

Top Sources of FDI within Maine, 2001

Country	FDI ($ Millions)
Canada	1,315
United Kingdom	661
France	172
Japan	162
Germany	149

Source: Bureau of Economic Analysis

Top European Export Markets, 2003

Country	Exports ($ Millions)
UK	133
Belgium	53
Netherlands	45
Italy	40
Germany	17

Source: Office of Trade and Economic Analysis

Top Ten Exports to Europe ($ Millions)

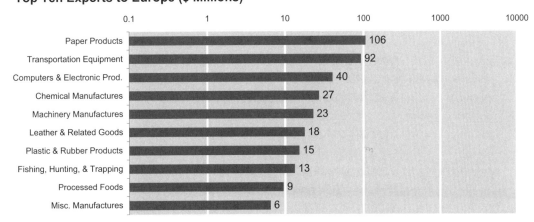

Source: Office of Trade and Economic Analysis

Maryland and Europe
Employment, Investment, and Trade Linkages

Employment

European investment in Maryland supported 88,000 jobs in 2001; the bulk of employment was in services.

Investment

Of the $13 billion invested in Maryland in 2001, 67%, or $8.7 billion came from Europe.

Trade

In 2003, Europe purchased $1.4 billion worth of goods from Maryland.

Top exports are transportation equipment, computers and chemicals.

Top Sources of FDI within Maryland, 2001

Country	FDI ($ Millions)
United Kingdom	3,549
Netherlands	1,621
France	1,332
Germany	1,194
Japan	1,142

Source: Bureau of Economic Analysis

Top European Export Markets, 2003

Country	Exports ($ Millions)
UK	324
Belgium	214
Netherlands	190
Germany	183
France	149

Source: Office of Trade and Economic Analysis

Top Ten Exports to Europe ($ Millions)

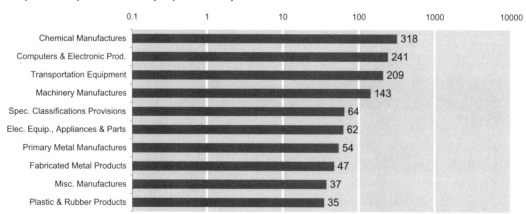

Source: Office of Trade and Economic Analysis

Massachusetts and Europe
Employment, Investment, and Trade Linkages

Employment

European investment in Massachusetts supported 155,000 jobs in 2001; one-in-five workers toiled in manufacturing.

Investment

Of the $25.7 billion invested in Massachusetts in 2001, 71%, or $18.3 billion came from Europe.

Trade

In 2003, Europe purchased $7.3 billion worth of goods from Massachusetts.

Nearly a third of exports to Europe consist of computers and electronic products.

Top Sources of FDI within Massachusetts, 2001

Country	FDI ($ Millions)
United Kingdom	8,886
France	3,745
Netherlands	2,605
Canada	2,396
Germany	1,999

Source: Bureau of Economic Analysis

Top European Export Markets, 2003

Country	Exports ($ Millions)
Netherlands	1,759
Germany	1,599
UK	1,430
France	619
Ireland	382

Source: Office of Trade and Economic Analysis

Top Ten Exports to Europe ($ Millions)

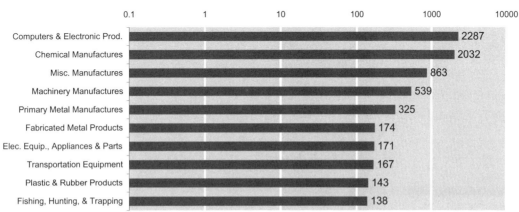

Source: Office of Trade and Economic Analysis

Michigan and Europe
Employment, Investment, and Trade Linkages

Employment

European investment in Michigan supported 172,000 jobs in 2001; more than half (54%) were related to manufacturing.

Investment

Of the $53.8 billion invested in Michigan in 2001, 73%, or $39.2 billion came from Europe.

Trade

In 2003, Europe purchased $4 billion worth of goods from Michigan.

Not surprisingly, transportation equipment is Michigan's top export to Europe.

Top Sources of FDI within Michigan, 2001

Country	FDI ($ Millions)
Germany	31,065
Japan	8,229
Canada	4,295
United Kingdom	3,591
France	1,608

Source: Bureau of Economic Analysis

Top European Export Markets, 2003

Country	Exports ($ Millions)
Germany	973
UK	706
Belgium	424
France	380
Austria	378

Source: Office of Trade and Economic Analysis

Top Ten Exports to Europe ($ Millions)

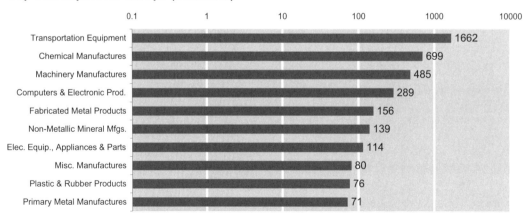

Source: Office of Trade and Economic Analysis

Minnesota and Europe
Employment, Investment, and Trade Linkages

Employment

European investment in Minnesota supported 59,000 jobs in 2001; roughly 30% were in manufacturing activities.

Investment

Of the $13.2 billion invested in Minnesota in 2001, 41%, or $5.4 billion came from Europe.

Trade

In 2003, Europe purchased $4.2 billion worth of goods from Minnesota.

Miscellaneous manufactures rank as the top export to Europe.

Top Sources of FDI within Minnesota, 2001

Country	FDI ($ Millions)
Canada	4,291
United Kingdom	1,800
Germany	1,475
Japan	952
Netherlands	800

Source: Bureau of Economic Analysis

Top European Export Markets, 2003

Country	Exports ($ Millions)
Ireland	1,204
UK	579
Netherlands	575
Germany	436
France	328

Source: Office of Trade and Economic Analysis

Top Ten Exports to Europe ($ Millions)

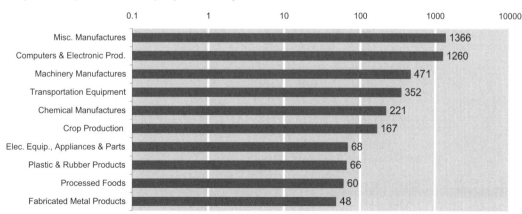

Source: Office of Trade and Economic Analysis

Mississippi and Europe
Employment, Investment, and Trade Linkages

Employment

European investment in Mississippi supported 15,000 jobs in 2001; 40.3% were in manufacturing activities.

Investment

Of the $4.9 billion invested in Mississippi in 2001, 47%, or $2.3 billion came from Europe.

Trade

In 2003, Europe purchased $677 million worth of goods from Mississippi.

Chemicals and paper rank as the top exports to Europe.

Top Sources of FDI within Mississippi, 2001

Country	FDI ($ Millions)
Canada	1,344
United Kingdom	881
France	559
Germany	340
Japan	323

Source: Bureau of Economic Analysis

Top European Export Markets, 2003

Country	Exports ($ Millions)
Belgium	208
UK	91
Germany	75
Italy	60
Spain	40

Source: Office of Trade and Economic Analysis

Top Ten Exports to Europe ($ Millions)

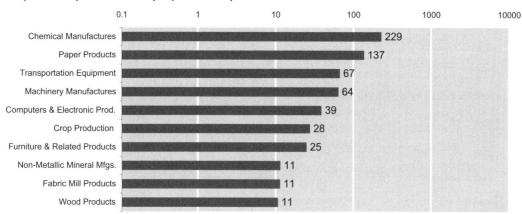

Source: Office of Trade and Economic Analysis

Missouri and Europe
Employment, Investment, and Trade Linkages

Employment

European investment in Missouri supported 75,000 jobs in 2001; 45% were in manufacturing.

Investment

Of the $15.1 billion invested in Missouri in 2001, 67%, or $10.1 billion came from Europe.

Trade

In 2003, Europe purchased $1.4 billion worth of goods from Missouri.

Top exports include chemicals, machinery and computers.

Top Sources of FDI within Missouri, 2001

Country	FDI ($ Millions)
Germany	3,845
United Kingdom	2,142
France	1,971
Canada	1,617
Japan	1,281

Source: Bureau of Economic Analysis

Top Sources of FDI within Missouri, 2001

Country	FDI ($ Millions)
Germany	3,845
United Kingdom	2,142
France	1,971
Canada	1,617
Japan	1,281

Source: Office of Trade and Economic Analysis

Top Ten Exports to Europe ($ Millions)

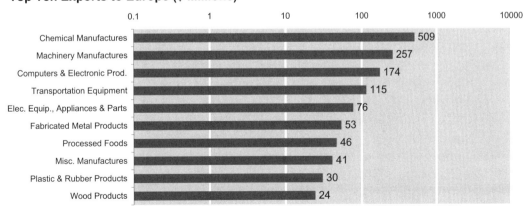

Export	$ Millions
Chemical Manufactures	509
Machinery Manufactures	257
Computers & Electronic Prod.	174
Transportation Equipment	115
Elec. Equip., Appliances & Parts	76
Fabricated Metal Products	53
Processed Foods	46
Misc. Manufactures	41
Plastic & Rubber Products	30
Wood Products	24

Source: Office of Trade and Economic Analysis

Montana and Europe
Employment, Investment, and Trade Linkages

Employment

European investment in Montana supported 5,000 jobs in 2001.

Investment

Of the $3.1 billion invested in Montana in 2001, 23%, or $0.7 billion came from Europe.

Trade

In 2003, Europe purchased $45 million worth of goods from Montana.

Exports are relatively small and skewed towards machinery goods.

Top Sources of FDI within Montana, 2001

Country	FDI ($ Millions)
Canada	1,227
United Kingdom	606
Japan	458
France	43
Germany	26

Source: Bureau of Economic Analysis

Top European Export Markets, 2003

Country	Exports ($ Millions)
Netherlands	12
UK	9
Germany	7
France	7
Belgium	3

Source: Office of Trade and Economic Analysis

Top Ten Exports to Europe ($ Millions)

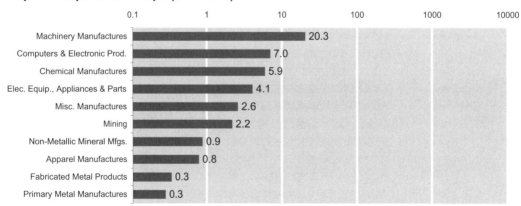

Source: Office of Trade and Economic Analysis

Nebraska and Europe
Employment, Investment, and Trade Linkages

Employment

European investment in Nebraska supported 13,000 jobs in 2001.

Investment

Of the $2.5 billion invested in Nebraska in 2001, 44%, or $1.1 billion came from Europe.

Trade

In 2003, Europe purchased $388 million worth of goods from Nebraska.

Top exports are chemicals and computers.

Top Sources of FDI within Nebraska, 2001

Country	FDI ($ Millions)
Japan	627
Canada	395
Switzerland	305
Germany	201
United Kingdom	195

Source: Bureau of Economic Analysis

Top European Export Markets, 2003

Country	Exports ($ Millions)
Netherlands	99
Italy	61
Germany	45
UK	45
Belgium	37

Source: Office of Trade and Economic Analysis

Top Ten Exports to Europe ($ Millions)

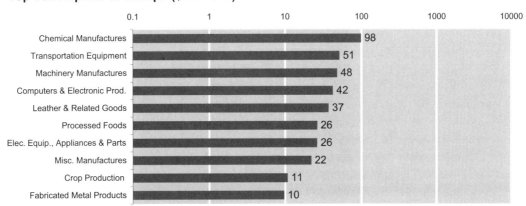

Export	$ Millions
Chemical Manufactures	98
Transportation Equipment	51
Machinery Manufactures	48
Computers & Electronic Prod.	42
Leather & Related Goods	37
Processed Foods	26
Elec. Equip., Appliances & Parts	26
Misc. Manufactures	22
Crop Production	11
Fabricated Metal Products	10

Source: Office of Trade and Economic Analysis

Nevada and Europe
Employment, Investment, and Trade Linkages

Employment

European investment in Nevada supported 17,000 jobs in 2001.

Investment

Of the $8.3 billion invested in Nevada in 2001, 25%, or $2.1 billion came from Europe.

Trade

In 2003, Europe purchased $949 million worth of goods from Nevada.

Manufactured goods, including computers, are the top exports to the EU.

Top Sources of FDI within Nevada, 2001

Country	FDI ($ Millions)
Canada	4,352
United Kingdom	1,179
Japan	1,045
Australia	424
Germany	236

Source: Bureau of Economic Analysis

Top European Export Markets, 2003

Country	Exports ($ Millions)
Switzerland	658
UK	79
Germany	52
France	37
Belgium	32

Source: Office of Trade and Economic Analysis

Top Ten Exports to Europe ($ Millions)

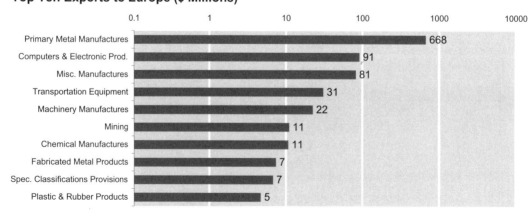

Source: Office of Trade and Economic Analysis

New Hampshire and Europe
Employment, Investment, and Trade Linkages

Employment

European investment in New Hampshire supported 27,000 jobs in 2001; half of these jobs were in manufacturing.

Investment

Of the $5.4 billion invested in New Hampshire in 2001, 70%, or $3.8 billion came from Europe.

Trade

In 2003, Europe purchased $681 million worth of goods from New Hampshire.

Computers and machinery are the top exports to Europe.

Top Sources of FDI within New Hampshire, 2001

Country	FDI ($ Millions)
United Kingdom	2,550
Germany	705
Japan	473
Canada	330
France	234

Source: Bureau of Economic Analysis

Top European Export Markets, 2003

Country	Exports ($ Millions)
UK	160
Netherlands	128
Germany	109
Italy	54
Ireland	53

Source: Office of Trade and Economic Analysis

Top Ten Exports to Europe ($ Millions)

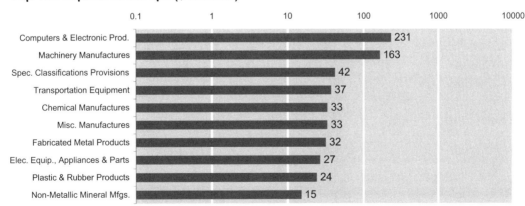

Computers & Electronic Prod.	231
Machinery Manufactures	163
Spec. Classifications Provisions	42
Transportation Equipment	37
Chemical Manufactures	33
Misc. Manufactures	33
Fabricated Metal Products	32
Elec. Equip., Appliances & Parts	27
Plastic & Rubber Products	24
Non-Metallic Mineral Mfgs.	15

Source: Office of Trade and Economic Analysis

New Jersey and Europe
Employment, Investment, and Trade Linkages

Employment

European investment in New Jersey supported 194,000 jobs in 2001; one-quarter of the workforce was involved in manufacturing.

Investment

Of the $38.6 billion invested in New Jersey in 2001, 65%, or $25.2 billion came from Europe.

Trade

In 2003, Europe purchased $5.8 billion worth of goods from New Jersey.

Exports consist of high-end goods, like chemicals (pharmaceuticals) and computers.

Top Sources of FDI within New Jersey, 2001

Country	FDI ($ Millions)
United Kingdom	6,188
Japan	5,906
Switzerland	5,584
Germany	4,993
France	4,163

Source: Bureau of Economic Analysis

Top European Export Markets, 2003

Country	Exports ($ Millions)
UK	1,407
Germany	1,022
France	602
Belgium	557
Italy	470

Source: Office of Trade and Economic Analysis

Top Ten Exports to Europe ($ Millions)

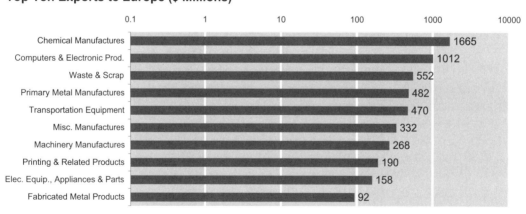

Source: Office of Trade and Economic Analysis

New Mexico and Europe
Employment, Investment, and Trade Linkages

Employment

European investment in New Mexico supported 8,000 jobs in 2001; one-quarter were in manufacturing activities.

Investment

Of the $5.6 billion invested in New Mexico in 2001, 25%, or $1.4 billion came from Europe.

Trade

In 2003, Europe purchased $177 million worth of goods from New Mexico.

Exports are relatively small and are skewed toward computers and related goods.

Top Sources of FDI within New Mexico, 2001

Country	FDI ($ Millions)
Japan	1,204
Netherlands	1,073
Australia	221
Germany	147
France	130

Source: Bureau of Economic Analysis

Top European Export Markets, 2003

Country	Exports ($ Millions)
Ireland	75
Germany	22
UK	20
France	18
Belgium	12

Source: Office of Trade and Economic Analysis

Top Ten Exports to Europe ($ Millions)

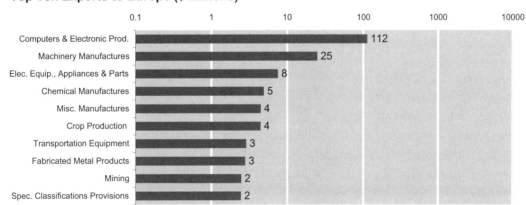

Source: Office of Trade and Economic Analysis

New York and Europe
Employment, Investment, and Trade Linkages

Employment

European investment in New York supported 337,000 jobs in 2001; most of the jobs (84%) were in services.

Investment

Of the $71.2 billion invested in New York in 2001, 55%, or $39 billion came from Europe.

Trade

In 2003, Europe purchased $13.1 billion worth of goods from New York.

Exports run the gamut—from computers to plastics.

Top Sources of FDI within New York, 2001

Country	FDI ($ Millions)
Japan	11,523
United Kingdom	10,855
Germany	9,904
Canada	8,932
France	7,941

Source: Bureau of Economic Analysis

Top European Export Markets, 2003

Country	Exports ($ Millions)
UK	3,283
Switzerland	1,770
Germany	1,723
Belgium	1,669
France	1,261

Source: Office of Trade and Economic Analysis

Top Ten Exports to Europe ($ Millions)

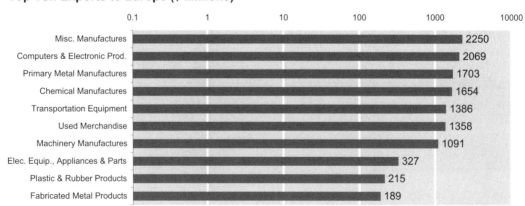

Misc. Manufactures	2250
Computers & Electronic Prod.	2069
Primary Metal Manufactures	1703
Chemical Manufactures	1654
Transportation Equipment	1386
Used Merchandise	1358
Machinery Manufactures	1091
Elec. Equip., Appliances & Parts	327
Plastic & Rubber Products	215
Fabricated Metal Products	189

Source: Office of Trade and Economic Analysis

North Carolina and Europe
Employment, Investment, and Trade Linkages

Employment

European investment in North Carolina supported 148,000 jobs in 2001; 44% of jobs were in manufacturing.

Investment

Of the $23.1 billion invested in North Carolina in 2001, 63%, or $14.6 billion came from Europe.

Trade

In 2003, Europe purchased $3.3 billion worth of goods from North Carolina.

Exports include such high-tech goods as computers, chemicals and machinery.

Top Sources of FDI within North Carolina, 2001

Country	FDI ($ Millions)
United Kingdom	4,200
Germany	3,971
Japan	3,113
Canada	2,293
Netherlands	1,845

Source: Bureau of Economic Analysis

Top European Export Markets, 2003

Country	Exports ($ Millions)
UK	687
Germany	611
France	360
Netherlands	329
Belgium	300

Source: Office of Trade and Economic Analysis

Top Ten Exports to Europe ($ Millions)

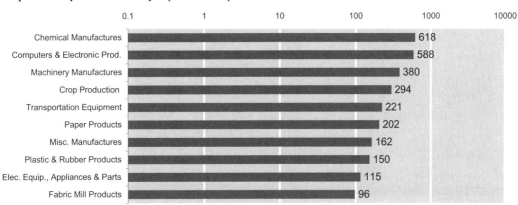

Source: Office of Trade and Economic Analysis

North Dakota and Europe
Employment, Investment, and Trade Linkages

Employment

European investment in North Dakota supported 4,000 jobs in 2001.

Investment

Of the $1.8 billion invested in North Dakota in 2001, 28%, or $0.5 billion came from Europe.

Trade

In 2003, Europe purchased $196 million worth of goods from North Dakota.

By a large percentage, the state's top export consists of machinery.

Top Sources of FDI within North Dakota, 2001

Country	FDI ($ Millions)
Canada	805
United Kingdom	285
Germany	166
Netherlands	47
France	29

Source: Bureau of Economic Analysis

Top European Export Markets, 2003

Country	Exports ($ Millions)
Belgium	101
Italy	21
Spain	18
UK	14
Germany	13

Source: Office of Trade and Economic Analysis

Top Ten Exports to Europe ($ Millions)

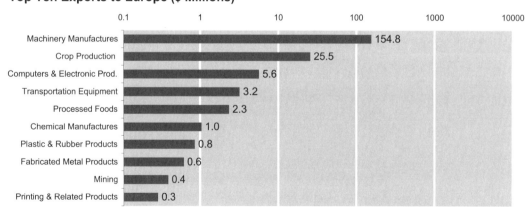

Source: Office of Trade and Economic Analysis

Ohio and Europe
Employment, Investment, and Trade Linkages

Employment

European investment in Ohio supported 149,000 jobs in 2001; four-in-ten workers were employed in manufacturing activities.

Investment

Of the $35.3 billion invested in Ohio in 2001, 55%, or $19.4 billion came from Europe.

Trade

In 2003, Europe purchased $5 billion worth of goods from Ohio.

Transportation equipment and machinery are the state's top exports to Europe.

Top Sources of FDI within Ohio, 2001

Country	FDI ($ Millions)
Japan	11,241
Germany	6,732
United Kingdom	6,152
France	2,324
Netherlands	2,213

Source: Bureau of Economic Analysis

Top European Export Markets, 2003

Country	Exports ($ Millions)
UK	1,242
France	768
Germany	727
Netherlands	512
Belgium	449

Source: Office of Trade and Economic Analysis

Top Ten Exports to Europe ($ Billions)

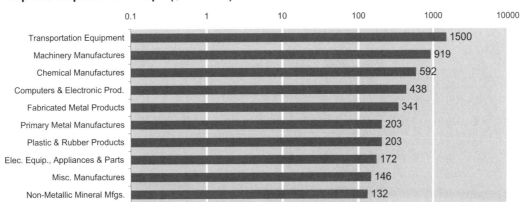

Transportation Equipment	1500
Machinery Manufactures	919
Chemical Manufactures	592
Computers & Electronic Prod.	438
Fabricated Metal Products	341
Primary Metal Manufactures	203
Plastic & Rubber Products	203
Elec. Equip., Appliances & Parts	172
Misc. Manufactures	146
Non-Metallic Mineral Mfgs.	132

Source: Office of Trade and Economic Analysis

Oklahoma and Europe
Employment, Investment, and Trade Linkages

Employment

European investment in Oklahoma supported 25,000 jobs in 2001; one-third of workers were in manufacturing activities.

Investment

Of the $7.9 billion invested in Oklahoma in 2001, 66%, or $5.2 billion came from Europe.

Trade

In 2003, Europe purchased $358 million worth of goods from Oklahoma.

Top exports include machinery, transportation equipment and computers.

Top Sources of FDI within Oklahoma, 2001

Country	FDI ($ Millions)
United Kingdom	2,633
Germany	884
Japan	816
Netherlands	662
France	641

Source: Bureau of Economic Analysis

Top European Export Markets, 2003

Country	Exports ($ Millions)
UK	79
Germany	54
France	50
Netherlands	44
Belgium	37

Source: Office of Trade and Economic Analysis

Top Ten Exports to Europe ($ Millions)

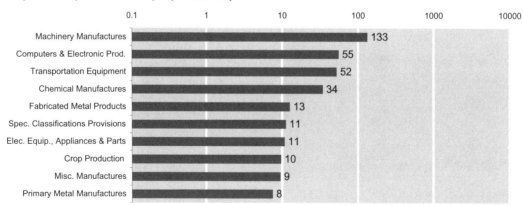

Source: Office of Trade and Economic Analysis

Oregon and Europe
Employment, Investment, and Trade Linkages

Employment

European investment in Oregon supported 31,000 jobs in 2001; one-in-five of these jobs was in manufacturing activities.

Investment

Of the $12 billion invested in Oregon in 2001, 48%, or $5.7 billion came from Europe.

Trade

In 2003, Europe purchased $1.6 billion worth of goods from Oregon.

Roughly half of Oregon's exports to Europe consist of computers and related products.

Top Sources of FDI within Oregon, 2001

Country	FDI ($ Millions)
United Kingdom	3,732
Japan	3,660
Germany	991
France	556
Canada	445

Source: Bureau of Economic Analysis

Top European Export Markets, 2003

Country	Exports ($ Millions)
Germany	322
UK	209
France	195
Ireland	176
Netherlands	175

Source: Office of Trade and Economic Analysis

Top Ten Exports to Europe ($ Millions)

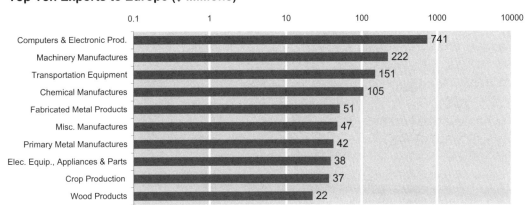

Source: Office of Trade and Economic Analysis

Pennsylvania and Europe
Employment, Investment, and Trade Linkages

Employment

European investment in Pennsylvania supported 191,000 jobs in 2001; one-third of total workers were involved in manufacturing.

Investment

Of the $34.2 billion invested in Pennsylvania in 2001, 72%, or $24.6 billion came from Europe.

Trade

In 2003, Europe purchased $3.9 billion worth of goods from Pennsylvania.

Exports are relatively diverse, ranging from chemicals to transportation equipment.

Top Sources of FDI within Pennsylvania, 2001

Country	FDI ($ Millions)
United Kingdom	7,872
Germany	7,090
France	4,830
Japan	2,895
Netherlands	2,069

Source: Bureau of Economic Analysis

Top European Export Markets, 2003

Country	Exports ($ Millions)
UK	846
Germany	751
Netherlands	477
France	372
Belgium	372

Source: Office of Trade and Economic Analysis

Top Ten Exports to Europe ($ Millions)

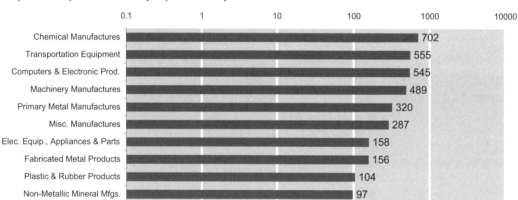

Source: Office of Trade and Economic Analysis

Rhode Island and Europe
Employment, Investment, and Trade Linkages

Employment

European investment in Rhode Island supported 16,000 jobs in 2001; roughly 19% were related to manufacturing.

Investment

Of the $3.9 billion invested in Rhode Island in 2001, 59%, or $2.3 billion came from Europe.

Trade

In 2003, Europe purchased $310 million worth of goods from Rhode Island.

Manufactured goods make up the bulk of exports.

Top Sources of FDI within Rhode Island, 2001

Country	FDI ($ Millions)
United Kingdom	1,497
Japan	692
Canada	590
Germany	284
Netherlands	265

Source: Bureau of Economic Analysis

Top European Export Markets, 2003

Country	Exports ($ Millions)
UK	51
Belgium	51
Germany	41
France	28
Sweden	22

Source: Office of Trade and Economic Analysis

Top Ten Exports to Europe ($ Millions)

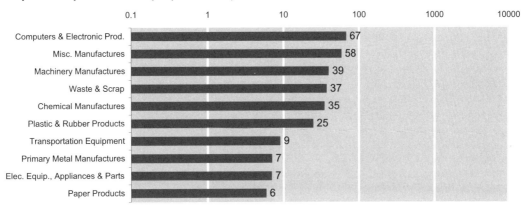

Source: Office of Trade and Economic Analysis

South Carolina and Europe
Employment, Investment, and Trade Linkages

Employment

European investment in South Carolina supported 104,000 jobs in 2001; just over 40% of jobs were in manufacturing.

Investment

Of the $23.2 billion invested in South Carolina in 2001, 68%, or $15.8 billion came from Europe.

Trade

In 2003, Europe purchased $5 billion worth of goods from South Carolina.

Well over half of the state's exports consist of transportation equipment.

Top Sources of FDI within South Carolina, 2001

Country	FDI ($ Millions)
Germany	4,088
Japan	3,731
United Kingdom	3,502
France	3,249
Switzerland	1,750

Source: Bureau of Economic Analysis

Top European Export Markets, 2003

Country	Exports ($ Millions)
Germany	2,703
UK	817
Netherlands	299
Belgium	291
France	275

Source: Office of Trade and Economic Analysis

Top Ten Exports to Europe ($ Millions)

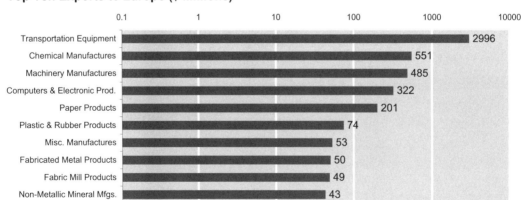

Source: Office of Trade and Economic Analysis

South Dakota and Europe
Employment, Investment, and Trade Linkages

Employment

European investment in South Dakota supported 3,000 jobs in 2001.

Investment

Of the $1 billion invested in South Dakota in 2001, 30%, or $0.3 billion came from Europe.

Trade

In 2003, Europe purchased $96 million worth of goods from South Dakota.

Computers are the state's top export to Europe.

Top Sources of FDI within South Dakota, 2001

Country	FDI ($ Millions)
Canada	461
United Kingdom	218
Japan	78
Germany	44
Netherlands	23

Source: Bureau of Economic Analysis

Top European Export Markets, 2003

Country	Exports ($ Millions)
UK	37
Germany	25
Italy	6
Netherlands	5
Spain	4

Source: Office of Trade and Economic Analysis

Top Ten Exports to Europe ($ Millions)

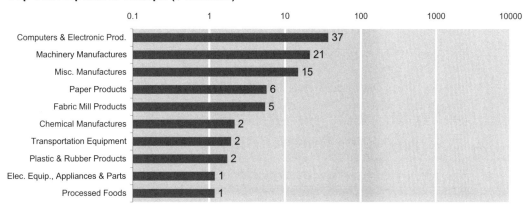

Source: Office of Trade and Economic Analysis

Tennessee and Europe
Employment, Investment, and Trade Linkages

Employment

European investment in Tennessee supported 83,000 jobs in 2001; just over one-third of the jobs were in manufacturing.

Investment

Of the $21.3 billion invested in Tennessee in 2001, 41%, or $8.8 billion came from Europe.

Trade

In 2003, Europe purchased $2.8 billion worth of goods from Tennessee.

Manufactured goods, ranging from chemicals to computers, make up the bulk of exports.

Top Sources of FDI within Tennessee, 2001

Country	FDI ($ Millions)
Japan	7,919
United Kingdom	3,111
Canada	2,037
Germany	1,659
Netherlands	1,117

Source: Bureau of Economic Analysis

Top European Export Markets, 2003

Country	Exports ($ Millions)
UK	646
Germany	440
Netherlands	400
Belgium	353
France	221

Source: Office of Trade and Economic Analysis

Top Ten Exports to Europe ($ Millions)

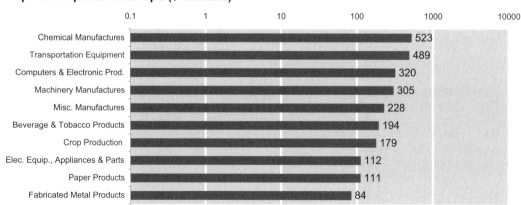

Source: Office of Trade and Economic Analysis

Texas and Europe
Employment, Investment, and Trade Linkages

Employment

European investment in Texas supported 252,000 jobs in 2001; roughly 30% of jobs were in manufacturing.

Investment

Of the $112.1 billion invested in Texas in 2001, 61%, or $68.3 billion came from Europe.

Trade

In 2003, Europe purchased $11.2 billion worth of goods from Texas.

Top exports include chemicals, computers and machinery.

Top Sources of FDI within Texas, 2001

Country	FDI ($ Millions)
United Kingdom	22,654
France	14,219
Germany	13,162
Netherlands	12,448
Japan	8,735

Source: Bureau of Economic Analysis

Top European Export Markets, 2003

Country	Exports ($ Millions)
UK	2,130
Netherlands	1,733
Belgium	1,631
Germany	1,583
France	905

Source: Office of Trade and Economic Analysis

Top Ten Exports to Europe ($ Billions)

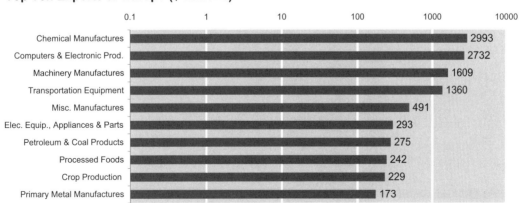

Source: Office of Trade and Economic Analysis

Utah and Europe
Employment, Investment, and Trade Linkages

Employment

European investment in Utah supported 24,000 jobs in 2001, with one-in-five workers involved in manufacturing.

Investment

Of the $13.7 billion invested in Utah in 2001, 81%, or $11.1 billion came from Europe.

Trade

In 2003, Europe purchased $2.1 billion worth of goods from Utah.

Primary metals dominate exports to Europe.

Top Sources of FDI within Utah, 2001

Country	FDI ($ Millions)
United Kingdom	9,876
Canada	1,016
Japan	810
Switzerland	447
Germany	325

Source: Bureau of Economic Analysis

Top European Export Markets, 2003

Country	Exports ($ Millions)
Switzerland	1,105
UK	487
Netherlands	124
Germany	119
Belgium	69

Source: Office of Trade and Economic Analysis

Top Ten Exports to Europe ($ Millions)

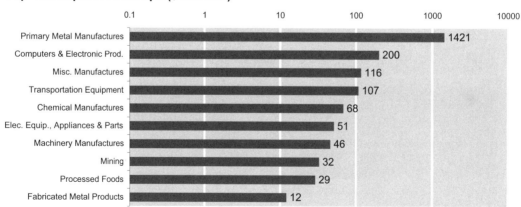

Source: Office of Trade and Economic Analysis

Vermont and Europe
Employment, Investment, and Trade Linkages

Employment

European investment in Vermont supported 7,000 jobs in 2001

Investment

Of the $2.6 billion invested in Vermont in 2001, 81%, or $2.1 billion came from Europe.

Trade

In 2003, Europe purchased $292 million worth of goods from Vermont.

By a wide margin, computers are the top export to Europe.

Top Sources of FDI within Vermont, 2001

Country	FDI ($ Millions)
United Kingdom	1,413
Switzerland	503
France	82
Japan	65
Germany	57

Source: Bureau of Economic Analysis

Top European Export Markets, 2003

Country	Exports ($ Millions)
Ireland	59
Netherlands	56
UK	53
Germany	31
Italy	26

Source: Office of Trade and Economic Analysis

Top Ten Exports to Europe ($ Millions)

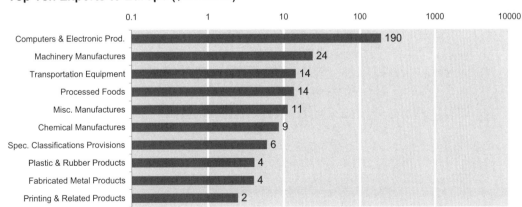

Source: Office of Trade and Economic Analysis

Virginia and Europe
Employment, Investment, and Trade Linkages

Employment

European investment in Virginia supported 104,000 jobs in 2001; roughly one-quarter were involved in manufacturing.

Investment

Of the $21.4 billion invested in Virginia in 2001, 59%, or $12.7 billion came from Europe.

Trade

In 2003, Europe purchased $3.8 billion worth of goods from Virginia.

Top exports include computers, chemicals and transportation equipment.

Top Sources of FDI within Virginia, 2001

Country	FDI ($ Millions)
Germany	5,162
United Kingdom	3,425
Japan	3,405
France	1,394
Canada	1,084

Source: Bureau of Economic Analysis

Top European Export Markets, 2003

Country	Exports ($ Millions)
Germany	990
UK	724
Belgium	474
Netherlands	389
Italy	224

Source: Office of Trade and Economic Analysis

Top Ten Exports to Europe ($ Millions)

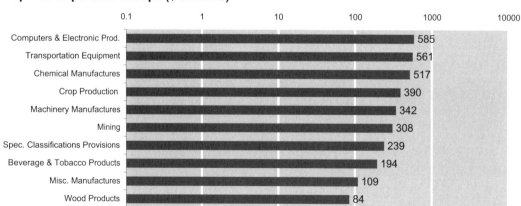

Source: Office of Trade and Economic Analysis

Washington and Europe
Employment, Investment, and Trade Linkages

Employment

European investment in Washington supported 57,000 jobs in 2001; the bulk of jobs were in services (82% of the total).

Investment

Of the $19.2 billion invested in Washington in 2001, 39%, or $7.5 billion came from Europe.

Trade

In 2003, Europe purchased $7.8 billion worth of goods from Washington.

Transportation equipment dominates exports to Europe.

Top Sources of FDI within Washington, 2001

Country	FDI ($ Millions)
Japan	4,861
Canada	3,652
United Kingdom	3,426
Netherlands	1,501
Germany	1,274

Source: Bureau of Economic Analysis

Top European Export Markets, 2003

Country	Exports ($ Millions)
Netherlands	1,739
UK	1,462
Italy	1,101
Ireland	843
Germany	786

Source: Office of Trade and Economic Analysis

Top Ten Exports to Europe ($ Billions)

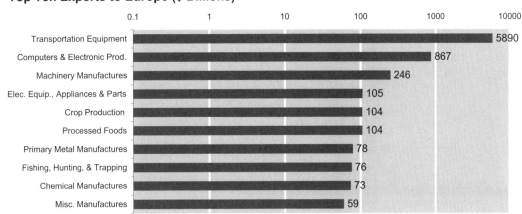

Transportation Equipment	5890
Computers & Electronic Prod.	867
Machinery Manufactures	246
Elec. Equip., Appliances & Parts	105
Crop Production	104
Processed Foods	104
Primary Metal Manufactures	78
Fishing, Hunting, & Trapping	76
Chemical Manufactures	73
Misc. Manufactures	59

Source: Office of Trade and Economic Analysis

West Virginia and Europe
Employment, Investment, and Trade Linkages

Employment

European investment in West Virginia supported 20,000 jobs in 2001; roughly half were in manufacturing.

Investment

Of the $7.1 billion invested in West Virginia in 2001, 76%, or $5.4 billion came from Europe.

Trade

In 2003, Europe purchased $622 million worth of goods from West Virginia.

Chemicals are the state's top export to Europe.

Top Sources of FDI within West Virginia, 2001

Country	FDI ($ Millions)
Germany	2,947
Japan	1,135
France	962
United Kingdom	515
Netherlands	508

Source: Bureau of Economic Analysis

Top European Export Markets, 2003

Country	Exports ($ Millions)
Belgium	236
Netherlands	80
UK	74
Italy	65
Germany	56

Source: Office of Trade and Economic Analysis

Top Ten Exports to Europe ($ Millions)

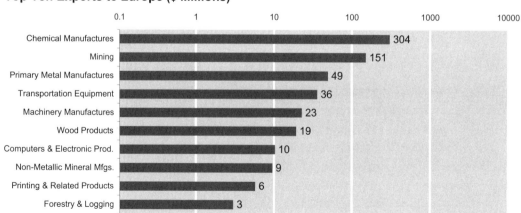

Chemical Manufactures	304
Mining	151
Primary Metal Manufactures	49
Transportation Equipment	36
Machinery Manufactures	23
Wood Products	19
Computers & Electronic Prod.	10
Non-Metallic Mineral Mfgs.	9
Printing & Related Products	6
Forestry & Logging	3

Source: Office of Trade and Economic Analysis

Wisconsin and Europe
Employment, Investment, and Trade Linkages

Employment

European investment in Wisconsin supported 64,000 jobs in 2001; manufacturing jobs accounted for roughly 45% of the total.

Investment

Of the $15.8 billion invested in Wisconsin in 2001, 41%, or $6.5 billion came from Europe.

Trade

In 2003, Europe purchased $2.5 billion worth of goods from Wisconsin.

Computers and machinery are the top exports to Europe.

Top Sources of FDI within Wisconsin, 2001

Country	FDI ($ Millions)
Canada	3,157
Germany	2,965
United Kingdom	993
France	935
Switzerland	709

Source: Bureau of Economic Analysis

Top European Export Markets, 2003

Country	Exports ($ Millions)
UK	494
Germany	448
France	371
Belgium	263
Netherlands	242

Source: Office of Trade and Economic Analysis

Top Ten Exports to Europe ($ Millions)

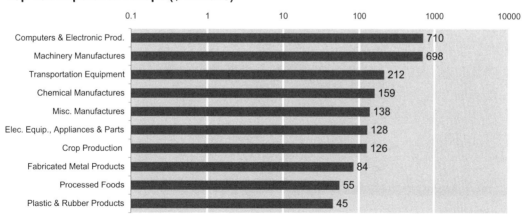

Source: Office of Trade and Economic Analysis

Wyoming and Europe
Employment, Investment, and Trade Linkages

Employment

European investment in Wyoming supported 5,000 jobs in 2001.

Investment

Of the $10.1 billion invested in Wyoming in 2001, 75%, or $7.6 billion came from Europe.

Trade

In 2003, Europe purchased $64 million worth of goods from Wyoming.

By a wide margin, chemicals are the top export to Europe.

Top Sources of FDI within Wyoming, 2001

Country	FDI ($ Millions)
United Kingdom	6,324
Canada	1,319
Belgium	748
Germany	298
France	167

Source: Bureau of Economic Analysis

Top European Export Markets, 2003

Country	Exports ($ Millions)
Belgium	17
Spain	13
Netherlands	13
UK	7
France	5

Source: Office of Trade and Economic Analysis

Top Ten Exports to Europe ($ Millions)

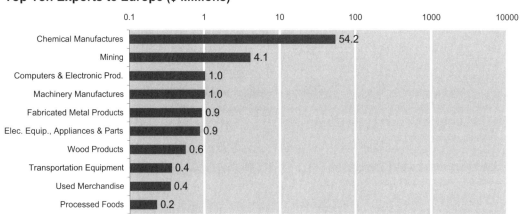

Source: Office of Trade and Economic Analysis

Chapter 5

U.S. Commerce and Europe:
A Country-by-Country Comparison

Commercial relations between the United States and Europe date back to the colonial period. Yet it was not until the second half of the 20th century that the transatlantic economy truly emerged as a cohesive and integrated economic entity.

In the aftermath of World War II, cross-border ties were bolstered by the establishment of the Bretton Woods system, the creation of various multilateral institutions like the World Bank and International Monetary Fund, and by such framework agreements as the General Agreement on Tariffs and Trade (GATT), now the World Trade Organization (WTO). These institutions and initiatives, complemented by transatlantic cooperation in defense and security matters, were the initial building blocks to what stands today as the largest bilateral commercial artery of the world economy.

In the aftermath of World War II, America's commercial presence in Europe was rather shallow. In fact, Europe's share of U.S. overseas investment was just 15% of the total in 1950, with U.S. overseas investment concentrated in the resource-rich locations like Canada and Latin America. Combined, Canada and Latin America represented roughly 70% of America's overseas presence at the outset of the Cold War. Mining and oil exploration were the principal sectors driving U.S. investment outflows, which helps explain the north-south concentration of U.S. investment flows in the early 1950s.

In the intervening decades, however, the motivations for investing overseas among U.S. firms shifted, as did the geographic composition of U.S. foreign direct investment. Access to markets, rather than raw materials, became the overriding determinant driving the overseas expansion of U.S. firms. As a result, Europe, after lagging behind Canada and Latin America in the early 1950s, emerged as the most favored destination of U.S. firms in the ensuing decades, a ranking the region has never relinquished.

As Europe rebuilt and recovered from the ravages of war in the late 1950s, and moved toward the creation of a common market, U.S. firms were quick to seize the opportunities across the Atlantic. While U.S. foreign investment outflows to Europe averaged just $400 million (in nominal terms) annually in the 1950s, the annual average more than quadrupled in the 1960s, jumping to $1.7 billion. Cumulative U.S. outflows to Europe totaled $16.6 billion over the 1960s. That represented nearly 40% of the U.S. total, up from a 20% share in the 1950s. In the 1970s, Europe's share rose to 47% of total U.S. FDI outflows, while over the 1980s and 1990s, Europe accounted for more than half of total U.S. investment outflows.

The 1990s, in particular, were an intense period of U.S. investment in Europe (and an intense period of European investment in the U.S.). Notwithstanding all the hype associated with globalization and the opening of untapped markets such as China, India and Poland, U.S. FDI outflows in the 1990s hardly deviated from the prior four decades. Europe remained the top destination of U.S. investment, a bias due in large part to transatlantic convergence in such key areas as industry deregulation (media, energy and telecoms), technology usage, and financial market liberalization. These variables, among others, helped to further align the macro policies and micro practices of the U.S. and Europe.

In the end, American firms invested more capital overseas in the 1990s—in excess of $750 billion—than in the prior four decades combined. But the surge in U.S. FDI did not gravitate towards the new and untapped markets of the developing nations, as many assume. Rather, the bulk of U.S. investment flows in the 1990s, or nearly half of the global total, went to the so-called "Old World," or Europe.

The current decade has been no different. In fact, Europe's share of U.S. investment outflows remains robust and has even accelerated, edging up to just over 55% of the global total over the 2000-03 period. In 2003 alone, Europe accounted for a staggering 64% of total U.S. outflows. That

Europe would consume the lion's share of U.S. investment in 2003 is surprising given transatlantic acrimony over the U.S.-led war in Iraq. This continuing, even deepening bias towards Europe is particularly counter-intuitive given the overriding notion conveyed in the media that U.S. firms are decamping America for low-wage destinations like Mexico, India and of course, China.

Reality is different. Ireland, for instance, attracted more than two-and-a-half times as much U.S. investment in 2003 than China. U.S. investment in Austria was more than three times greater than U.S. levels in India. Combined, India and China attracted only $1.9 billion in U.S. investment in 2003, *less* than total U.S. flows to Sweden. Granted, one year hardly makes a trend, but even after aggregating U.S. investment outflows for the decade, from 2000-03, the picture does not change.

Over the 2000-03 period, for instance, cumulative U.S. foreign direct investment in Ireland was nearly $20 billion versus just $5.6 billion in U.S. investment in China.

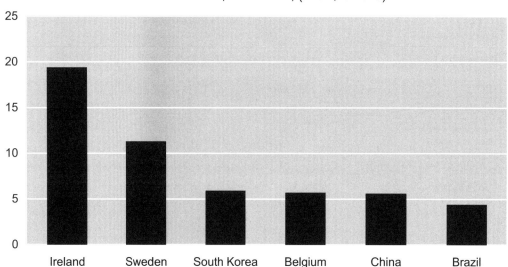

U.S. Foreign Direct Investment Outflows
Cumulative totals, 2002-2003, (U.S. $ billions)

Source: Bureau of Economic Analysis

Over the same time frame, U.S. firms invested more capital in Sweden ($11.3 billion) and Belgium ($5.7 billion) than not only China but also in other key emerging markets like Brazil ($4.4 billion) and South Korea ($5.9 billion). Meanwhile, cumulative U.S. investment flows to Denmark in the first four years of this decade ($4.1 billion) were nearly three times greater than U.S. flows to India ($1.5 billion).

U.S. Investment in Services vs. Manufacturing

That Europe continues to attract a dominant share of U.S. investment flows is due in part to the changing composition of U.S. investment to Europe. While still a significant destination for U.S. manufacturing investment, Europe's primary attraction to U.S. firms lies now in service activities like financial services, transportation, research and development, consulting, insurance, education, medical services, and related functions. Over the past decade, these markets have become more accessible to U.S. firms on account of greater market liberalization across various European nations. In addition, lower transatlantic communication costs, the proliferation of the Internet and greater utilization of information technology have also played a key role in expanding market opportunities in Europe's service economy. As outlined in Chapter 1, asset-augmenting strategies of companies seeking a competitive edge in the global knowledge economy point toward deeper investments in other knowledge economies. On the whole, those are to be found in Europe.

Against this backdrop, America's investment profile in Europe underwent a dramatic change over the 1990s. While in the early 1990s U.S. foreign direct investment in Europe (based on a historical cost basis) was roughly balanced between manufacturing and services, one decade later America's

investment in Europe was overwhelmingly geared toward services. Indeed, the U.S. investment stake in Europe totaled nearly $800 billion in 2002, with nearly three-fourths of the total in service activities. In 1994, in contrast, services accounted for 58% of America's total investment position in Europe.

Reflecting this shift towards more service-related investment, the employment profile of U.S. affiliates in Europe has changed dramatically as well over the past decade. In 1993, for instance, of the 2.4 million European workers on the payrolls of U.S. affiliates, 1.6 million workers, or two-thirds of the total, were employed in manufacturing activities. Thereafter, manufacturing employment among U.S. affiliates expanded by only 21.2% between 1993 and 2001, the last year of available data. In contrast, service employment among U.S. affiliates more than doubled, to 1.85 million in 2001 versus 849,000 in 1993, as more U.S. service leaders like Wal-Mart, AOL, Citgroup and others penetrated deeper and deeper into the European market. Presently, U.S. affiliate employment is virtually split between manufacturing and service –related activities. Meanwhile, the greater the penetration of U.S. service firms into Europe, the greater the level of U.S. foreign affiliate sales in services, which is discussed further in chapter 7.

U.S. Manufacturing Investment Remains Key in Europe

Despite the shift to more service investment, Europe continues to attract a large share of U.S. manufacturing investment. Europe, in fact, remains the primary destination of U.S. manufacturers—notwithstanding rising angst in America over U.S. manufacturing jobs being lost to such low-cost nations as Mexico and China. These nations have attracted more U.S. manufacturing investment over the past decade. Yet over the 1998-02 period, with 2002 being the last year of available data, Europe still accounted for nearly 52% of total U.S. manufacturing capital outflows. Measured another way, on a historic cost basis, Europe accounted for 51.2% of all U.S. manufacturing investment in 2002, *up* from 48.7% at the start of the decade.

While Europe continues to attract U.S. manufacturing investment, the geographic nature of this investment in Europe continues to change and evolve, a dynamic at work since the 1950s. Then, the bulk of America's European manufacturing base was in the United Kingdom, with the latter accounting for roughly 58% of total U.S. manufacturing investment in Europe in 1956. Germany and France were a distant second, with a share of 10.5%, respectively.

The gap, however, narrowed dramatically the next decade on account of the formation of the European Economic Community, which acted to divert U.S. investment from the United Kingdom to the continent. By 1966, the UK's share of

U.S. manufacturing had declined to 41.6%, while Germany's share more than doubled from the prior decade, to 20.2%. In the intervening decade, U.S. manufacturing investment in Europe was concentrated in the "Big Three," or the UK, Germany and France. Combined, the trio accounted for 65% of total U.S. manufacturing in Europe in 1980, although their collective share has steadily decreased since then.

As more U.S. manufacturing investment has gravitated towards Europe's periphery, namely to nations like Ireland, Sweden and Spain, the share of U.S. manufacturing to the UK, Germany and France has declined. In fact, the collective share of U.S. manufacturing investment in the "Big Three" dropped below 50% of the European total in 2002.

Since 1996, Germany, France and the United Kingdom have all seen their respective share of U.S. manufacturing investment in Europe decline. The UK's share dropped from 24.3% in 1996 to 23.6% in 2002. Over the same period, Germany's share fell by 1.6 percentage points, from 15.5% to 13.9%, while France's share

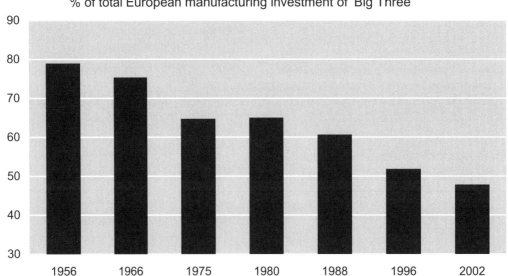

U.S. Manufacturing Investment in Europe
% of total European manufacturing investment of 'Big Three'

Note: 'Big Three' composed of United Kingdom, Germany, and France. Source: Bureau of Economic Analysis

slipped 1.7 percentage points, from 12% to 10.3%. Spain and Belgium also registered sizable drops, with Spain's share of U.S. manufacturing investment dropping to 3.5% in 2002 from 4.9% in 1996. Belgium's share decreased to 4.3%, down from 6%.

The most significant winners, in contrast, have been Ireland and Sweden. More liberal and investor-friendly investment polices have helped bolster investment flows to both nations. Ireland has become a favorite of U.S. technology firms on account of its large, English-speaking labor force. Favorable tax rates and Ireland's preferential access to the European Union have also been drawing cards, with such technology leaders like Intel and Microsoft significantly expanding their presence in-country in the past few years. As a result, Ireland has emerged as a leading exporter of software and information technology products over the past decade. Roughly two-thirds of Ireland's top 100 exporters are foreign affiliates, mostly U.S. affiliates.

Sweden has also become a favorite location for U.S. investment, due in large part to the nation's more liberal foreign investment climate, including the removal of exchange controls, tax reform, the relaxation of restrictions on foreign participation in financial services, and industry deregulation in a number of industries like telecom, transport and electricity. A skilled labor force, plenty of technological capabilities (Sweden spends some 3.4% of GDP on research, the highest in the world) and first-class infrastructure only add to Sweden's attractiveness. So does Sweden's proximity, and trade and investment linkages with eastern Europe, which make the country a natural bridge.

U.S. foreign affiliate sales in Sweden used to be geared mainly to the local market, with the latter accounting for roughly 79% of total affiliate sales in 1990. The rest, or 21% of the total, consisted of U.S. affiliate exports to third markets and to the U.S. One decade later, however, affiliate sales to the local market accounted for just 51% of total affiliate sales, while the share of sales to third markets (namely affiliate exports to the EU and lately, central Europe and the Baltic states) jumped to

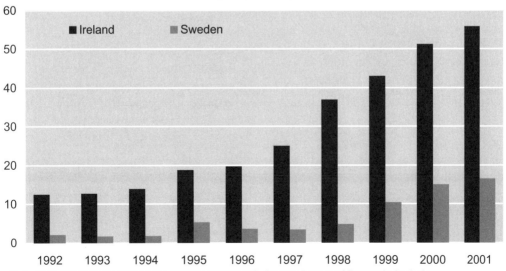

U.S. Affiliate Exports from Ireland and Sweden
(U.S.$ billions)

Note: Data includes exports to third markets and the U.S. Source: Bureau of Economic Analysis

35% of the total in 2001 from 19% in 1990. Exports to the U.S., meanwhile, surged to 14.4% of the total in 2001 from just 2.1% as more and more of U.S. affiliate production in Sweden became more globalized, or suitable for markets anywhere in the world.

So much of U.S. production in Sweden has become globalized over the past decade that by 2001, U.S. affiliate exports from Sweden to the U.S. ($4.9 billion) were some 40% larger than U.S. affiliate exports from China ($3.4 billion). The bulk of these exports consisted of high-end technology and pharmaceutical goods. The shift in foreign affiliate sales in Sweden, in turn, underscores the dynamic and ever-changing nature and strategies of U.S. foreign affiliates operating in Europe. Indeed, unbeknownst to many, U.S. motivations for investing in Europe continue to be altered by various macro circumstances in Europe, making U.S. investment flows to Europe far more dynamic than is generally understood.

Europe's Allure: More Than a Large, Wealthy Market

No other economic entity in the world can match the size, the output and the wealth of the United States other than the European Union. The Union's population of 454 million is 163 million more than America's. The total output of the European Union (including its ten new member states) in 2002 of €9.613 trillion compares to €11.084 trillion for the United States.

In the map section of the appendix we offer some new maps of Europe weighted according to investment and trade flows with the United States.

Given the overall size and wealth of an integrated European Union, market-seeking investment—or investment intended to exploit new market opportunities or protect an existing market position—has been the primary motivation of U.S. foreign direct investment in Europe for decades. Reinforcing this trend, of total U.S. foreign affiliate sales in Europe of $1.3 trillion in 2001 (majority-owned foreign affiliates), 62.1% were for the local market, not far from the global norm (65.2%) and not far from the levels registered in 1990 (64.8%) and 1983 (61.4%). In other words, what motivates U.S. firms to invest in Europe—large integrated markets—has not changed all that much over the past few decades. However, a country-by-country analysis reveals much more and underscores the fact that U.S. investment in Europe is more complex and less homogenous than many believe. The motives and activities of U.S. affiliates vary greatly across Europe, with U.S. firms leveraging and exploiting each host nation's endowment, whether that is skilled labor, technology capabilities, geographic proximity to central Europe or other factors.

The Netherlands and Switzerland, for instance, play important roles for U.S. affiliates in a number of non-manufacturing functions such as finance, wholesale trade, insurance and related functions. Reflecting these activities, roughly 60% of total U.S. foreign affiliate sales in the Netherlands were for export in 2001, while more than 75% of Switzerland's affiliate sales were for export in the same year.

Ireland and Sweden and to a lesser extent, Finland, Austria and Belgium serve as export platforms for U.S. affiliates. Ireland serves as a gateway to the broader European market. Sweden and Finland increasingly act as bridges to the Baltic states and Russia. Austria plays a similar role in providing access to the central European markets of Hungary, the Czech Republic and Slovakia. Affiliates in Belgium, meanwhile, are increasingly woven into the integrated European production networks of U.S. firms, and assembly and manufacturing parts and components that are then exported to various locations across Europe. In general, across the region and across national boundaries, U.S. affiliates act less as separate national operations and more as integrated operations, with each plant performing a specific role or function in the greater European production network of U.S. multinationals.

U.S. affiliates in Germany, the United Kingdom and France play similar integrated roles and U.S. affiliate exports from all three nations are significant. In fact, exports from the UK totaled $98.6 billion in 2001, exports from Germany totaled $68.2 billion, and exports from France totaled $33 billion. Yet it is the large and wealthy markets of all three nations that primarily attract the investment of U.S. firms. The same is true of Italy, where local sales of affiliates accounted for 79% of total sales in 2001, among the highest percentages in Europe. In Germany, local sales accounted for 66% of the total in 2001, 76.3% of the total in the United Kingdom and 73% of total sales in France. Local affiliate sales in Spain accounted for over 70% of the total in 2001.

Regions of Europe are critical engines of transatlantic economic prosperity. The map section of the appendix compares the transatlantic economic ties of the British, French and German regions. Many of these regions have deeper economic ties with the United States than do many countries of the world. The chart section of the appendix documents U.S. investment projects by sector in the British, French and German regions between 1997-2003.

In general, U.S. firms view and approach Europe less as a single market and more as a heterogeneous entity, with each nation, and even regions within nations, offering varying strategic endowments. The motivations for investing in Europe have pivoted on market-seeking and efficiency-seeking investment for decades, although central Europe's accession into the European Union presents new opportunities and motivations to U.S. firms. These states have much lower wage costs than their European counterparts and not surprisingly, have attracted more U.S. foreign direct investment based on favorable international-factor cost considerations. But this picture is also changing rapidly. More on this subject in the next chapter.

U.S. Affiliate Sales in Europe By Destination
% of total

Region	Calendar 1983: Local Market	Calendar 1983: Exports to 3rd Market	Calendar 1983: Exports to U.S.	Calendar 1990: Local Market	Calendar 1990: Exports to 3rd Market	Calendar 1990: Exports to U.S.	Calendar 2001: Local Market	Calendar 2001: Exports to 3rd Market	Calendar 2001: Exports to U.S.
World	63.7%	25.6%	10.7%	67.0%	22.8%	10.2%	65.2%	24.0%	10.8%
Europe	61.4%	35.0%	3.6%	64.8%	31.2%	4.0%	62.1%	32.6%	5.3%
Austria	na	na	na	77.8%	21.1%	1.1%	57.4%	28.9%	13.7%
Belgium	39.7%	57.2%	3.1%	41.5%	55.5%	3.0%	47.0%	50.4%	2.6%
Denmark	na	na	na	75.7%	20.0%	4.3%	na	23.2%	na
Finland	97.6%	na	na	97.4%	0.2%	2.4%	75.8%	20.7%	3.5%
France	74.1%	24.0%	1.9%	72.4%	24.6%	3.0%	72.9%	23.7%	3.4%
Germany	69.8%	28.1%	2.1%	68.4%	29.0%	2.6%	65.8%	30.2%	4.0%
Ireland	na	na	5.3%	29.3%	64.9%	5.8%	22.0%	63.8%	14.2%
Italy	83.0%	16.0%	1.0%	82.3%	16.2%	1.5%	79.0%	18.3%	2.7%
Netherlands	44.1%	53.0%	2.9%	41.8%	55.7%	2.5%	40.1%	53.6%	6.3%
Norway	45.7%	41.7%	12.6%	na	37.7%	na	na	32.2%	na
Portugal	76.6%	22.8%	0.6%	79.5%	20.1%	0.4%	80.5%	18.1%	1.4%
Spain	72.9%	25.8%	1.3%	74.7%	23.7%	1.6%	71.0%	27.7%	1.3%
Sweden	81.0%	18.1%	0.9%	78.8%	19.1%	2.1%	50.9%	34.7%	14.4%
Switzerland	12.4%	81.3%	6.3%	25.4%	63.5%	11.1%	24.5%	69.5%	6.0%
United Kingdom	68.3%	26.4%	5.3%	74.6%	20.3%	5.1%	76.3%	18.9%	4.8%

Source: Bureau of Economic Analysis

Austria & the United States
Investment and Trade Figures

Investment

Not surprisingly, America's investment position in Austria exceeded Austria's investment stakes in the U.S. Total assets of U.S. affiliates were three times larger than Austria's assets in the U.S. U.S. foreign affiliate sales in Austria were roughly four times greater than comparable affiliate sales in the U.S.

Trade

On a global basis, the U.S. accounted for 4.9% of Austria's exports in 2002, although America's export share rises to 12.8% when intra-EU trade is subtracted from the total. Machinery was Austria's top export to the U.S. Of Austria's total imports of $78 billion in 2002, the U.S. accounted for 3.5% of the total and 10.7% of total imports excluding intra-EU trade.

Austria–U.S. Global Linkages, 2001
($ Billions)

	United States in Austria	Austria in United States
Foreign Direct Investment*	4.0	3.4
Total Assets of Affiliates	15.6	4.6
Gross Product of Affiliates	3.4	0.5
Foreign Affiliate Sales	13.4	3.4
Affiliate Employees ('000)	36.2	12.8

*Based on a historical-cost basis, data for 2002; gross product for majority-owned affiliates

Top Ten U.S. Imports from Austria, 2003 (in $millions)

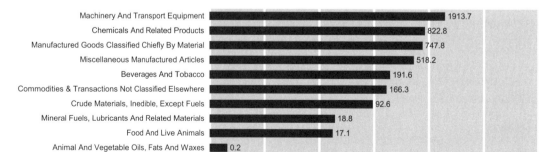

Sources: BEA; IMF; International Trade Administration

U.S. Capital Expenditure in Austria
(1997-2003)

Number of Capital Expenditure Projects	
Year	**Tally**
1997	5
1998	13
1999	13
2000	12
2001	6
2002	3
2003	3

Overall Sources of Foreign Projects in Austria (1997-2003)

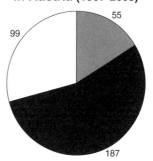

■ EU Projects ■ USA Projects □ Other Projects

Type of U.S. Capital Expenditure: New vs. Expansionary Ventures

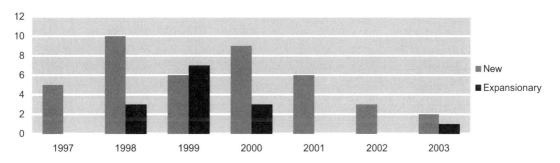

Industry Specific U.S. Capital Expenditure Activity

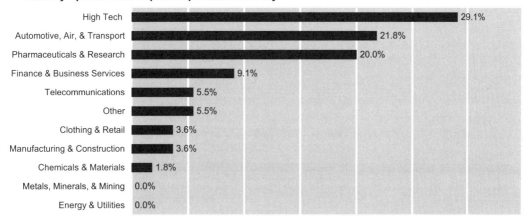

High Tech	29.1%
Automotive, Air, & Transport	21.8%
Pharmaceuticals & Research	20.0%
Finance & Business Services	9.1%
Telecommunications	5.5%
Other	5.5%
Clothing & Retail	3.6%
Manufacturing & Construction	3.6%
Chemicals & Materials	1.8%
Metals, Minerals, & Mining	0.0%
Energy & Utilities	0.0%

Source: Ernst & Young

Belgium & the United States
Investment and Trade Figures

Investment

America's investment position in Belgium was more than double Belgium's investment stakes in the U.S. However, affiliate employment levels were about equal in 2001. The gross product of U.S. affiliates in Belgium totaled nearly $13 billion in 2001, roughly double the gross product of U.S. affiliates in China.

Trade

The U.S. accounted for 7.9% of Belgium's total exports in 2002, but a share of 28.7% of total exports when intra-EU trade is excluded. Manufactured goods lead the way as top exports. Regarding imports, the U.S. supplied 6.4% of Belgium's total imports in 2002, although the share rises to 22% excluding intra-EU trade.

Belgium–U.S. Global Linkages, 2001
($ Billions)

	United States in Belgium	Belgium in United States
Foreign Direct Investment*	24.1	9.6
Total Assets of Affiliates	123.4	40.4
Gross Product of Affiliates	12.7	6.3
Foreign Affiliate Sales	60.1	25.4
Affiliate Employees ('000)	145.2	145.6

*Based on a historical-cost basis, data for 2002; gross product for majority-owned affiliates

Top Ten U.S. Imports from Belgium, 2003 (in $millions)

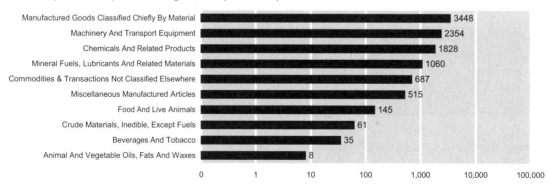

Sources: BEA; IMF; International Trade Administration

U.S. Capital Expenditure in Belgium
(1997-2003)

Number of Capital Expenditure Projects	
Year	Tally
1997	39
1998	66
1999	46
2000	40
2001	40
2002	21
2003	17

Overall Sources of Foreign Projects in Belgium (1997-2003)

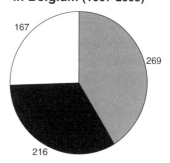

■ EU Projects ▨ USA Projects □ Other Projects

Type of U.S. Capital Expenditure: New vs. Expansionary Ventures

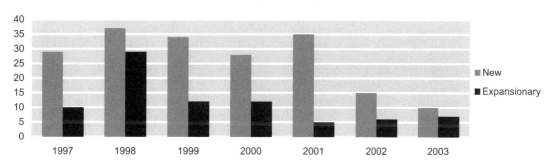

Industry Specific U.S. Capital Expenditure Activity

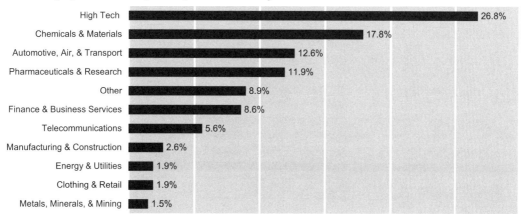

Source: Ernst & Young

Denmark & the United States
Investment and Trade Figures

Investment

The investment balance favored Denmark, with America's investment position in Denmark nearly four times larger than Denmark's comparable position in the U.S. Interestingly, U.S. foreign affiliate sales in Denmark were 35% larger than affiliate sales in India in 2001. The affiliate employment balance favored Denmark.

Trade

Denmark's exports to the U.S. totaled $3.6 billion in 2002, or 6.4% of the global total. Excluding intra-EU trade, the share of exports to the U.S. rises to 18.1%. Denmark's imports from the U.S. totaled $1.9 billion in 2002, 3.9% of the global total and 13.8% excluding intra-EU trade.

Denmark–U.S. Global Linkages, 2001
($ Billions)

	United States in Denmark	Denmark in United States
Foreign Direct Investment*	7.7	1.9
Total Assets of Affiliates	36.9	13.9
Gross Product of Affiliates	3.3	1.3
Foreign Affiliate Sales	–	7.2
Affiliate Employees ('000)	–	17.9

*Based on a historical-cost basis, data for 2002; gross product for majority-owned affiliates

Top Ten U.S. Imports from Denmark, 2003 (in $millions)

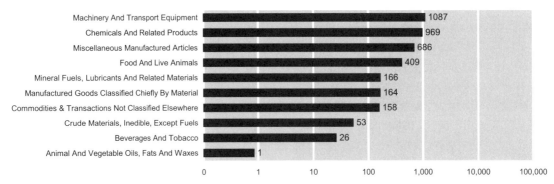

Sources: BEA; IMF; International Trade Administration

U.S. Capital Expenditure in Denmark
(1997-2003)

Number of Capital Expenditure Projects	
Year	Tally
1997	5
1998	14
1999	13
2000	12
2001	8
2002	16
2003	3

Overall Sources of Foreign Projects in Denmark (1997-2003)

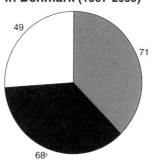

■ EU Projects ▨ USA Projects □ Other Projects

Type of U.S. Capital Expenditure: New vs. Expansionary Ventures

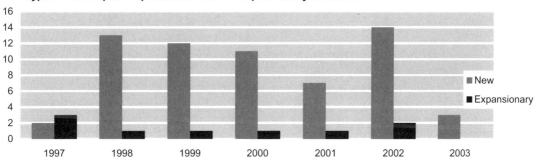

Industry Specific U.S. Capital Expenditure Activity

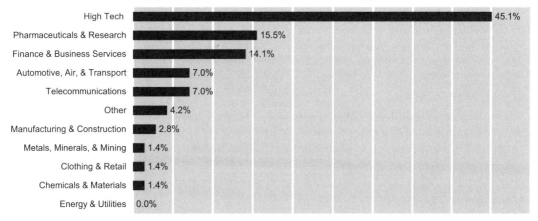

Source: Ernst & Young

Finland & the United States
Investment and Trade Figures

Investment

The investment balance favored the United States, with Finnish investment in the U.S. totaling $7.2 billion in 2002 versus $1.4 billion of U.S. investment in Finland. Finland's asset base in the U.S. is roughly double America's asset base in Finland. The affiliate employment balance favored the U.S.

Trade

Exports to the U.S. amounted to $4 billion in 2002, representing 9% of the global total. Excluding intra-EU trade flows, the U.S. accounted for 19.3% of total exports. Imports from the U.S. totaled just $1.2 billion, 3.7% of the global total, or 8% excluding intra-EU trade flows.

Finland–U.S. Global Linkages, 2001
($ Billions)

	United States in Finland	Finland in United States
Foreign Direct Investment*	1.4	7.2
Total Assets of Affiliates	8.0	16.7
Gross Product of Affiliates	1.9	3.5
Foreign Affiliate Sales	7.4	18.1
Affiliate Employees ('000)	19.7	48.7

*Based on a historical-cost basis, data for 2002; gross product for majority-owned affiliates

Top Ten U.S. Imports from Finland, 2003 (in $millions)

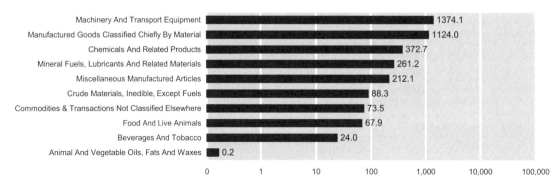

Machinery And Transport Equipment	1374.1
Manufactured Goods Classified Chiefly By Material	1124.0
Chemicals And Related Products	372.7
Mineral Fuels, Lubricants And Related Materials	261.2
Miscellaneous Manufactured Articles	212.1
Crude Materials, Inedible, Except Fuels	88.3
Commodities & Transactions Not Classified Elsewhere	73.5
Food And Live Animals	67.9
Beverages And Tobacco	24.0
Animal And Vegetable Oils, Fats And Waxes	0.2

Sources: BEA; IMF; International Trade Administration

U.S. Capital Expenditure in Finland
(1997-2003)

Number of Capital Expenditure Projects	
Year	Tally
1997	4
1998	6
1999	1
2000	7
2001	8
2002	3
2003	1

Overall Sources of Foreign Projects
in Finland (1997-2003)

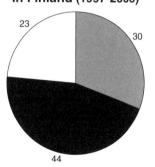

■ EU Projects ▨ USA Projects □ Other Projects

Type of U.S. Capital Expenditure: New vs. Expansionary Ventures

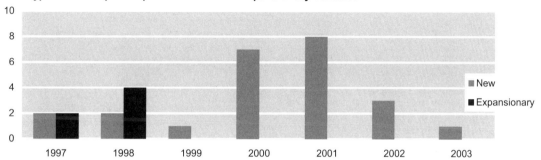

Industry Specific U.S. Capital Expenditure Activity

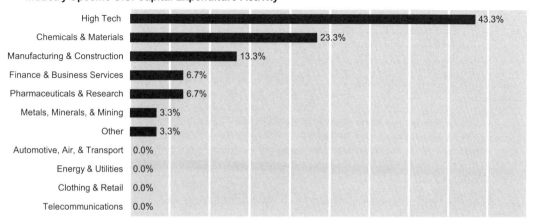

Source: Ernst & Young

France & the United States
Investment and Trade Figures

Investment

The investment balance favored the U.S., with U.S. investment in France ($43.4 billion) just 25% of total French investment in the U.S. in 2002 ($171 billion). The U.S. is a significant market for French firms, with U.S. affiliates of French firms recording nearly $190 billion in foreign affiliate sales in 2001. Affiliate employment levels were roughly equal at 578,00 each.

Trade

Exports to the United States amounted to $26 billion in 2002, or 7.8% of the global total and 20.1% of the total excluding intra-EU trade. The composition of exports runs the gamut— from machinery to food. France's imports from the U.S. totaled $22.3 billion in 2002— that represented 6.8% of the global total. Excluding intra-EU imports, the U.S. share of imports rises to nearly 20%.

France–U.S. Global Linkages, 2001
($ Billions)

	United States in France	France in United States
Foreign Direct Investment*	43.4	170.6
Total Assets of Affiliates	190.6	534.5
Gross Product of Affiliates	34.4	40.0
Foreign Affiliate Sales	134.9	188.1
Affiliate Employees ('000)	578.3	578.6

*Based on a historical-cost basis, data for 2002; gross product for majority-owned affiliates

Top Ten U.S. Imports from France, 2003 (in $millions)

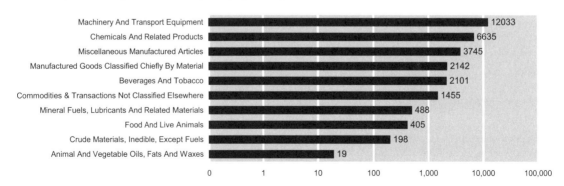

Sources: BEA; IMF; International Trade Administration

U.S. Capital Expenditure in France
(1997-2003)

Number of Capital Expenditure Projects	
Year	Tally
1997	110
1998	114
1999	147
2000	162
2001	118
2002	115
2003	65

Overall Sources of Foreign Projects in France (1997-2003)

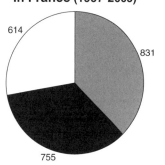

■ EU Projects ■ USA Projects □ Other Projects

Type of U.S. Capital Expenditure: New vs. Expansionary Ventures

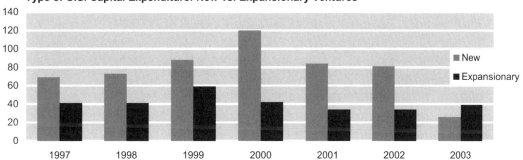

Industry Specific U.S. Capital Expenditure Activity

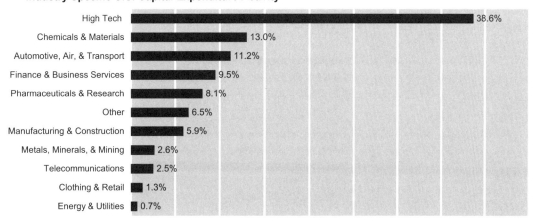

Industry	Percent
High Tech	38.6%
Chemicals & Materials	13.0%
Automotive, Air, & Transport	11.2%
Finance & Business Services	9.5%
Pharmaceuticals & Research	8.1%
Other	6.5%
Manufacturing & Construction	5.9%
Metals, Minerals, & Mining	2.6%
Telecommunications	2.5%
Clothing & Retail	1.3%
Energy & Utilities	0.7%

Source: Ernst & Young

Germany & the United States
Investment and Trade Figures

Investment

The investment balance favored the U.S., with U.S. investment in Germany totaling $65 billion in 2002 versus $137 billion of German investment in the U.S. Germany's asset base in the U.S. is roughly double America's asset base in Germany, although the gross product of U.S. affiliates in Germany ($58 billion in 2001) exceeded the total output of German affiliates in the United States. The employment balance favored the U.S.

Trade

Germany is the largest European exporter to the U.S., with exports to the U.S. totaling over $62 billion in 2002. The U.S. accounted for just over 10% of total German exports, but nearly 23% when intra-EU trade flows are excluded. Germany's imports from the U.S. totaled $37.5 billion—that equated to 7.7% of total German imports or 15.9% excluding intra-EU trade.

Germany–U.S. Global Linkages, 2001
($ Billions)

	United States in Germany	Germany in United States
Foreign Direct Investment*	64.7	137.1
Total Assets of Affiliates	320.8	687.8
Gross Product of Affiliates	57.7	50.2
Foreign Affiliate Sales	240.7	313.9
Affiliate Employees ('000)	652.6	734.8

*Based on a historical-cost basis, data for 2002; gross product for majority-owned affiliates

Top Ten U.S. Imports from Germany, 2003 (in $millions)

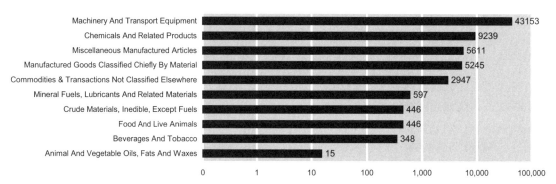

Sources: BEA; IMF; International Trade Administration

U.S. Capital Expenditure in Germany
(1997-2003)

Number of Capital Expenditure Projects	
Year	Tally
1997	74
1998	89
1999	111
2000	83
2001	78
2002	67
2003	15

Overall Sources of Foreign Projects in Germany (1997-2003)

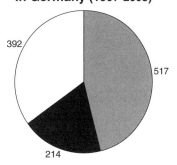

■ EU Projects ▨ USA Projects □ Other Projects

Type of U.S. Capital Expenditure: New vs. Expansionary Ventures

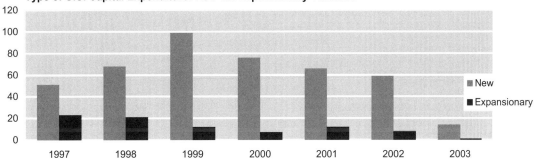

Industry Specific U.S. Capital Expenditure Activity

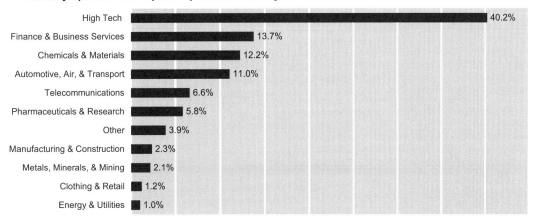

Source: Ernst & Young

Top German Regional Commercial Partners of the United States*

State	Total Commerce (millions of dollars)
1. Baden-Württemberg	97,297
2. North Rhine-Westfalia	88,264
3. Hesse	84,322
4. Bavaria	56,116
5. Lower Saxony	13,457
6. Hamburg	10,952
7. Rhineland-Palatinate	10,025
8. Berlin	3,981
9. Saxony	3,927
10. Bremen	2,968
11. Schleswig-Holstein	2,162
12. Thuringia	1,134
13. Saarland	978
14. Brandenburg	879
15. Saxony-Anhalt	372
16. Mecklenburg-Vorpommern	90

*Combines 2001 investment data (outward and inward) and 2002 trade data (exports and imports), which may include some double counting. Our intention is to provide an overall picture rather than a precise accounting.

Source: Deutsche Bundesbank; Federal Statistical Office Germany

2001 Inward Foreign Direct Investment from the U.S.
(millions of dollars)

1. North Rhine-Westfalia	9,257
2. Bavaria	6,768
3. Baden-Württemberg	4,565
4. Lower Saxony	1,672
5. Rhineland-Palatinate	1,472
6. Berlin	1,388
7. Hamburg	912
8. Hesse	854
9. Schleswig-Holstein	639
10. Thuringia	597
11. Saxony	578
12. Saxony-Anhalt	202
13. Saarland	136
14. Bremen	100
15. Brandenburg	–
15. Mecklenburg-Vorpommern	–

2001 Outward Foreign Direct Investment to the United States
(millions of dollars)

1. Hesse	75,482
2. Baden-Württemberg	72,480
3. North Rhine-Westfalia	66,368
4. Bavaria	27,347
5. Rhineland-Palatinate	5,725
6. Lower Saxony	4,995
7. Hamburg	3,093
8. Berlin	1,009
9. Schleswig-Holstein	322
10. Saarland	73
11. Bremen	36
12. Saxony	18
13. Thuringia	15
14. Saxony-Anhalt	–
14. Brandenburg	–
14. Mecklenburg-Vorpommern	–

Source: Deutsche Bundesbank; Federal Statistical Office Germany

2002 Exports to the U.S.
(millions of dollars)

1. Bavaria	14,377
2. Baden-Württemberg	13,231
3. North Rhine-Westfalia	7,658
4. Lower Saxony	3,817
5. Hamburg	3,073
6. Hesse	2,681
7. Saxony	2,391
8. Bremen	2,355
9. Rhineland-Palatinate	1,804
10. Berlin	667
11. Schleswig-Holstein	632
12. Brandenburg	603
13. Thuringia	408
14. Saarland	332
15. Saxony-Anhalt	127
16. Mecklenburg-Vorpommern	61

Source: Deutsche Bundesbank; Federal Statistical Office Germany

The United States is the #1 investment location for 8 of the 16 German states.

Three German states register greater investments in the United States than in the entire EU14 outside Germany:

State	Investment in U.S.	Investment in EU14 (excluding Germany)
Hesse	75,482	36,343
Baden-Württemberg	72,480	29,082
North Rhine-Westfalia	66,368	64,059
(millions of dollars, 2001)		

Source: Deutsche Bundesbank

Greece & the United States
Investment and Trade Figures

Investment

America's investment position in Greece totaled $1.1 billion in 2002. No data is available regarding the investment position of Greece in the U.S. U.S. affiliate sales of $7.5 billion in 2001 ranked among the lowest in Europe.

Trade

Exports to the U.S. totaled just $500 million in 2002. That represented 5.3% of total Greek exports, but the share rises to 8.5% excluding intra-EU trade. Imports from the U.S. totaled $1.5 billion, with the U.S. accounting for 4.7% of total Greek imports in 2002, and nearly 10% excluding intra-EU trade.

Greece–U.S. Global Linkages, 2001
($ Billions)

	United States in Greece	Greece in United States
Foreign Direct Investment*	1.1	–
Total Assets of Affiliates	8.9	–
Gross Product of Affiliates	0.8	–
Foreign Affiliate Sales	7.5	–
Affiliate Employees ('000)	–	–

*Based on a historical-cost basis, data for 2002; gross product for majority-owned affiliates

Top Ten U.S. Imports from Greece, 2003 (in $millions)

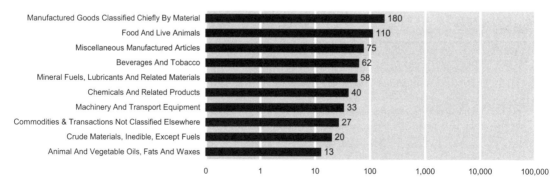

Sources: BEA; IMF; International Trade Administration

U.S. Capital Expenditure in Greece
(1997-2003)

Number of Capital Expenditure Projects	
Year	Tally
1997	0
1998	2
1999	3
2000	3
2001	2
2002	2
2003	1

Overall Sources of Foreign Projects
in Greece (1997-2003)

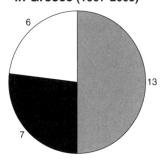

■ EU Projects ▨ USA Projects □ Other Projects

Type of U.S. Capital Expenditure: New vs. Expansionary Ventures

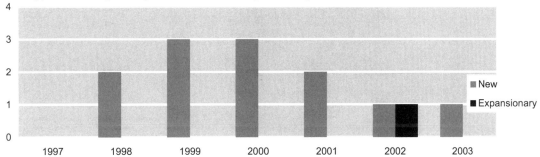

Industry Specific U.S. Capital Expenditure Activity

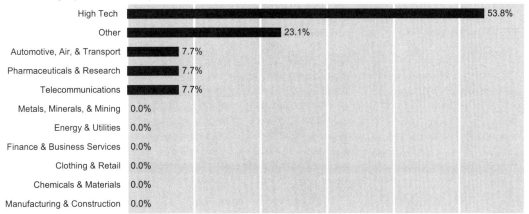

High Tech	53.8%
Other	23.1%
Automotive, Air, & Transport	7.7%
Pharmaceuticals & Research	7.7%
Telecommunications	7.7%
Metals, Minerals, & Mining	0.0%
Energy & Utilities	0.0%
Finance & Business Services	0.0%
Clothing & Retail	0.0%
Chemicals & Materials	0.0%
Manufacturing & Construction	0.0%

Source: Ernst & Young

Ireland & the United States
Investment and Trade Figures

Investment

The investment balance favored Ireland, with U.S. investment in Ireland totaling $42 billion in 2002 versus $26 billion of Ireland's investment in the U.S. The gross product of U.S. affiliates totaled 16.5 billion in 2001, accounting for around 16% of Ireland's total GDP. The employment balance favored Ireland.

Trade

The U.S. is a key export destination for Ireland, with Ireland's exports to the U.S. totaling $14.6 billon in 2002. The U.S. accounted for 16.7% of total exports of Ireland; when intra-EU exports are excluded from the total, the share of exports to the U.S. jumps to 45.7%. Top exports to the U.S. include machinery and chemicals. The U.S. is also a key supplier to Ireland, with the U.S. accounting for 15.3% of total imports of Ireland in 2002 and 42% excluding intra-EU trade.

Ireland–U.S. Global Linkages, 2001
($ Billions)

	United States in Ireland	Ireland in United States
Foreign Direct Investment*	41.6	26.2
Total Assets of Affiliates	192.1	23.9
Gross Product of Affiliates	16.5	5.8
Foreign Affiliate Sales	72.0	17.7
Affiliate Employees ('000)	89	66.9

*Based on a historical-cost basis, data for 2002; gross product for majority-owned affiliates

Top Ten U.S. Imports from Ireland, 2003 (in $millions)

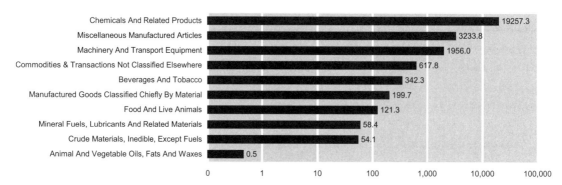

Sources: BEA; IMF; International Trade Administration

U.S. Capital Expenditure in Ireland
(1997-2003)

Number of Capital Expenditure Projects	
Year	Tally
1997	99
1998	60
1999	63
2000	78
2001	36
2002	32
2003	21

Overall Sources of Foreign Projects in Ireland (1997-2003)

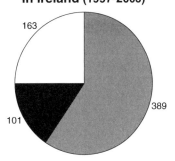

■ EU Projects ■ USA Projects □ Other Projects

Type of U.S. Capital Expenditure: New vs. Expansionary Ventures

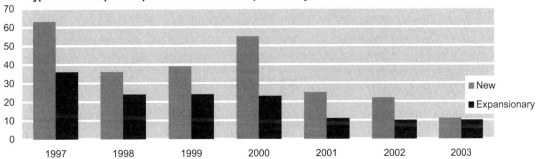

Industry Specific U.S. Capital Expenditure Activity

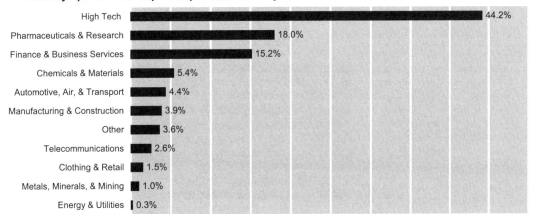

High Tech 44.2%
Pharmaceuticals & Research 18.0%
Finance & Business Services 15.2%
Chemicals & Materials 5.4%
Automotive, Air, & Transport 4.4%
Manufacturing & Construction 3.9%
Other 3.6%
Telecommunications 2.6%
Clothing & Retail 1.5%
Metals, Minerals, & Mining 1.0%
Energy & Utilities 0.3%

Source: Ernst & Young

Italy & the United States
Investment and Trade Figures

Investment

The investment balance favored Italy—U.S. investment totaled $28.5 billion in Italy in 2002, versus the $6.7 billion invested by Italian firms in the U.S. for the same period. U.S. foreign affiliates in Italy produced roughly four times as much output in 2001 as Italian affiliates produced in the U.S. The employment balance favored Italy, with U.S. foreign affiliates employing nearly 240,000 workers in 2001.

Trade

The U.S. is a significant export market for Italy, with Italy's exports to the U.S. totaling $24.5 billion in 2002. The U.S. accounted for nearly 10% of Italy's total global exports and for nearly 21% excluding intra-EU trade. Manufactured goods were the top exports to the U.S. Italy's imports from the U.S. amounted to $11.8 billion in 2002, with the U.S. accounting for 4.9% of the global total and 11.3% of the total excluding intra-EU trade.

Italy–U.S. Global Linkages, 2001
($ Billions)

	United States in Italy	Italy in United States
Foreign Direct Investment*	28.5	6.7
Total Assets of Affiliates	89.4	36.9
Gross Product of Affiliates	20.7	5.1
Foreign Affiliate Sales	78.3	22.9
Affiliate Employees ('000)	238.5	101.3

*Based on a historical-cost basis, data for 2002; gross product for majority-owned affiliates

Top Ten U.S. Imports from Italy, 2003 (in $millions)

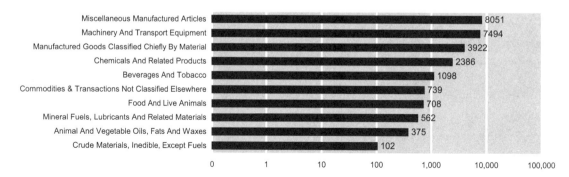

Sources: BEA; IMF; International Trade Administration

U.S. Capital Expenditure in Italy
(1997-2003)

Number of Capital Expenditure Projects	
Year	Tally
1997	12
1998	11
1999	16
2000	16
2001	21
2002	12
2003	5

Overall Sources of Foreign Projects in Italy (1997-2003)

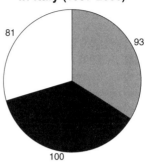

■ EU Projects ■ USA Projects □ Other Projects

Type of U.S. Capital Expenditure: New vs. Expansionary Ventures

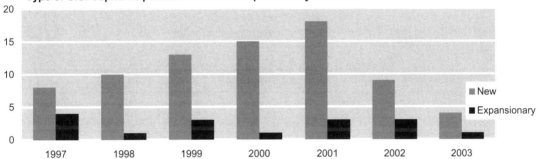

Industry Specific U.S. Capital Expenditure Activity

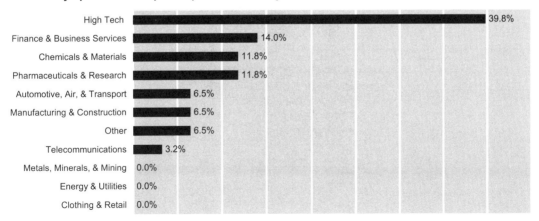

Source: Ernst & Young

Luxembourg & the United States
Investment and Trade Figures

Investment

Investment between the U.S. and Luxembourg is fairly balanced, although most U.S. investment in Luxembourg is indirectly tied to other nations. The bulk of bilateral investment flows is in financial services and related industries.

Trade

Trade volumes are small—with exports to the U.S. totaling just $300 million in 2002, while imports from the U.S. amounted to $500 million. The U.S. accounted for less than 3% of total exports but for nearly 18% excluding intra-EU trade. Imports from the U.S. accounted for 3.9% of the total in 2002 and for 18.1% excluding intra-EU trade.

Luxembourg–U.S. Global Linkages, 2001
($ Billions)

	United States in Luxembourg	Luxembourg in United States
Foreign Direct Investment*	–	–
Total Assets of Affiliates	–	–
Gross Product of Affiliates	–	–
Foreign Affiliate Sales	–	–
Affiliate Employees ('000)	–	–

*Based on a historical-cost basis, data for 2002; gross product for majority-owned affiliates

Top Ten U.S. Imports from Luxembourg, 2003 (in $millions)

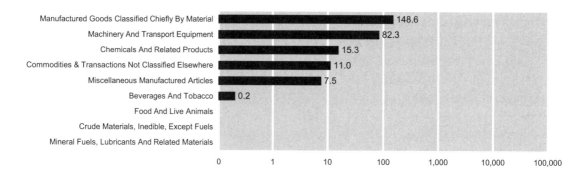

Sources: BEA; IMF; International Trade Administration

U.S. Capital Expenditure in Luxembourg
(1997-2003)

Number of Capital Expenditure Projects	
Year	Tally
1997	5
1998	0
1999	2
2000	0
2001	2
2002	1
2003	1

Overall Sources of Foreign Projects in Luxembourg (1997-2003)

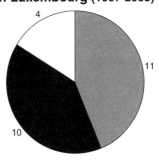

■ EU Projects ■ USA Projects □ Other Projects

Type of U.S. Capital Expenditure: New vs. Expansionary Ventures

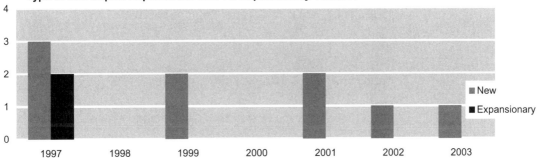

Industry Specific U.S. Capital Expenditure Activity

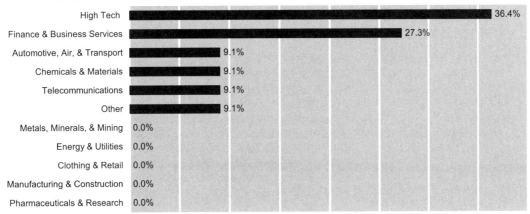

Industry	Percent
High Tech	36.4%
Finance & Business Services	27.3%
Automotive, Air, & Transport	9.1%
Chemicals & Materials	9.1%
Telecommunications	9.1%
Other	9.1%
Metals, Minerals, & Mining	0.0%
Energy & Utilities	0.0%
Clothing & Retail	0.0%
Manufacturing & Construction	0.0%
Pharmaceuticals & Research	0.0%

Source: Ernst & Young

Netherlands & the United States
Investment and Trade Figures

Investment

Investment between the U.S. and the Netherlands is fairly balanced, with America's investment stake in the Netherlands totaling $146 billion in 2002, versus $155 billion of Dutch investment in the U.S. The U.S. is a prime foreign destination for Dutch firms, with Dutch firms producing some $45 billion in output in the U.S. in 2001. That was more than double the level of output of U.S. affiliates in the Netherlands. The employment balance favored the U.S. by a wide margin.

Trade

Exports to the U.S. amounted to $11.1 billion in 2002, with the U.S. accounting for 4.6% of the global total. Excluding intra-EU trade, the U.S. share of the global total rises to nearly 20%. Machinery and chemicals were among the top exports to the U.S. Imports from the U.S. totaled nearly $20 billion, roughly 9% of the global total or 18.7% excluding intra-EU trade.

Netherlands–U.S. Global Linkages, 2001
($ Billions)

	United States in Netherlands	Netherlands in United States
Foreign Direct Investment*	145.5	154.7
Total Assets of Affiliates	423.5	620.0
Gross Product of Affiliates	20.4	44.7
Foreign Affiliate Sales	141.2	244.6
Affiliate Employees ('000)	230	571.9

*Based on a historical-cost basis, data for 2002; gross product for majority-owned affiliates

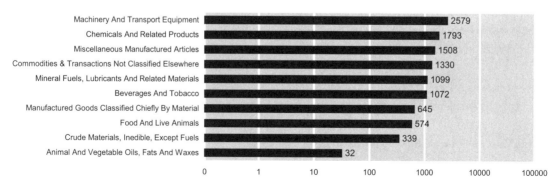

Top Ten U.S. Imports from the Netherlands, 2003 (in $millions)

Machinery And Transport Equipment	2579
Chemicals And Related Products	1793
Miscellaneous Manufactured Articles	1508
Commodities & Transactions Not Classified Elsewhere	1330
Mineral Fuels, Lubricants And Related Materials	1099
Beverages And Tobacco	1072
Manufactured Goods Classified Chiefly By Material	645
Food And Live Animals	574
Crude Materials, Inedible, Except Fuels	339
Animal And Vegetable Oils, Fats And Waxes	32

Sources: BEA; IMF; International Trade Administration

U.S. Capital Expenditure in the Netherlands
(1997-2003)

Number of Capital Expenditure Projects	
Year	Tally
1997	42
1998	42
1999	46
2000	61
2001	32
2002	26
2003	13

Overall Sources of Foreign Projects in the Netherlands (1997-2003)

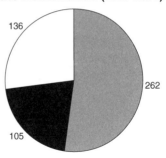

■ EU Projects   ▨ USA Projects   ▢ Other Projects

Type of U.S. Capital Expenditure: New vs. Expansionary Ventures

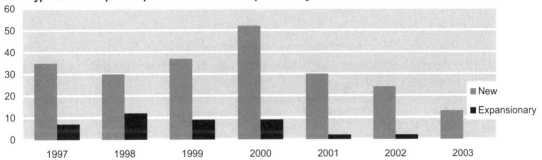

Industry Specific U.S. Capital Expenditure Activity

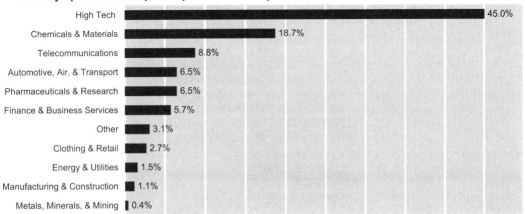

High Tech	45.0%
Chemicals & Materials	18.7%
Telecommunications	8.8%
Automotive, Air, & Transport	6.5%
Pharmaceuticals & Research	6.5%
Finance & Business Services	5.7%
Other	3.1%
Clothing & Retail	2.7%
Energy & Utilities	1.5%
Manufacturing & Construction	1.1%
Metals, Minerals, & Mining	0.4%

Source: Ernst & Young

Norway & the United States
Investment and Trade Figures

Investment

The investment balance favored Norway, with U.S. investment totaling $7.4 billion in 2002 versus $3.4 billion of Norwegian investment in the U.S. U.S. assets in Norway were roughly three times larger than Norway's assets in the United States. The employment balance favored Norway, with U.S. foreign affiliates employing over 31,000 workers in 2001.

Trade

Exports to the United States totaled $5.2 billion in 2002, which was about 8.6% of Norway's total global exports and 35% of exports excluding those destined for the EU. The bulk of U.S.-bound exports were in materials and synthetic derivatives. Imports from the U.S. totaled $2.1 billion in 2002, or 6.1% of Norway's global imports, and 19.2% of imports originating from regions outside the EU.

Norway–U.S. Global Linkages, 2001
($ Billions)

	United States in Norway	Norway in United States
Foreign Direct Investment*	7.4	3.4
Total Assets of Affiliates	21.7	7.7
Gross Product of Affiliates	8.6	1.5
Foreign Affiliate Sales	18.4	9.7
Affiliate Employees ('000)	31.3	20.8

*Based on a historical-cost basis, data for 2002; gross product for majority-owned affiliates

Top Ten U.S. Imports from Norway, 2003 (in $millions)

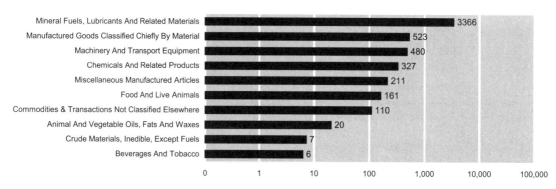

Sources: BEA; IMF; International Trade Administration

U.S. Capital Expenditure in Norway
(1997-2003)

Number of Capital Expenditure Projects	
Year	Tally
1997	2
1998	1
1999	4
2000	0
2001	4
2002	1
2003	1

Overall Sources of Foreign Projects in Norway (1997-2003)

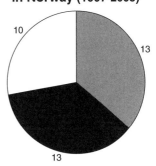

■ EU Projects ▨ USA Projects □ Other Projects

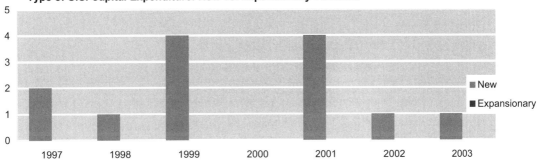

Type of U.S. Capital Expenditure: New vs. Expansionary Ventures

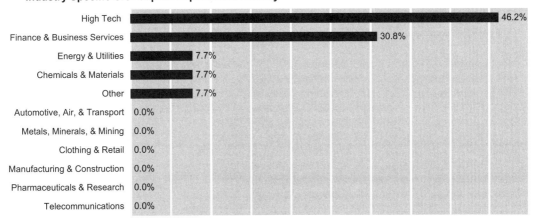

Industry Specific U.S. Capital Expenditure Activity

- High Tech — 46.2%
- Finance & Business Services — 30.8%
- Energy & Utilities — 7.7%
- Chemicals & Materials — 7.7%
- Other — 7.7%
- Automotive, Air, & Transport — 0.0%
- Metals, Minerals, & Mining — 0.0%
- Clothing & Retail — 0.0%
- Manufacturing & Construction — 0.0%
- Pharmaceuticals & Research — 0.0%
- Telecommunications — 0.0%

Source: Ernst & Young

Portugal & the United States
Investment and Trade Figures

Investment

U.S. investment in Portugal totaled $3.4 billion in 2002. Comparable data showing Portugal's investment in the U.S. are not available.

Trade

Portugal's exports to the U.S. totaled just $1.5 billion in 2002. That represents just under 6% of the global total yet nearly 29% when intra-EU trade is excluded from the total. Imports from the U.S. were small—$800 million in 2002—accounting for just 2.2% of the global total. Excluding intra-EU trade, the share from the U.S. rises to 9.4%.

Portugal–U.S. Global Linkages, 2001
($ Billions)

	United States in Portugal	Portugal in United States
Foreign Direct Investment*	3.4	–
Total Assets of Affiliates	10.4	–
Gross Product of Affiliates	3.2	–
Foreign Affiliate Sales	8.4	–
Affiliate Employees ('000)	40.9	–

*Based on a historical-cost basis, data for 2002; gross product for majority-owned affiliates

Top Ten U.S. Imports from Portugal, 2003 (in $millions)

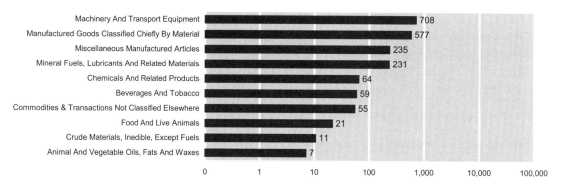

Sources: BEA; IMF; International Trade Administration

U.S. Capital Expenditure in Portugal (1997-2003)

Number of Capital Expenditure Projects

Year	Tally
1997	5
1998	13
1999	6
2000	2
2001	3
2002	6
2003	3

Overall Sources of Foreign Projects in Portugal (1997-2003)

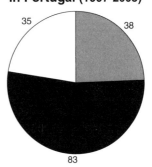

■ EU Projects ▨ USA Projects □ Other Projects

Type of U.S. Capital Expenditure: New vs. Expansionary Ventures

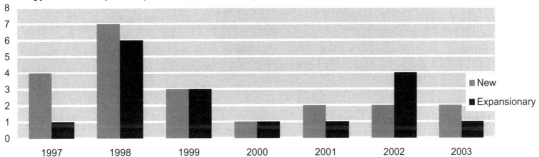

Industry Specific U.S. Capital Expenditure Activity

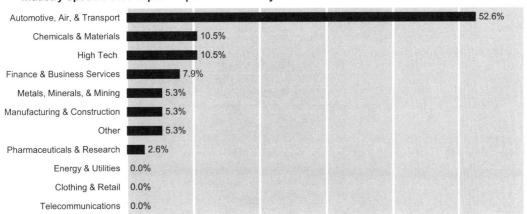

Industry	Percentage
Automotive, Air, & Transport	52.6%
Chemicals & Materials	10.5%
High Tech	10.5%
Finance & Business Services	7.9%
Metals, Minerals, & Mining	5.3%
Manufacturing & Construction	5.3%
Other	5.3%
Pharmaceuticals & Research	2.6%
Energy & Utilities	0.0%
Clothing & Retail	0.0%
Telecommunications	0.0%

Source: Ernst & Young

Spain & the United States
Investment and Trade Figures

Investment

The investment balance favored Spain, with U.S. investment in Spain ($24 billion) some five times larger than Spain's investment in the U.S. ($4.7 billion). Spanish assets in the U.S. totaled $7.9 billion in 2001, while affiliate sales in the U.S. totaled just $4.7 billion. The employment balance was heavily skewed in favor of Spain.

Trade

Spain's exports to the U.S. amounted to $5.4 billion in 2002, with the U.S. accounting for 4.6% of the global total, but 15% of the total excluding intra-EU trade. Imports from the U.S. represented 3.7% of the global total or 14.5% excluding intra-EU trade.

Spain–U.S. Global Linkages, 2001
($ Billions)

	United States in Spain	Spain in United States
Foreign Direct Investment*	23.9	4.7
Total Assets of Affiliates	66.9	7.9
Gross Product of Affiliates	10.6	0.8
Foreign Affiliate Sales	52.9	4.7
Affiliate Employees ('000)	202.1	14.8

*Based on a historical-cost basis, data for 2002; gross product for majority-owned affiliates

Top Ten U.S. Imports from Spain, 2003 (in $millions)

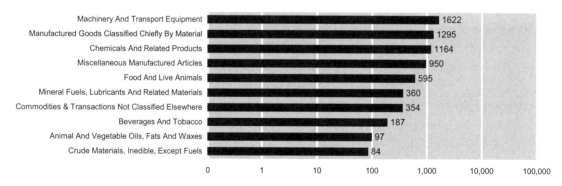

Sources: BEA; IMF; International Trade Administration

U.S. Capital Expenditure in Spain
(1997-2003)

Number of Capital Expenditure Projects	
Year	Tally
1997	18
1998	26
1999	39
2000	43
2001	42
2002	34
2003	10

Overall Sources of Foreign Projects in Spain (1997-2003)

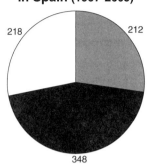

■ EU Projects   ■ USA Projects   ☐ Other Projects

Type of U.S. Capital Expenditure: New vs. Expansionary Ventures

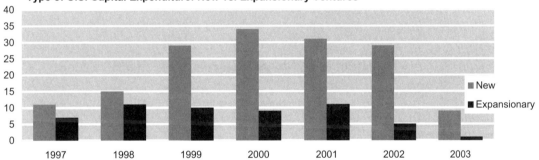

Industry Specific U.S. Capital Expenditure Activity

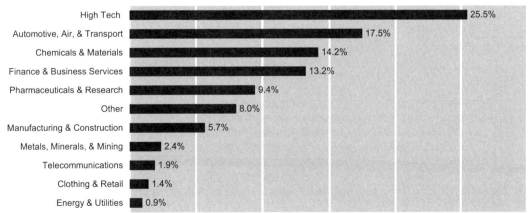

Source: Ernst & Young

Sweden & the United States
Investment and Trade Figures

Investment

The investment balance favored the U.S., with U.S. investment of $19 billion in Sweden slightly less than the $22 billion Swedish firms had invested in the U.S. as of 2002. The asset base between the U.S. and Sweden is roughly balanced, although Swedish firms produce more output in the U.S. than U.S. affiliates produce in Sweden. The employment balance was heavily in favor of the United States, with Sweden employing some 248,000 workers in 2001.

Trade

The U.S. is a fairly large export market for Sweden, with exports to the U.S. ($9.3 billion in 2002) accounting for 11.6% of the global total and nearly 25% of the total excluding intra-EU trade. U.S. imports accounted for 5% of Sweden's total imports in 2002, although the share rises to 14.5% excluding intra-EU trade.

Sweden–U.S. Global Linkages, 2001
($ Billions)

	United States in Sweden	Sweden in United States
Foreign Direct Investment*	19.0	22.0
Total Assets of Affiliates	60.7	65.5
Gross Product of Affiliates	5.7	10.5
Foreign Affiliate Sales	33.7	41.0
Affiliate Employees ('000)	90.7	248.8

*Based on a historical-cost basis, data for 2002; gross product for majority-owned affiliates

Top Ten U.S. Imports from Sweden, 2003 (in $millions)

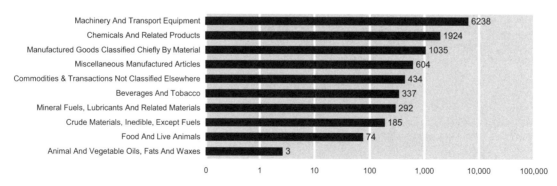

Sources: BEA; IMF; International Trade Administration

U.S. Capital Expenditure in Sweden
(1997-2003)

Number of Capital Expenditure Projects

Year	Tally
1997	8
1998	14
1999	18
2000	24
2001	36
2002	23
2003	10

Overall Sources of Foreign Projects in Sweden (1997-2003)

■ EU Projects ■ USA Projects □ Other Projects

Type of U.S. Capital Expenditure: New vs. Expansionary Ventures

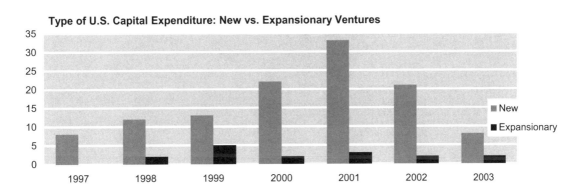

Industry Specific U.S. Capital Expenditure Activity

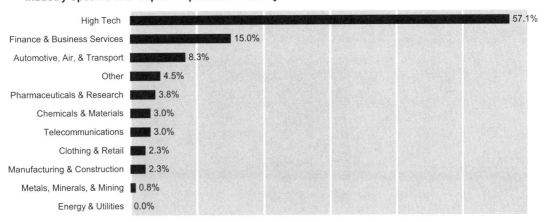

Industry	Percentage
High Tech	57.1%
Finance & Business Services	15.0%
Automotive, Air, & Transport	8.3%
Other	4.5%
Pharmaceuticals & Research	3.8%
Chemicals & Materials	3.0%
Telecommunications	3.0%
Clothing & Retail	2.3%
Manufacturing & Construction	2.3%
Metals, Minerals, & Mining	0.8%
Energy & Utilities	0.0%

Source: Ernst & Young

Switzerland & the United States
Investment and Trade Figures

Investment

The investment balance favored the U.S.—U.S. investment in Switzerland totaled $70 billion in 2002 vs. $113 billion of Swiss investment in the U.S. in the same year. Switzerland's asset base in the U.S. (mainly in services such as insurance and financial services) is much larger than America's asset base in Switzerland. The employment balance was heavily in favor of the U.S.

Trade

Swiss exports to the U.S. totaled $10.5 billion in 2002, representing 12% of all Swiss exports, and 29.2% when taken as a share of exports to regions outside the EU. In the same year, Switzerland imported U.S. goods worth $5.5 billion, approximately 7% of the global total, yet when imports from the EU were excluded, U.S. goods comprised over 30% of Swiss imports.

Switzerland–U.S. Global Linkages, 2001
(\$ Billions)

	United States in Switzerland	Switzerland in United States
Foreign Direct Investment*	70.1	113.2
Total Assets of Affiliates	168.0	818.2
Gross Product of Affiliates	2.2	36.1
Foreign Affiliate Sales	84.1	127.7
Affiliate Employees ('000)	60	546.8

*Based on a historical-cost basis, data for 2002; gross product for majority-owned affiliates

Top Ten U.S. Imports from Switzerland, 2003 (in $millions)

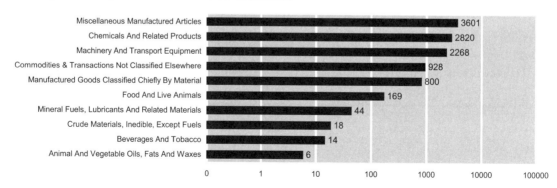

Sources: BEA; IMF; International Trade Administration

U.S. Capital Expenditure in Switzerland
(1997-2003)

Number of Capital Expenditure Projects	
Year	Tally
1997	19
1998	20
1999	24
2000	32
2001	10
2002	9
2003	6

Overall Sources of Foreign Projects in Switzerland (1997-2003)

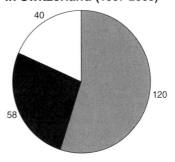

■ EU Projects ■ USA Projects □ Other Projects

Type of U.S. Capital Expenditure: New vs. Expansionary Ventures

Industry Specific U.S. Capital Expenditure Activity

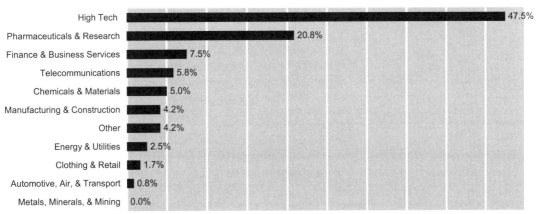

High Tech	47.5%
Pharmaceuticals & Research	20.8%
Finance & Business Services	7.5%
Telecommunications	5.8%
Chemicals & Materials	5.0%
Manufacturing & Construction	4.2%
Other	4.2%
Energy & Utilities	2.5%
Clothing & Retail	1.7%
Automotive, Air, & Transport	0.8%
Metals, Minerals, & Mining	0.0%

Source: Ernst & Young

United Kingdom & the United States
Investment and Trade Figures

Investment

The U.S.-UK investment balance was fairly even, with the U.S. enjoying a slight edge in 2002. The gross product of both U.S. and British affiliates is large, exceeding $100 billion, respectively, in 2001. U.S. foreign affiliate sales in the United Kingdom totaled over $425 billion, the largest country total in the world. Affiliate employment between the U.S. and UK is robust, with affiliates on both sides of the Atlantic each employing more than 1 million workers in 2001.

Trade

The U.S. is a key export market for the United Kingdom, with the U.S. accounting for 15.5% of total global exports of the UK. Excluding intra-EU trade, America's export share rises to over 35%. The U.S. is also a key provider of imports to the UK, with imports from the U.S. accounting for nearly 12% of the global total in 2002, and nearly 24% excluding intra-EU trade.

United Kingdom–U.S. Global Linkages, 2001
($ Billions)

	United States in United Kingdom	United Kingdom in United States
Foreign Direct Investment*	255.4	283.3
Total Assets of Affiliates	1,423.1	841.1
Gross Product of Affiliates	103.1	100.3
Foreign Affiliate Sales	428.2	353.9
Affiliate Employees ('000)	1,280	1,120.7

*Based on a historical-cost basis, data for 2002; gross product for majority-owned affiliates

Top Ten U.S. Imports from the United Kingdom, 2003 (in $millions)

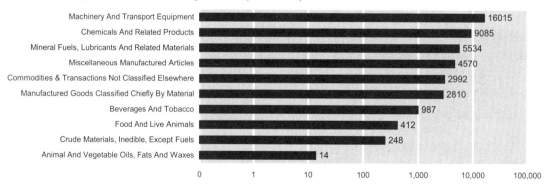

Sources: BEA; IMF; International Trade Administration

U.S. Capital Expenditure in the United Kingdom (1997-2003)

Number of Capital Expenditure Projects

Year	Tally
1997	377
1998	299
1999	269
2000	329
2001	203
2002	181
2003	126

Overall Sources of Foreign Projects in the United Kingdom (1997-2003)

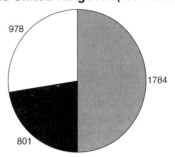

978   1784   801

■ EU Projects   ▨ USA Projects   ☐ Other Projects

Type of U.S. Capital Expenditure: New vs. Expansionary Ventures

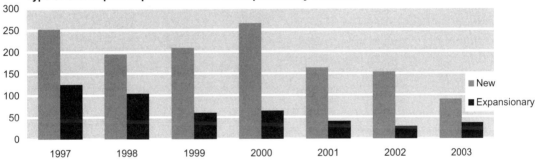

Industry Specific U.S. Capital Expenditure Activity

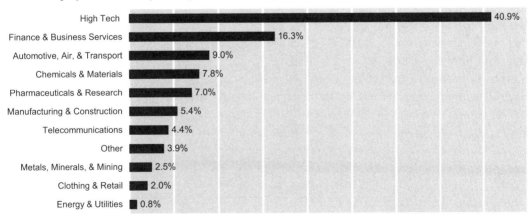

High Tech	40.9%
Finance & Business Services	16.3%
Automotive, Air, & Transport	9.0%
Chemicals & Materials	7.8%
Pharmaceuticals & Research	7.0%
Manufacturing & Construction	5.4%
Telecommunications	4.4%
Other	3.9%
Metals, Minerals, & Mining	2.5%
Clothing & Retail	2.0%
Energy & Utilities	0.8%

Source: Ernst & Young

Chapter 6

European Enlargement and the Transatlantic Economy

The accession of ten countries (Cyprus, Czech Republic, Estonia, Hungary, Lithuania, Latvia, Malta, Poland, Slovenia, and Slovakia) to the European Union (EU) in May 2004 presents a host of new and promising strategic opportunities for U.S. multinationals. Accession has fully integrated these countries into the mainstream of transatlantic commerce and expanded the size of the Single European Market. This round of enlargement has increased the number of EU member nations by two-thirds, from 15 to 25; boosted the EU's population by 74 million (almost 20%), from 381 million to 455 million; doubled its territory to 2.5 million square miles; nearly doubled its official languages from 11 to 20; and widened the gap in income distribution by about 20%—twice as much as the increase when the EU took in Greece, Spain, and Portugal in the 1980s.

The GDP per capita of the ten new members on average is only about 35% that of the other fifteen. While the ten new members add only about 5% to the overall output of the EU, they have been registering annual growth rates of 5% to 8%, far outstripping those of the EU 15, and are likely to do so for the next decade. The new members have also enjoyed an "accession premium" with bonds trading at tighter spreads than equally rated countries from other parts of the world.

Accession has not been accompanied by any economic "Big Bang." The central and eastern European nations have been reorienting their trade and investment patterns for more than a decade. Trade and investment linkages between older EU nations and the accession states have been expanding for years. Indeed, multinationals from Europe, the United States and Asia have been preparing for EU accession since the collapse of communism in the early 1990s.

Fusing East and West

Trade between central, eastern and western Europe has flourished over the past decade as various tariffs on goods have been either reduced or removed. Early in the 1990s, so-called "Europe Agreements" removed all tariffs on industrial goods traded between the EU and many accession nations. In 1997, tariffs on most industrial goods exports from central and eastern Europe were trimmed, while tariffs on EU exports to the region were removed by January 2002. As a result, cross-border

The Larger EU and the U.S.

	Total Population Jan. 2004 (millions)	GDP (billion euros, 2002)
EU 25	454.9	9,613
EU 15	380.8	9,169
U.S.	291.4	11,084

Source: Eurostat

trade between east and west Europe soared over the past decade, with EU exports to central Europe in general rising by an average annual rate of 12% between 1994 and 2002. Over the last decade, EU exports to the region increased fourfold while EU imports from the region more than trebled. This means that central Europe is now more important to the EU than either Asia or Latin America as a trading partner. Germany, Austria and Italy represent more than three-quarters of total trade flows between eastern and western Europe.

Foreign direct investment flows have also been key to integrating the accession states into the EU. Low corporate taxes, access to new markets, cheap yet skilled labor, above-trend growth prospects—all of these determinants helped boost the stock of foreign direct investment in central and eastern Europe over the past decade. Favorable policies have also been key to attracting the investment of multinationals, with the various nations of central Europe signators to hundreds of bilateral investment treaties and double taxation treaties since the early 1990s.

EU enlargement has been a major policy decision facilitating investment flows to central Europe. Preparing for accession has been a massive undertaking for the accession states. They have had to adapt laws and regulations, adopt new policy goals, and further restructure industries. Preparing for accession has also been a challenge for the EU 15 who, in order to accommodate their new partners, have had to reexamine a variety of common EU policies.

The region of central and eastern Europe is viewed increasingly from abroad as one of the most promising geographies of an integrated Europe. The accession states continued to attract FDI inflows

right through the steep global downturn of foreign direct investment over 2001-02. In 2001, for instance, FDI inflows to central and eastern Europe ($25 billion) were relatively unchanged from the prior year, versus a 41% plunge in global foreign direct investment. In 2002, FDI inflows to the region rose nearly 15%, to a record $28.7 billion, while global FDI flows fell by another 20%. Total inflows in 2002 were more than three times larger than annual average inflows of $8.2 billion over the 1991-96 period.

Not unexpectedly, surging investment inflows have dramatically raised the level of FDI stock in central and eastern Europe. In fact, from a total FDI stock base of just $2 billion in 1990, the region's stock of FDI topped nearly $188 billion in 2002, with Poland ($45.2 billion), the Czech Republic ($38.5 billion) and Hungary ($24.4 billion) the largest accumulators of FDI stock in the region. Combined, the three nations represented nearly 60% of all the FDI stock of central and eastern Europe in 2002. If Russia, a non-accession nation, is included, the share rises to 70%, highlighting the fact that FDI flows to central and eastern Europe are rather concentrated. The stock of FDI is presently skewed towards the first wave of economic reformers such as Poland, Hungary and Czech Republic, whose embrace of privatization-led FDI early in the 1990s helped jumpstart the FDI investment cycle and promote the integration of central Europe into the EU.

Poland, Hungary and the Czech Republic have garnered a solid share of FDI among accession states. Yet viewed from another perspective—the ratio of FDI stock to GDP, a better gauge of multinational penetration in the host nation—the integration of the accession nations into the world economy has been more broadly based. According to this measurement, Estonia and the Czech Republic stand out, with the ratio of FDI to GDP averaging roughly 65% in 2001, versus less than 15% in 1995. Slovakia (43%), Hungary (38%), Latvia (32%) and Lithuania (29%) follow. The figure for Poland is on the low side—24% in 2001, while Slovenia's ratio of FDI stock to GDP is the lowest among accession nations, 23%, but nevertheless above the global average of 22%.

The upshot is that the accession states were already integrated into the production networks and operating frameworks of multinationals well ahead of the May 2004 accession date. By sector, investment inflows run the gamut—from automobiles and consumer electronics, to various service activities such as telecoms, financial services and retail. Recent FDI inflows in more advanced accession states such as Hungary and the Czech Republic have been in higher value-added activities such as logistics and R&D functions. In general, FDI to the accession nations is becoming more specialized as various nations, with varying degrees of capabilities, become more integrated into the operations of multinationals.

During the 1990s European multinationals began to use central and eastern Europe as a base from which to produce parts and components as part of their broad internal production networks. This pattern of trade in parts and components between central and eastern European countries and the EU is similar to the pattern within Nafta. The EU accounts for the bulk of central and eastern European trade in parts and components, just as the U.S. and Canada account for the bulk of Mexico's trade in parts and components. This early pattern resulted from the comparative advantage of the central and eastern European countries in the labor-intensive stage of production, which is the assembling of components.

Not all of the countries participate fully or evenly in these networks, however. Hungary and Estonia are particularly engaged in electronics and Slovakia, Poland and the Czech Republic in the automotive industry. This underscores the point that the availability of cheap labor, while important, is often not a sufficient condition for countries to participate competitively within intra-firm production networks, particularly in relatively skill intensive industries. Recent years, in fact, have seen an increasing specialization of FDI between the accession nations (upper to middle income states, with a more advanced skilled labor force) and non-accession countries (lower income nations, with cheaper labor). Multinationals have already begun to shift more labor-intensive activities to the non-

More Globally Integrated: Inward FDI Stock as a Percentage of GDP

Country	1995	2001
Estonia	14	66
Czech Republic	14	64
Slovakia	4	43
Hungary	27	38
Latvia	13	32
Lithuania	6	29
Poland	6	24
Slovenia	9	23
Malta	28	74
Cyprus	18	48
World	**10**	**22**

Source: Unctad

accession nations (and to China), while boosting their level of efficiency-seeking FDI in the more developed and skilled states of Hungary, the Czech Republic, Slovakia, Slovenia and Estonia.

The European Union is by far the dominant source of foreign direct investment in central and eastern Europe, due to its proximity and strong historical and cultural ties. According to figures from the United Nations, the EU accounts for 68% of the region's total inflows, with German firms leading the way. Between 1990 and 2000 German investment in central Europe totaled nearly $24 billion, well ahead of the second largest investor in the region, the Netherlands, whose firms ploughed some $10 billion into central Europe over the same period. France ($9.9 billion), the United Kingdom ($7 billion), and Austria ($6.1 billion) round out the top five European investors in the region.

U.S. multinationals have been just as active as many European firms in the accession states. Indeed, U.S. companies worked just as quickly as their west European counterparts to integrate various accession states into their European operations shortly after the Berlin Wall was breached. U.S. firms have factored EU enlargement in their decisions to invest in eastern and central Europe for a decade.

U.S. Linkages with the Accession Countries

U.S. multinationals have been very active in the accession states over the past decade, and are already well integrated into central and eastern Europe. This is best illustrated by the fact that while U.S. exports were the primary means by which U.S. firms delivered goods to central Europe in 1990, with exports totaling $5.2 billion, by the middle of the decade foreign affiliate sales had

emerged as the primary mode of delivery of goods and services.

In terms of transatlantic trade, the new EU nations have brought their tariffs in line with the EU's Common External Tariff, the schedule of tariffs that U.S. and other third-nation products face when exporting to the EU. The extension of the EU's external tariff to the new member states has led to a decrease of their previous average tariff of 9% to an average of 4%. While this overall decrease in average industrial tariff rates promises benefits for third-nation traders, and while the harmonization of commercial laws and regulations has facilitated the creation of a more predictable business environment in central and eastern Europe, the U.S. lost market access and market share as a result of differential tariff treatment when these countries entered into preferential agreements with the EU in the early 1990s. U.S. agricultural exporters will lose further market access as a result of the EU's restrictive Common Agricultural Policy.

During past rounds of EU enlargement, the U.S. engaged the European Commission in compensation negotiations regarding these trade effects of enlargement. The U.S. and EU are already discussing possible levels of compensation, as provided by the WTO. But once again, while trade is important, an inordinate focus on this element diverts attention from the more dynamic process underway—that of investment.

In 1990, U.S. foreign affiliate sales in central and eastern Europe totaled just $500 million, not surprising given corporate America's nominal investment position in the region. Subsequently, however, as U.S. foreign investment rose in the region over the 1990s, so did foreign affiliate sales. The latter topped nearly $35 billion in

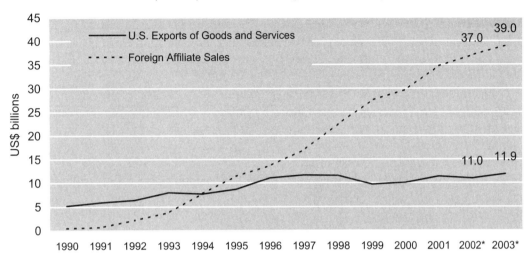

U.S. Sales to Eastern Europe[1]

(U.S. exports vs. U.S. foreign affiliate sales[2])

* Estimate. 1. Includes Russia. 2. Foreign Affiliate Sales for majority-owned foreign affiliates.
Source: Bureau of Economic Analysis

2001, roughly triple the level of U.S. exports to central and eastern Europe in the same year ($11.4 billion). No better figure captures the penetration of U.S. multinationals into the region.

Initially, U.S. foreign direct investment was primarily privatization-led as various governments in central and eastern Europe shifted from a command economy to a free-market economy by hiving off state enterprises to private investors. More recently, the enlargement process itself has been key in attracting more greenfield investment (namely in automobiles and electronics) and more investment in various service activities, by giving newcomers preferential access to one of the largest markets in the world

U.S. multinational strategies in the accession states vary by country. In Poland, for instance, the key motivation of firms is to gain access to Poland's consumer market, the largest among the accession states. Investment in Hungary, in contrast, has been geared more towards exploiting the nation's low wage costs and proximity to the

markets of developed Europe. These two variables have made Hungary a central European export platform in the overall European networks of U.S. multinationals.

While the strategic goals of U.S. firms toward the accession states continue to evolve, it is readily apparent that the determinants of U.S. investment in the region are more complex and less homogenous then generally recognized. Each nation offers different endowments and attributes—some are important to multinationals, some are not. How best to meld and integrate these endowments effectively into broader, pre-existing European production networks is the key challenge for many U.S. multinationals.

In the decade prior to accession, the United States concluded a series of bilateral investment treaties with EU candidate countries. These have been extended but modified to ensure that after accession U.S. investors continue to enjoy a level "investment playing field" with EU investors in all member states.

America's Bias: Poland, Hungary, the Czech Republic

U.S. multinationals have been particularly focused on three of the ten accession states—Poland, Hungary and the Czech Republic. In 2001, these three nations combined accounted for nearly 95% of total U.S. investment in the ten new EU nations (based on a historic cost basis). Poland has attracted the largest share of U.S. investment in the region, a distinction stemming from the country's rather large, young and educated consumer market. With a total population of nearly 40 million, the nation is not only among the most populous in eastern Europe but in all of Europe itself. In eastern Europe alone, the country is the second largest market after Russia in terms of GDP and third largest after Russia and Ukraine in terms of population.

U.S. foreign affiliate sales in Poland totaled nearly $11 billion in 2001, greater than affiliate sales in a handful of older EU members such as Portugal ($8.4 billion), Finland ($7.4 billion), and Greece ($7.5 billion). Reflecting the market-seeking nature of U.S. investment in Poland, roughly 76% of total affiliate sales were for the local market, well above the global average of roughly 65% and the regional average for all of eastern Europe of 61%.

Hungary, the second most popular destination for U.S. investment, stands in sharp contrast to Poland. U.S. multinationals have been attracted by the nation's low wages and preferential access to the European Union. Accordingly, 60% of total U.S. foreign affiliate sales of $8.2 billion in 2001 consisted of exports to EU markets. Less than 40% of U.S. affiliate sales were for the local Hungarian market.

On balance, from the perspective of U.S. multinationals, Hungary's role in the greater EU market is not unlike the role played by Ireland, which emerged as a key low-cost, export platform to the EU for U.S. multinationals during the 1990s. Hungary is playing a similar role today, a point underscored by the fact that multinationals (from the U.S., Europe and Asia) accounted for roughly four-fifths of the nation's total exports in 2000, with the share of high tech exports in

America's Foreign Investment in EU Accession Countries

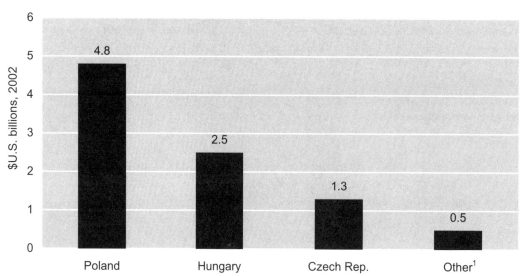

1. Cyprus, Estonia, Latvia, Lithuania, Malta, Slovakia, Slovenia. Source: Bureau of Economic Analysis.

total exports rising from 4% in 1985 to 25% in 2000. Key exports shipped by affiliates include internal combustion piston engines, automatic data processing machines, passenger cars, sound equipment, and telecom equipment.

Even though the Czech Republic is similar in size (GDP) and population to Hungary, it is leveraged more by U.S. foreign affiliates for the local market or for local sales than for export to third markets. Roughly 75% of total U.S. foreign affiliate sales were for the local market in 2001. U.S. foreign affiliate exports from the Czech Republic totaled $1.3 billion in 2001, versus affiliate exports of $4.8 billion from Hungary and $2.1 billion from Poland. Combined, U.S. foreign affiliate exports from the three nations—$8.2 billion—were not that far below U.S. affiliate exports from China in the same year ($9.4 billion).

If one includes the other central and eastern European nations (accession and non-accession countries), it is interesting to note that U.S. affiliates have long exported

more goods from eastern Europe ($13.5 billion in 2001) than from China. This reflects the strategic thrust of U.S. multinationals: investment in China is geared primarily for the local market, not for export. Meanwhile, central and eastern Europe's inexpensive yet skilled labor force, along with its proximity to—and now membership in—the European Union, makes the region an ideal export platform to one of the largest markets in the world.

Comparing U.S. Investment Stakes in Eastern Europe and China

The premium that U.S. multinationals have attached to eastern Europe in general, and to a few key accession nations in particular, becomes clearer when comparing the investment stakes of U.S. multinationals in eastern Europe with U.S. investment stakes in China. Despite the size of China relative to eastern Europe, and despite ever mounting fears that U.S. firms are increasingly decamping the United States for China, America's investment stakes in eastern

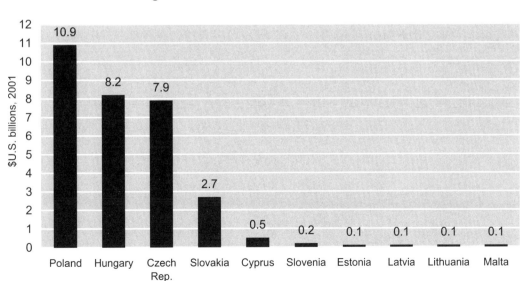

U.S. Foreign Affiliate Sales in the EU Accession Countries

Source: Bureau of Economic Analysis

Europe (accession plus non-accession nations) surprisingly superceded those in China in 2001, the last year of available data.

America's investment stakes in eastern Europe totaled $16.7 billion on a historic cost basis in 2001, against an investment position of $10.3 billion in China. U.S. assets in eastern Europe were some 50% larger than America's asset base in China in 2001. For the same year, U.S. affiliates in eastern Europe generated some $9.3 billion in output against $6 billion in China. Similarly, U.S. foreign affiliate sales in eastern Europe ($42.5 billion) were nearly 17% greater than sales in China ($36.4 billion). In terms of affiliate employment, the edge goes to China, with U.S. foreign affiliates employing nearly 315,000 workers in China in 2001 to roughly 294,000 workers in eastern Europe. In sum, however, U.S. multinationals are more entrenched in eastern Europe than China, a fact little appreciated or understood by many. As a side note, large investments in the oil rich nations of central Asia and Russia have been impor-

tant in boosting U.S. investment flows to eastern Europe. Yet, looking at the accession nations in isolation, China only holds a slight edge when it comes to U.S. foreign direct investment.

The United States and the Other EU Accession Countries

U.S. multinational linkages with the rest of the accession states are small but growing. The Baltic states of Estonia, Latvia and Lithuania have yet to garner significant amounts of U.S. investment, although U.S. investment levels are expected to rise as these Baltic nations incorporate elements of Scandinavian success and innovation and become more of a gateway to the EU, Russia, eastern and northern Europe.

U.S. investment in Cyprus and Malta is sparse and is expected to remain so due to each state's small local markets and lack of hinterland, which inhibit U.S. foreign affiliate exports. The investment outlook for Slovenia is better, assuming the nation emerges both in its own right and as a

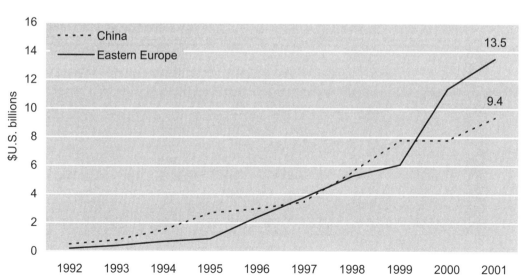

U.S. Affiliate Exports from Eastern Europe vs. China

Source: Bureau of Economic Analysis

bridge to southeastern Europe over the next few years. The picture is also bright in Slovakia. Centered in the heart of Europe, the nation is well positioned to capture more U.S. investment in distribution, transportation, wholesale trade and other service-related activities.

The Bottom Line

U.S. multinationals are already well entrenched in the key accession states of Poland, Hungary and the Czech Republic, and are likely to continue to expand and adjust their strategies towards the entire region over the next decade.

In general, the enlargement process makes the European Union all the more attractive to U.S. multinationals, an assumption that runs counter to fashionable notions that U.S. firms are poised to give up on Europe for faster growth markets of Asia. To the contrary, the steady march of European integration translates into larger and deeper pan-European markets for U.S. firms, and a deeper and more integrated transatlantic economy. It translates into more resources, notably innovative capabilities so prized by U.S. multinationals. Finally, the accession nations are not only well positioned to serve as a bridge to the wealthy markets of western Europe—they are also positioned to someday serve as a springboard to the more underdeveloped regions and fringes of eastern Europe.

In the end, integration between U.S. firms and the accession states is well underway. Barring an unforeseen shock, the process will continue and reflect the prevailing local attributes and endowments of each individual nation. While the strategies of multinationals in any particular country will ebb and flow, corporate America's underlying commitment to the new member states is expected to grow only stronger in coming years.

Czech Republic & the United States
Investment and Trade Figures

Investment

America's investment base is small in the Czech Republic but expanding owing to the nation's skilled labor pool and low wages. U.S. foreign direct investment totaled $1.3 billion on a historic cost basis in 2002. Gross product of affiliates totaled $1.6 billion. U.S. affiliate employment in the Czech Republic (57,400 workers) is larger than affiliate employment in Russia.

Trade

U.S. imports from the Czech Republic totaled $1.3 billion in 2003, more than double the level of 1997. Imports consist of high-end goods like parts and components for nuclear reactors and electronic machinery.

Overall Sources of Foreign Projects in the Czech Republic (1997-2003)

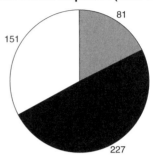

81
151
227

■ EU Projects ■ USA Projects □ Other Projects

Czech Republic–U.S. Global Linkages, 2001
($ Billions)

	U.S. in Czech Republic	Czech Republic in U.S.
Foreign Direct Investment*	1.3	–
Total Assets of Affiliates	8.3	–
Gross Products of Affiliates	1.6	–
Foreign Affiliate Sales	7.9	–
Affiliate Employees ('000)	57.4	–

*Based on a historical-cost basis, data for 2002; gross product for majority-owned affiliates

Top Ten U.S. Imports from the Czech Republic, 2003 ($ Millions)

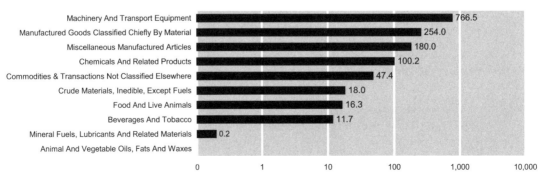

Machinery And Transport Equipment	766.5
Manufactured Goods Classified Chiefly By Material	254.0
Miscellaneous Manufactured Articles	180.0
Chemicals And Related Products	100.2
Commodities & Transactions Not Classified Elsewhere	47.4
Crude Materials, Inedible, Except Fuels	18.0
Food And Live Animals	16.3
Beverages And Tobacco	11.7
Mineral Fuels, Lubricants And Related Materials	0.2
Animal And Vegetable Oils, Fats And Waxes	

Sources: BEA; IMF; International Trade Administration

Cyprus & the United States
Investment and Trade Figures

Investment

Inadequate data limits observation of Cyprus' pattern of global direct investment. Given ongoing political uncertainty in Cyprus, and the country's small market, the nation has not attracted much in the way of U.S. investment.

Trade

Cyprus is an insignificant supplier of goods to the United States, with U.S. imports from the country totaling just $24 million in 2003.

Cyprus–U.S. Global Linkages, 2001
($ Billions)

	United States in Cyprus	Cyprus in United States
Foreign Direct Investment*	0.2	–
Total Assets of Affiliates	0.6	–
Gross Products of Affiliates	–	–
Foreign Affiliate Sales	0.5	–
Affiliate Employees ('000)	2.1	–

*Based on a historical-cost basis, data for 2002; gross product for majority-owned affiliates

Top Ten U.S. Imports from Cyprus, 2003 ($ Millions)

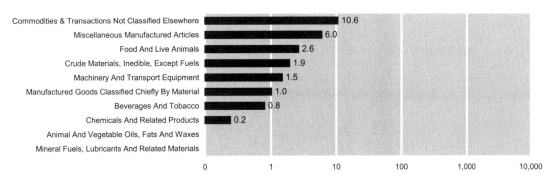

Sources: BEA; IMF; International Trade Administration

Estonia & the United States
Investment and Trade Figures

Investment

America's investment base in Estonia is rather small but expected to expand as the Baltic states emerge as a key gateway to Russia and northern Europe.

Trade

U.S. imports from Estonia totaled $181 million in 2003, a rebound from 2002 ($163 million) but well off the peak levels of 2000, when imports topped $500 million. The decline reflects the sharp fall in U.S. imports of mineral fuel over the past few years.

Overall Sources of Foreign Projects in Estonia (1997-2003)

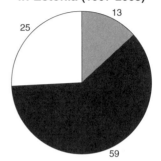

■ EU Projects ▨ USA Projects ☐ Other Projects

Estonia–U.S. Global Linkages, 2001
($ Billions)

	United States in Estonia	Estonia in United States
Foreign Direct Investment*	0.03	–
Total Assets of Affiliates	0.1	–
Gross Products of Affiliates	–	–
Foreign Affiliate Sales	0.1	–
Affiliate Employees ('000)	1.9	–

*Based on a historical-cost basis, data for 2002; gross product for majority-owned affiliates

Top Ten U.S. Imports from Estonia, 2003 ($ Millions)

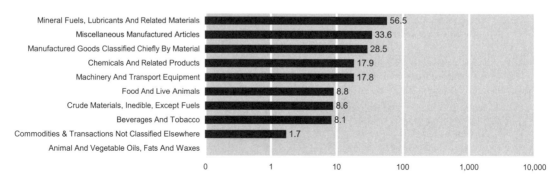

Sources: BEA; IMF; International Trade Administration

Hungary & the United States
Investment and Trade Figures

Investment

America's investment base in Hungary is among the largest in central Europe, with U.S.'s FDI totaling $2.5 billion in 2002. Total affiliate assets amounted to $6.3 billion in 2001, on par with U.S. assets in Russia. U.S. affiliates employed more than 52,000 workers in 2001, far more the number of workers employed next door in Austria.

Trade

U.S. imports from Hungary totaled $2.7 billion in 2003, up from $1.8 billion in 1997. The bulk of imports consist of parts and components, including those used in nuclear reactors. Vehicle and electronic shipments have increased along with greater affiliate production in the nation.

Overall Sources of Foreign Projects in Hungary (1997-2003)

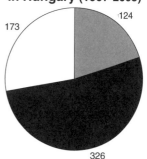

173 124 326

■ EU Projects ■ USA Projects □ Other Projects

Hungary–U.S. Global Linkages, 2001
($ Billions)

	United States in Hungary	Hungary in United States
Foreign Direct Investment*	2.5	–
Total Assets of Affiliates	6.3	–
Gross Products of Affiliates	1.2	–
Foreign Affiliate Sales	8.2	–
Affiliate Employees ('000)	52.6	–

*Based on a historical-cost basis, data for 2002; gross product for majority-owned affiliates

Top Ten U.S. Imports from Hungary, 2003 ($ Millions))

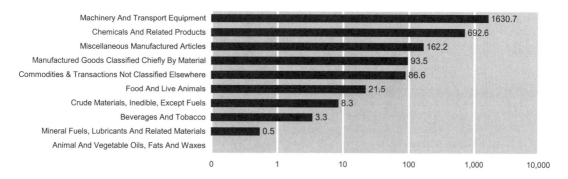

Sources: BEA; IMF; International Trade Administration

Latvia & the United States
Investment and Trade Figures

Investment

Latvia has yet to attract much foreign direct investment from the United States. Investment linkages are shallow but expected to gradually expand over the next decade. The nation is well positioned to serve as an export bridge to Russia.

Trade

U.S. imports from Latvia have increased steadily over the past few years, rising from $148 million in 1997 to $377 million last year. Imports consist mainly of primary commodities like mineral fuels, chemicals, iron and steel.

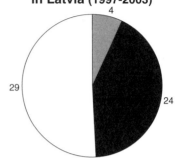

Overall Sources of Foreign Projects in Latvia (1997-2003)

■ EU Projects   ▨ USA Projects   ☐ Other Projects

Latvia–U.S. Global Linkages, 2001
($ Billions)

	United States in Latvia	Latvia in United States
Foreign Direct Investment*	0	–
Total Assets of Affiliates	0.1	–
Gross Products of Affiliates	–	–
Foreign Affiliate Sales	0.1	–
Affiliate Employees ('000)	0.4	–

*Based on a historical-cost basis, data for 2002; gross product for majority-owned affiliates

Top Ten U.S. Imports from Latvia, 2003 ($ Millions)

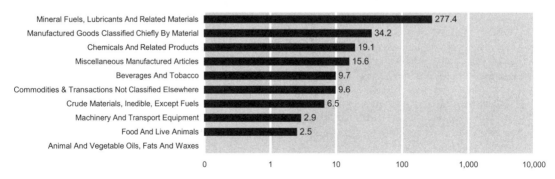

Sources: BEA; IMF; International Trade Administration

Lithuania & the United States
Investment and Trade Figures

Investment

Lithuania has yet to attract significant levels of U.S. foreign direct investment. However, as the Baltic states develop and become more integrated into the greater European market, U.S. investment flows are expected to increase.

Trade

U.S. imports from Lithuania soared over the past few years, rising from just $79 million in 1997 to nearly $350 million in 2003. Rising shipments of mineral fuel led the import surge.

Overall Sources of Foreign Projects in Lithuania (1997-2003)

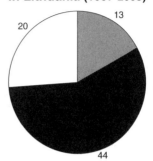

■ EU Projects ■ USA Projects □ Other Projects

Lithuania–U.S. Global Linkages, 2001
($ Billions)

	United States in Lithuania	Lithuania in United States
Foreign Direct Investment*	0.07	–
Total Assets of Affiliates	–	–
Gross Products of Affiliates	–	–
Foreign Affiliate Sales	–	–
Affiliate Employees ('000)	–	–

*Based on a historical-cost basis, data for 2002; gross product for majority-owned affiliates

Top Ten U.S. Imports from Lithuania, 2003 ($ Millions)

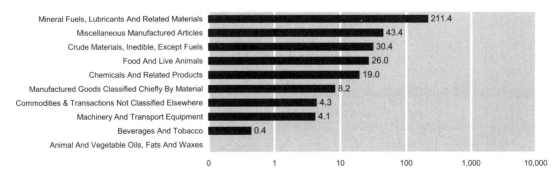

Sources: BEA; IMF; International Trade Administration

Malta & the United States
Investment and Trade Figures

Investment

Given its small size, Malta has not attracted much U.S. foreign direct investment over the past few decades.

Trade

U.S. imports from Malta totaled $373 million in 2003 and consisted of a wide variety of goods--electronic machinery, rubber and mineral fuels.

Malta–U.S. Global Linkages, 2001
($ Billions)

	United States in Malta	Malta in United States
Foreign Direct Investment*	0.07	–
Total Assets of Affiliates	1.1	–
Gross Products of Affiliates	–	–
Foreign Affiliate Sales	0.1	–
Affiliate Employees ('000)	1.2	–

*Based on a historical-cost basis, data for 2002; gross product for majority-owned affiliates

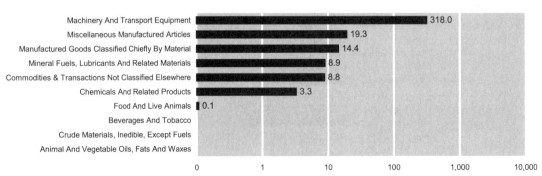

Top Ten U.S. Imports from Malta, 2003 ($ Millions)

Sources: BEA; IMF; International Trade Administration

Poland & the United States
Investment and Trade Figures

Investment

As one of the largest markets in central Europe, Poland has attracted significant sums of market-seeking U.S. foreign direct investment. The U.S. asset base in Poland is larger than America's asset base in Portugal, Finland, Greece and other smaller developed nations. The U.S. affiliate work force of more than 76,000 workers is among the largest in central Europe.

Trade

U.S. imports from Poland increased sharply over the past few years, rising to $1.3 billion in 2003 from $700 million in 1997. Imports ran the gamut—from heavy machinery, to electronic goods, to iron and steel.

Overall Sources of Foreign Projects in Poland (1997-2003)

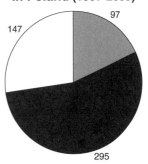

97
147
295

■ EU Projects ■ USA Projects □ Other Projects

Poland–U.S. Global Linkages, 2001
($ Billions)

	United States in Poland	Poland in United States
Foreign Direct Investment*	4.8	–
Total Assets of Affiliates	11.5	–
Gross Products of Affiliates	1.2	–
Foreign Affiliate Sales	10.9	–
Affiliate Employees ('000)	76.9	–

*Based on a historical-cost basis, data for 2002; gross product for majority-owned affiliates

Top Ten U.S. Imports from Poland, 2003 ($ Millions)

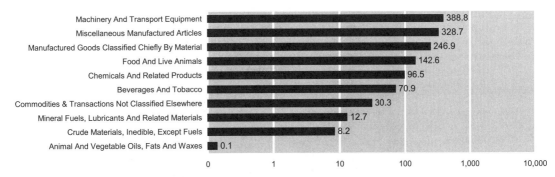

Machinery And Transport Equipment	388.8
Miscellaneous Manufactured Articles	328.7
Manufactured Goods Classified Chiefly By Material	246.9
Food And Live Animals	142.6
Chemicals And Related Products	96.5
Beverages And Tobacco	70.9
Commodities & Transactions Not Classified Elsewhere	30.3
Mineral Fuels, Lubricants And Related Materials	12.7
Crude Materials, Inedible, Except Fuels	8.2
Animal And Vegetable Oils, Fats And Waxes	0.1

Sources: BEA; IMF; International Trade Administration

Slovakia & the United States
Investment and Trade Figures

Investment

America's asset base in Slovakia is small but expanding. Centered in the heart of Europe, Slovakia is well positioned to capture U.S. investment in distribution, transporation, whole sale trade and other service-like activities. Total assets of U.S. affiliates amounted to $2.4 billion in 2001, while foreign affiliate sales totaled $2.7 billion. Affiliates employed over 25,000 workers in 2001, among the largest work forces in central and eastern Europe.

Overall Sources of Foreign Projects in Slovakia (1997-2003)

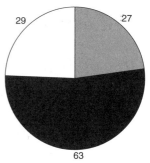

■ EU Projects ▧ USA Projects □ Other Projects

Trade

U.S. imports from Slovakia have surged, rising to $1.3 billion in 2003 from levels under $200 million in the late 1990s. Accounting for the surge has been rising vehicle imports from foreign affiliates producing in the country. Other imports include nuclear reactors, footwear and rubber.

Slovakia–U.S. Global Linkages, 2001
($ Billions)

	United States in Slovakia	Slovakia in United States
Foreign Direct Investment*	0.1	–
Total Assets of Affiliates	2.4	–
Gross Products of Affiliates	–	–
Foreign Affiliate Sales	2.7	–
Affiliate Employees ('000)	25.2	–

*Based on a historical-cost basis, data for 2002; gross product for majority-owned affiliates

Top Ten U.S. Imports from the Slovakia, 2003 ($ Millions)

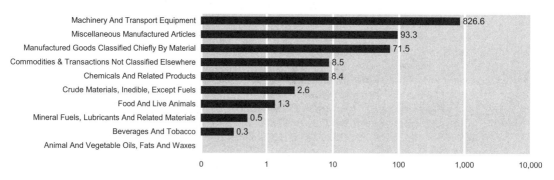

Sources: BEA; IMF; International Trade Administration

Slovenia & the United States
Investment and Trade Figures

Investment

Slovenia has experienced a gradual rise in U.S. foreign investment over the past few years. Total assets of affiliates amounted to $500 million in 2001. The country is expected to emerge as a bridge to Southeastern Europe over the next decade.

Trade

U.S. imports from Slovenia totaled $140 million in 2003, a gradual rise from the levels of the late 1990s. Imports include chemicals, furniture and glassware.

Overall Sources of Foreign Projects in Slovenia (1997-2003)

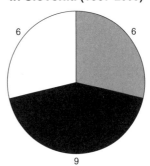

6   6

9

■ EU Projects   ■ USA Projects   □ Other Projects

Slovenia–U.S. Global Linkages, 2001
($ Billions)

	United States in Slovenia	Slovenia in United States
Foreign Direct Investment*	0.07	–
Total Assets of Affiliates	0.5	–
Gross Products of Affiliates	–	–
Foreign Affiliate Sales	0.2	–
Affiliate Employees ('000)	3.7	–

*Based on a historical-cost basis, data for 2002; gross product for majority-owned affiliates

Top Ten U.S. Imports from Slovenia 2003 ($ Millions)

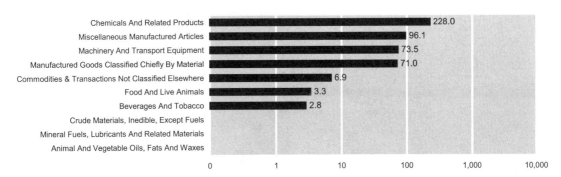

Sources: BEA; IMF; International Trade Administration

Chapter 7
Services and Connectivity in the Transatlantic Economy

"In the Cold War, the most frequently asked question was: "Whose side are you on?" In globalization, the most frequently asked question is, "To what extent are you connected to everyone?"
—Thomas Friedman, *The Lexus and the Olive Tree*

It is fashionable to argue that America's weighty commercial ties with Europe are a legacy of the past, and that the future is in "big emerging markets" or in mass economies such as China or India. There is no doubt that the integration of billions of workers and consumers more fully into the global economy will change the world. But economics is not a zero-sum game, and the rise of new economic relationships does not mean that the European and American economies will be less deeply entwined. In fact, the U.S. and Europe are setting the global pace when it comes to such future-oriented aspects of the global economy as the integration of services industries, transcontinental connectivity via the internet or telecommunications, or better corporate governance. Europe and America are likely to remain the pathfinders of the global economy, pushing the frontiers where the rest of world is likely to follow.

The Transatlantic Service Economy

Service activities are rapidly being reshaped on a global basis. Functions that were once considered nontradable (data processing, education, medical services) are now being traded regularly. Activities long classified as domestic endeavors (advertising, legal services, consulting) today easily take place across borders. And industries that were once the domain of the overregulated public sector (telecommunications, insurance, electric utilities) have been privatized and, in many cases, opened to foreign competition. Consequently, service activities have spread globally—but most notably across the Atlantic.

The global role of services has been recast in large part because of the accelerating pace of technological change. In Europe and many other parts of the world, technological advances have appreciably lowered the cost of communications, making it more feasible and efficient to retrieve, process and disseminate multiple forms of information. Just as container ships made the physical export of goods possible in the past, fiber-optic cables have made it possible to export more data, information, and other knowledge-based services that used to be considered nontradable. In short, communications technology increasingly allows firms to split and disperse parts of service functions to foreign affiliates or to non-equity joint partners.

Across the Atlantic, as communication costs have fallen, the information infrastructure has expanded, the internet has proliferated, the knowledge-based services of both the United States and Europe have become more linked, promoting more trade and foreign investment in services. Industry deregulation, a more liberal investment environment, falling communication costs —all of these variables and more converged in the 1990s to drive a transatlantic investment boom in services. The upshot—the service economies of the United States and Europe have never been as intertwined as they are today, notably in such activities as financial services, telecommunications, utilities, insurance, advertising, computer services and other related functions.

Following in the footsteps of manufacturers, U.S. and European service companies now deliver their services more through foreign affiliate sales than trade. Firms used to deliver services primarily via trade in the 1970s and 1980s, although foreign affiliate sales became the chief mode of delivery in the 1990s. Sales of services by U.S. foreign affiliates in Europe soared from $85 billion in 1994 to roughly $234 billion in 2001, the last year of available data. That marks a 175% increase, well ahead of the 64% rise in U.S. service exports to Europe over the same period.

Against this backdrop, U.S. foreign affiliate sales of services in Europe—after being roughly equal to U.S. service exports to Europe in 1992—were more than double the value of U.S. service exports in 2001.

On a global basis, Europe leads the way in terms of U.S. foreign affiliate sales of services, just as it does in global U.S. affiliate sales of goods. Indeed, of total U.S. affiliate sales of $432 billion in 2001, Europe accounted for 54% of the total, with Asia (with a 20% share) and Latin America (13%), a distant second and third, respectively. By country, the United Kingdom, whose various service sectors are most aligned with those of the U.S., accounted for the largest share of U.S. affiliate sales not only in Europe but also the world. In fact, foreign affiliate service sales of $124 billion in the UK in 2001 were greater than foreign affiliate service sales in all of Asia ($87 billion) and Latin America ($54 billion). In Europe, Germany ($26.3 billion), France ($20 billion) and the Netherlands ($8 billion) trailed the UK.

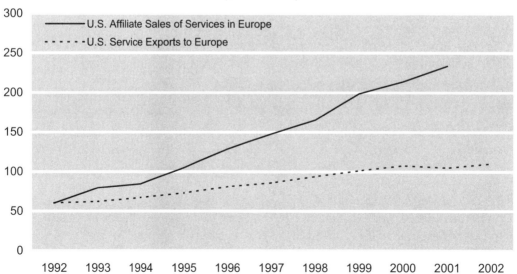

U.S. - Europe Service Linkages
($U.S. billions)

Source: Bureau of Economic Analysis

Sales of services by U.S. affiliates of European firms have also soared over the past decade. As Europe's investment position in services has expanded in the U.S., so have Europe's foreign affiliate sales of services in the U.S. The latter totaled $249 billion in 2001 versus $86 billion in 1994, a jump of 190%. U.S. service imports from Europe expanded over the same period, by 83%, well below the rate of growth of affiliate sales of services. Leading the way were British service firms, whose U.S. affiliate sales in services totaled $64.6 billion in 2001, or 26% of total European affiliate sales. German, French and Dutch affiliates in the U.S. posted substantial sales of services as well, totaling $42 billion, $43 billion and $31 billion, respectively, in 2001.

In short, foreign affiliate sales of services on both sides of the Atlantic have exploded over the past decade. In fact, affiliate sales of services have not only become a viable second channel of delivery for U.S. and European multinationals, they have become the overwhelming mode of delivery in a rather short period of time. Nothing better illustrates the ever-deepening integration of the transatlantic service economy.

Intercontinental Connectivity: Who's Connected to Whom?

Another indicator of deeper integration, and an increasingly vital node of the global economy, is intercontinental connectivity in terms of telecommunications and the internet. The map on the following page underscores in graphic fashion the thick linkages connecting the European and North American continents, particularly in comparison with the relatively thin connections between other continents.

An examination of interregional internet bandwidth underscores the "thick" nature of transatlantic connectivity. Between 2001 and 2003 transatlantic internet bandwidth doubled, to more than three times that of North American connections to Asia and the Pacific, 7½ times that between North America, Latin America and the Caribbean, and 87 times that of European connections to Asia and the Pacific.

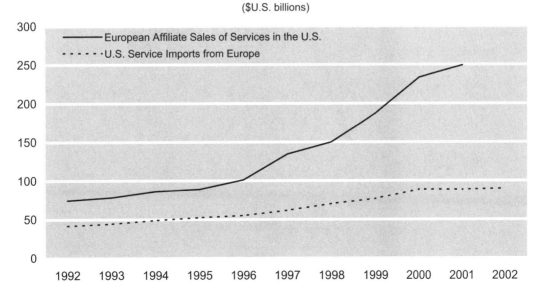

Europe - U.S. Service Linkages
($U.S. billions)

Source: Bureau of Economic Analysis

Interregional Internet Bandwidth, 2003

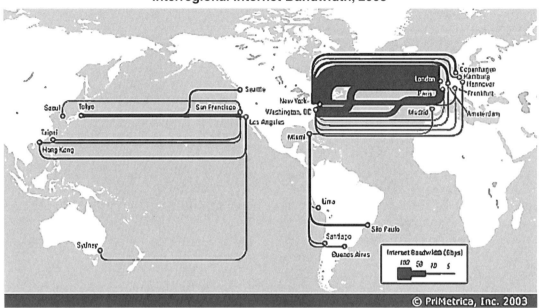

Interregional Internet Bandwidth, 2003

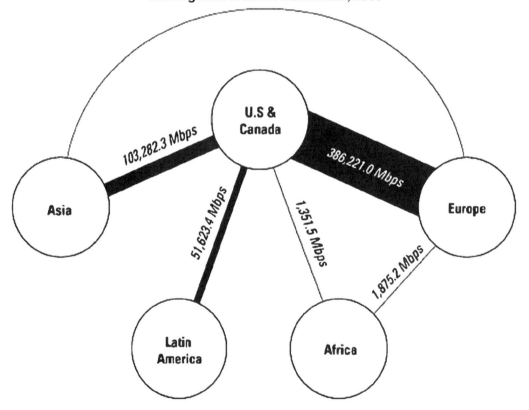

Source: Telegeography Research © PriMetrica, Inc., 2004

TeleGeography Research estimates that as of early 2003 international internet traffic was growing at an annual rate of 67%. If this trend continues, this means that international internet traffic would double every 16 months. Telegeography estimates that transatlantic internet bandwith will increase to over 1 terabit per second by 2005 to keep pace with traffic growth, while transpacific internet bandwidth will increase to slightly more than 400 gigabits per second by 2005, less than half of transatlantic connectivity.

Submarine bandwith figures are similar, with transatlantic connectivity twice as "thick" as transpacific links and more than three times as thick as intra-Asian connections.

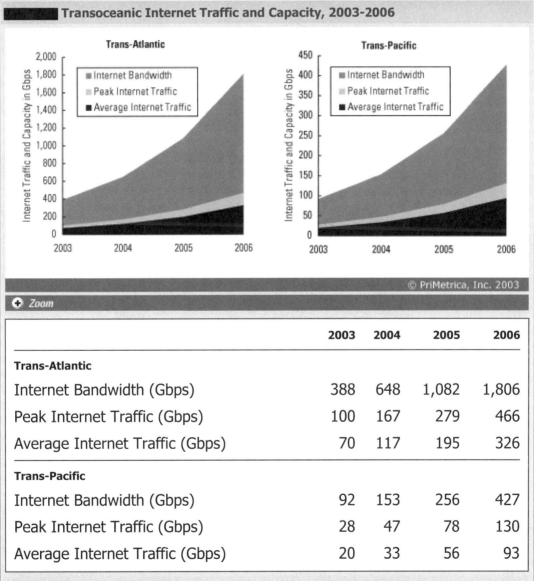

Transoceanic Internet Traffic and Capacity, 2003-2006

© PriMetrica, Inc. 2003

	2003	2004	2005	2006
Trans-Atlantic				
Internet Bandwidth (Gbps)	388	648	1,082	1,806
Peak Internet Traffic (Gbps)	100	167	279	466
Average Internet Traffic (Gbps)	70	117	195	326
Trans-Pacific				
Internet Bandwidth (Gbps)	92	153	256	427
Peak Internet Traffic (Gbps)	28	47	78	130
Average Internet Traffic (Gbps)	20	33	56	93

Notes: Traffic projections beyond 2003 assume 67 percent annual average traffic growth and constant peak-to-average traffic ratios. Internet capacity estimates assume 67 percent annual growth.

Source: TeleGeography research

© PriMetrica, Inc. 2004

In terms of international switched traffic—in other words, who talks to whom—Europe and North America generate 75 percent of the world's international traffic, according to Telegeography Research, and, thus, "drive global trends" (See pie chart illustration, International Traffic Volumes by Region, on following page).

Intra-European telecommunications traffic is of course particularly dense, and also tracks the continuing yet uneven integration of the European continent. The accompanying chart reflects the deeper integration of the older 15 EU member states as well as the new connections being made to the 10 new member states.

Submarine Bandwidth, 2003

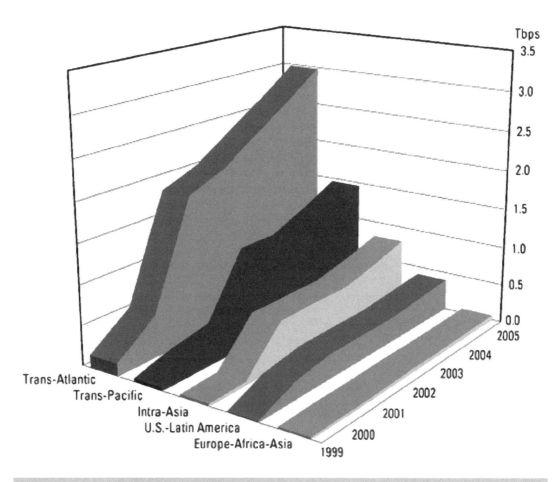

© 2003 TeleGeography, Inc.

Source: Telegeography Research © PriMetrica, Inc., 2003

International Traffic Volumes by Region

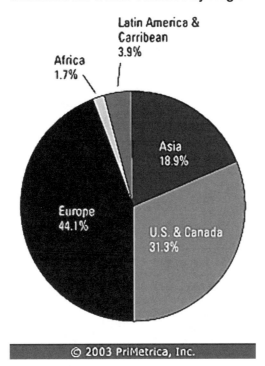

© 2003 PriMetrica, Inc.

European Telecommunications Traffic Flows, 2002

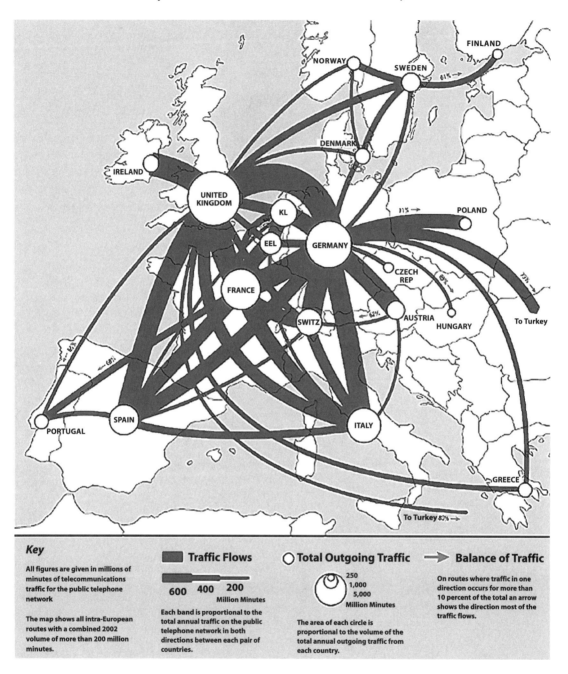

Key

All figures are given in millions of minutes of telecommunications traffic for the public telephone network

The map shows all intra-European routes with a combined 2002 volume of more than 200 million minutes.

Traffic Flows

600   400   200
Million Minutes

Each band is proportional to the total annual traffic on the public telephone network in both directions between each pair of countries.

⭘ **Total Outgoing Traffic**

250
1,000
5,000
Million Minutes

The area of each circle is proportional to the volume of the total annual outgoing traffic from each country.

➝ **Balance of Traffic**

On routes where traffic in one direction occurs for more than 10 percent of the total an arrow shows the direction most of the traffic flows.

Source: Telegeography Research © PriMetrica, Inc., 2003

Chapter 8
The Continuing Primacy of the Transatlantic Economy

The transatlantic partnership was pushed to the brink in 2003. The U.S.-led war in Iraq triggered a virulent wave of protests across Europe not seen in decades. In the United States, resentment swelled towards some Europeans—notably the French. Consumer boycotts emerged on both sides of the Atlantic. Restaurant owners in the United States were filmed pouring French wine down the drains of city streets. In Europe, McDonalds were vandalized and many bars and restaurants refused to serve Coca-Cola, Marlboro cigarettes and other popular U.S. brands.

Such symbolic acts only stoked anti-American and anti-European feelings and emboldened many to opine that the transatlantic partnership was doomed, that Europe and the United States no longer shared common values and that the two parties no longer needed each other. The transatlantic crisis of 2003, many proclaimed, was the prelude to a regrettable but inevitable transatlantic divorce.

Given the considerable list of current transatlantic differences, why don't Europeans and Americans just part company? The simple answer is that we simply can't afford it. A weaker transatlantic bond would render Americans and Europeans less safe, less prosperous, less free, and less able to advance either their ideals or their interests in the wider world.

Europeans who believe that the end of the Cold War means that they are no longer dependent on American success couldn't be more wrong. Europe cannot afford transatlantic divorce. European economies have never been as exposed to the North American market as they are today. Healthy transatlantic commerce has literally become the economic lifeblood of some European companies, countries and regions. Dense transatlantic networks of production and innovation are critical for European jobs and for Europe's ability to remain competitive in the global knowledge economy. Many of Europe's largest firms are more at home in the United States than in Europe itself. Some American states have stronger economic ties with Europe than do many countries. As the recent U.S. economic rebound and profits recovery make clear, what is good for America is also largely good for much of Europe.

Moreover, Iraq underscored that efforts by some in Europe to go it alone are more likely to split Europeans than unite them. If EU members were forced to choose between their incomplete European foreign and security project and alliance with the U.S., most would choose the latter. Europe would lose its voice in the U.S. debate and abdicate its ability to influence the world's only superpower. Finally, Europe has yet to translate its considerable political and economic weight into strategic power; it remains hampered by its lack of military clout, its highly inefficient way of decision-making, and the absence of any real ambition among wide swaths of European publics to play a strategic role. In some distant future the European Union may become an effective strategic player, but even then it is still likely to share more interests than differences with the United States.

Those Americans who have become so intoxicated by their country's "superpower" status that they actually believe they no longer need partners, or those who have become so mesmerized by the rhetoric and superficial hype of beckoning "emerging markets" that they believe they can afford to neglect the transatlantic underpinnings of American prosperity, are shortchanging America's own vital self interests. By a wide yet underappreciated margin, Europe is the most important commercial market in the world for corporate America. The region is not only a critical source of revenue for such leading U.S. firms as General Electric, IBM and Procter & Gamble. It is also a key supplier of capital for the debt-stretched United States. With their massive investment positions in the U.S., many European firms are key sources of employment and wages for U.S. workers, and essential sources of taxes for state and local governments. Some regions of Europe have a stronger commercial relationship with the United States than do most countries. Despite all the hype about "Asian tigers," just three German states—Bavaria, Baden-Württemberg and North-Rhine Westfalia—have a higher GDP than the four Asian tigers—South Korea, Taiwan, Singapore and Hong Kong. Growth of just 3% in Europe would create a new market the size of the entire country of Argentina for companies and investors from the U.S. and other countries. Just as Europe was the pivot for American security during the Cold War, Europe today is the geoeconomic base for American prosperity in the global knowledge economy.

Few great goals in this world can be reached without America, but few can be reached by America alone. In this era of shadowy networks and bioterrorists, failed states and recession, the only way we can grow our economy, share our burdens, protect our society, and advance our values is to band together with others, particularly our core allies and economic partners. In the post-Cold War, post-9/11 world, the relationship between the United States and Europe remains distinctive in this one sense: When both partners agree, they are the core of any effective global coalition. When they disagree, no global coalition is likely to be effective.

Neither party can afford a transatlantic split. Nor can the rest of the world. The global economy will suffer if the U.S. and Europe become regional antagonists rather than global collaborators. Together, the U.S. and Europe account for roughly 40% of world GDP and over one-third of global trade. That is why transatlantic disputes invariably take on global dimensions. Without U.S.-European cooperation, the Doha global trade round is destined to fail. Aid and assistance to developing nations will falter. Efforts to counter disease, fight terrorists or stop the spread of weapons of mass destruction will flounder. The peaceful transformation of the Greater Middle East, including Iraq, will remain elusive. The last thing American or European workers, consumers, companies and investors need is a transatlantic divorce that endangers their jobs, raises prices, undermines the value of their investments, or threatens their profound and mutual stake in each other's economic health.

We do not mean to gloss over significant difficulties facing both partners. Many European economies remain plagued by slow growth, aging societies, chronic unemployment, rigid labor laws, difficult regulatory environments, and weaker productivity. Americans face a mounting federal budget deficit, daunting social security and Medicare liabilities, jobless growth, and accelerating domestic and foreign debt. Policymakers on both sides of the Atlantic face a host of contentious economic issues, ranging from export subsidies and currency levels to corporate governance standards and genetically modified organisms.

These differences of perspective and policy are powerful. But the history of European-American relations has often been the history of difference. Merely asserting difference or reciting lists of tough issues does not make the case for divergence or divorce.

In fact, 2003 suggests that transatlantic commerce, fuelled by the deep integrating forces of mutual investment, remains strong, dynamic and—thankfully—more attuned to good economics than bad diplomacy. But this does not mean that the transatlantic economy is impervious to the sour and strained mood of the moment. In fact, that is our concern—that in an increasingly context-free debate more Europeans and Americans have come to believe they have little to lose by looser transatlantic bonds. As we have argued throughout this volume, talk of no-cost transatlantic divorce is dangerously myopic.

Our effort is intended simply to inject what we believe to be a sorely needed sense of perspective. Pouring French wine down the drain or vandalizing McDonalds may make for splashy headlines, but the more significant development is the accelerating integration and cohesion of the transatlantic economy—particularly since the end of the Cold War. Contrary to expectations, these bonds only tightened in 2003.

In fact, what is most striking about the Iraq debate and the raft of differences currently afflicting transatlantic relations is the degree to which they are accompanied by a host of other trends, documented in this study, that point to ever-deepening interactions between Americans and Europeans. In this world of uneven globalization, our societies and our economies are not drifting apart, they are colliding. American and European economies and societies have become so intertwined that in a number of specific areas they have transcended "foreign" relations and moved into a new arena of "transatlantic domestic policy"—a new frontier in which specific social and economic concerns and transnational and even regional actors often jump formal borders, override national policies, and challenge traditional forms of governance throughout the Atlantic world.

Transatlantic governance today is being defined as much by webs as by walls, as much by networked cooperation among private and regional actors as by hierarchical rules set by central governments. The Cold War image of a two pillar Atlantic world is being challenges by dense transatlantic networks within a common Atlantic space that has no center. These networks of interdependence have, in fact, attained a quality far different than those either continent has with any other. We have only begun to understand the many dimensions of this phenomenon.

Many of the issues confronting European and American policymakers today are those of deep integration, a new closeness that strikes at core issues of domestic governance, and that is of a qualitatively different nature than the "shallow integration" model of the Bretton Woods-GATT system established during the Cold War.

This is what makes current trade squabbles so discouraging. The EU, for instance, has imposed trade sanctions against U.S. goods because the U.S. Congress has failed to eliminate or amend the Foreign Sales Corporation (FSC) law that was declared illegal by the World Trade Organization in

2002. The EU intends to impose its sanctions carefully and gradually. Yet the very fact that the U.S. and Europe are headed down a protectionist path is dangerous. At risk are the supply chains and profits of U.S. and European companies and the general health of the transatlantic economy. Moreover, the tough issue behind the current EU sanctions is not "unfair U.S. competition" due to FSC but how differing domestic tax regimes on both sides of the Atlantic distort free flows of trade and investment in a global economy.

Deep integration is generating new transatlantic networks and new economic opportunities. But because it reaches into traditionally domestic areas it can also generate social dislocation, anxiety and friction, for instance on such issues as food safety, competition policies, religious cults, privacy protection, civil liberties or the death penalty.

Our societies are interacting so closely that many of these issues are debated as quasi-domestic controversies. Such controversies, rather than differences between "European" or "American" values themselves, reflect different perspectives on what tradeoffs are politically or socially acceptable when values widely shared across the Atlantic collide with each other. On many of these issues, in fact, differences within the U.S. and within Europe are more serious than those between Americans and Europeans. In fact, perhaps the strangest aspect about the "values" debate is that it is happening at the very time when values shared by Europeans and Americas are not only ascendant but again under threat. What is different today is not that we agree less with each other but that so much more of the world agrees with us. Those who do not agree are not just issuing manifestos, they are killing our citizens and threatening our societies.

Neither the framework for our relationship—which in many respects remains rooted in Cold War structures—nor the way our governments are currently organized adequately capture these new realities. On the economic front, for instance, opinion shapers need to look more closely at the intersection between deep Atlantic integration and traditional areas of domestic regulation. There is considerable need to work more concertedly to identify "best practices" for governance that could improve coordination and create safety valves for political and social pressures resulting from deep integration. In democratic societies controversial domestic issues are decided by elections or court rulings. When such issues transcend the border and enter the realm of transatlantic domestic policy, however, such avenues do not exist, and so these types of issues need to be managed through new forms of transatlantic regulatory and parliamentary consultation and coordination and more innovative diplomacy that takes account of the growing role of private actors.

The cutting edge of the transatlantic agenda, in fact, transcends current international mechanisms. Even a successful Doha global trade round, for example, will not address such pressing "deep integration" issues affecting the European and American economies as competition policies, standardized corporate governance, more effective regulatory cooperation, tax harmonization and other issues. Nor will it address issues raised by European and American scientists and entrepreneurs, who are pushing the frontiers of human discovery in such fields as genetics, nanotechnology and electronic commerce where there are neither global rules nor transatlantic mechanisms to sort out the complex legal, ethical and commercial tradeoffs posed by such innovation. In such areas the difficulty is less that there are different "European" or

"American" answers to these challenges and more that neither side has even sorted out the appropriate questions, much less the answers.

Transatlantic leadership is needed, not to challenge or replace multilateral efforts such as Doha with such competitive regional arrangements such as a Transatlantic Free Trade Agreement (TAFTA), but to be true pathfinders of the global economy by energizing Doha globally while charting a Doha-plus agenda transatlantically.

This is a challenging agenda on its own, but it has become more difficult because of the changing relationship between the transatlantic strategic and economic agendas. During the Cold War, leaders worked hard to keep transatlantic economic conflicts from spilling over to damage our core political alliance. Today, the growing challenge is to keep transatlantic political disputes from damaging our core economic relationship.

The real possibility we face is not transatlantic divorce but rather transatlantic dysfunction, in which growing transatlantic political disagreements spill over into our increasingly networked economic relationship, swamping efforts to cope with the consequences of deep transatlantic integration and blocking progress on a range of global challenges neither Europeans nor Americans will be able to tackle alone.

Policy decisions and media reporting continue to overlook or underestimate the nature and degree of these changes. Yet a fuller appreciation of the depth and breadth of transatlantic economic ties is perhaps more important than ever, given that emotions have been rubbed raw by transatlantic disputes over Iraq and by festering trade squabbles. In the end, cracks in the transatlantic economy represent a clear and present danger to Americans, to Europeans, and to the wider world. Transatlantic divorce? Transatlantic dysfunction? We literally cannot afford either.

Appendix

**Figures and Graphs
Charts and Maps**

Figures and Graphs

Figure 1

EU Exports to the U.S. vs. EU Exports to the World

	Total U.S. ($ Bil.)	1999 Share of Extra-EU Total	Share of World Total	Total U.S. ($ Bil.)	2000 Share of Extra-EU Total	Share of World Total
Austria	3.0	12.4%	4.6%	3.4	12.9%	5.0%
Belgium	9.4	22.1%	5.4%	10.9	23.4%	5.9%
Denmark	2.7	16.1%	5.5%	3.0	18.0%	5.9%
Finland	3.4	18.6%	8.0%	3.4	16.6%	7.4%
France	25.7	20.9%	7.9%	28.1	22.4%	8.7%
Germany	54.8	23.8%	10.2%	56.4	23.6%	10.3%
Greece	0.6	11.8%	5.7%	0.6	9.7%	5.5%
Ireland	10.9	42.9%	15.2%	12.9	42.3%	17.0%
Italy	21.9	22.3%	9.3%	24.5	23.0%	10.4%
Luxembourg	0.3	25.6%	3.7%	0.3	25.4%	4.1%
Netherlands	8.7	18.7%	4.0%	10.0	20.5%	4.4%
Norway	3.7	32.0%	8.3%	4.6	34.1%	7.9%
Portugal	1.2	29.4%	4.9%	1.4	29.2%	6.0%
Spain	4.7	15.8%	4.6%	5.5	16.2%	5.0%
Sweden	7.8	20.9%	9.2%	8.2	21.5%	9.7%
Switzerland	9.9	31.9%	12.4%	10.6	31.9%	13.1%
United Kingdom	40.0	35.7%	14.8%	44.8	36.7%	15.8%
Europe Total	208.7			228.5		

*Through the first 10 months of the year
Source: IMF Department of Trade Statistics, March 2004

EU Imports from the U.S. vs. EU Imports from the World

	Total U.S. ($ Bil.)	1999 Share of Extra-EU Total	Share of World Total	Total U.S. ($ Bil.)	2000 Share of Extra-EU Total	Share of World Total
Austria	2.9	14.8%	4.1%	2.9	13.1%	4.1%
Belgium	11.9	25.4%	7.5%	13.3	24.2%	7.6%
Denmark	2.0	16.0%	4.5%	1.9	13.5%	4.3%
Finland	1.8	15.1%	5.6%	1.6	11.9%	4.8%
France	25.1	23.8%	8.0%	24.6	20.9%	7.4%
Germany	38.8	17.9%	8.3%	42.8	17.7%	8.6%
Greece	1.5	16.0%	5.4%	0.9	7.9%	3.3%
Ireland	7.4	36.9%	15.6%	8.2	36.7%	16.2%
Italy	10.7	12.6%	4.9%	12.5	12.1%	5.3%
Luxembourg	1.0	48.1%	8.8%	0.4	19.8%	3.4%
Netherlands	19.6	20.6%	9.4%	21.9	20.7%	10.2%
Norway	2.5	23.8%	7.4%	2.2	20.5%	6.9%
Portugal	1.1	12.9%	2.8%	1.2	11.9%	3.1%
Spain	6.5	15.4%	4.8%	6.6	12.9%	4.6%
Sweden	4.0	16.6%	6.3%	4.9	19.6%	7.0%
Switzerland	5.7	31.9%	7.1%	6.5	30.7%	7.8%
United Kingdom	41.3	27.4%	12.9%	45.0	26.7%	13.4%
Europe Total	183.8			197.3		

*Through the first 10 months of the year
Source: IMF Department of Trade Statistics, March 2004

Figure 1—Continued

EU Exports to the U.S. vs. EU Exports to the World

Total U.S. ($ Bil.)	2001 Share of Extra-EU Total	Share of World Total	Total World ($ Bil.)	2002 Share of Extra-EU Total	Share of World Total	Total U.S. ($ Bil.)	2003 Share of Extra-EU Total	Share of World Total
3.6	13.4%	5.1%	3.9	12.8%	4.9%	3.9	12.5%	4.9%
10.6	23.2%	5.6%	16.8	28.7%	7.9%	8.6	19.5%	5.1%
3.5	19.5%	6.9%	3.6	18.1%	6.4%	2.9	16.5%	6.1%
4.2	20.8%	9.8%	4.0	19.3%	9.0%	3.7	18.1%	8.5%
27.7	21.9%	8.6%	26.0	20.1%	7.8%	21.6	18.2%	6.9%
60.3	23.6%	10.6%	62.3	22.8%	10.3%	52.2	20.9%	9.4%
0.5	9.8%	5.6%	0.5	8.5%	5.3%	0.8	13.0%	7.0%
13.9	42.2%	16.8%	14.6	45.7%	16.7%	15.8	53.2%	20.8%
23.5	21.1%	9.7%	24.5	20.8%	9.8%	20.8	18.6%	8.7%
0.3	16.4%	2.8%	0.3	17.6%	2.7%	0.2	14.1%	2.1%
9.7	19.7%	4.2%	11.1	19.9%	4.6%	10.9	19.8%	4.5%
4.6	35.1%	8.0%	5.2	35.0%	8.6%	4.2	31.4%	8.3%
1.4	28.4%	5.8%	1.5	28.5%	5.8%	1.5	28.1%	5.8%
5.0	15.0%	4.6%	5.4	15.0%	4.6%	5.2	14.5%	4.2%
8.0	23.2%	10.7%	9.3	24.9%	11.6%	8.5	25.1%	11.6%
9.6	29.2%	11.6%	10.5	29.2%	11.9%	8.2	25.6%	10.0%
42.8	35.0%	15.9%	42.9	35.1%	15.5%	39.8	34.6%	15.8%
229.2			242.3			208.8		

*Through the first 10 months of the year
Source: IMF Department of Trade Statistics, March 2004

EU Imports from the U.S. vs. EU Imports from the World

Total U.S. ($ Bil.)	2001 Share of Extra-EU Total	Share of World Total	Total World ($ Bil.)	2002 Share of Extra-EU Total	Share of World Total	Total U.S. ($ Bil.)	2003 Share of Extra-EU Total	Share of World Total
2.9	12.1%	3.8%	2.7	10.7%	3.5%	1.9	7.3%	2.4%
12.4	22.9%	7.0%	12.6	22.0%	6.4%	13.7	24.7%	7.1%
2.0	14.5%	4.4%	1.9	13.8%	3.9%	1.4	10.7%	3.0%
1.4	9.0%	4.2%	1.2	8.0%	3.7%	1.3	10.2%	3.9%
24.2	21.1%	7.4%	22.3	19.9%	6.8%	17.6	16.5%	5.5%
40.7	17.3%	8.3%	37.5	15.9%	7.7%	29.2	13.0%	5.8%
1.0	7.7%	3.5%	1.5	9.9%	4.7%	1.4	9.0%	4.0%
7.6	38.0%	15.0%	7.9	41.9%	15.3%	6.6	38.0%	15.3%
11.5	11.3%	4.9%	11.8	11.3%	4.9%	9.9	9.5%	4.2%
0.6	22.8%	4.9%	0.5	18.1%	3.9%	0.3	8.6%	2.0%
20.7	19.8%	9.9%	19.8	18.7%	9.1%	16.7	16.4%	7.8%
2.2	21.0%	6.9%	2.1	19.2%	6.1%	1.3	14.5%	4.2%
1.4	14.6%	3.8%	0.8	9.4%	2.2%	1.3	14.5%	4.2%
6.0	11.8%	4.2%	5.7	10.5%	3.7%	5.0	9.0%	3.1%
3.4	16.3%	5.7%	3.2	14.5%	5.0%	2.9	14.3%	4.4%
5.7	28.3%	6.7%	5.5	30.2%	6.6%	8.0	31.6%	8.5%
45.1	26.4%	14.0%	39.9	23.7%	11.9%	33.2	21.8%	10.5%
188.6			177.0			151.8		

*Through the first 10 months of the year
Source: IMF Department of Trade Statistics, March 2004

Figure 2

The Ties that Bind—Top Ten FDI Destinations and Investors

U.S. FDI by Country, Top Ten Destinations, 2002
(% share in historic cost basis)

Rank	Country	% Share
1	United Kingdom	16.8%
2	Canada	10.0%
3	Netherlands	9.6%
4	Switzerland	4.6%
5	Japan	4.3%
6	Germany	4.3%
7	Singapore	4.0%
8	Belgium/Luxembourg	3.9%
9	Mexico	3.8%
10	France	2.9%
	Total	64.2%

Source: Bureau of Economic Analysis

FDI Positions in U.S., Top Ten Investors, 2002
(% share in historic cost basis)

Rank	Country	% Share
1	United Kingdom	21.0%
2	France	12.7%
3	Netherlands	11.5%
4	Japan	11.3%
5	Germany	10.2%
6	Switzerland	8.4%
7	Canada	6.8%
8	Belgium/Luxembourg	3.3%
9	Ireland	1.9%
10	Australia	1.8%
	Total	88.9%

Source: Bureau of Economic Analysis

Figure 3

America's FDI Roots in Europe

US$ Billions	US FDI to Europe	% of US Total
European Total	796.9	52.4%
Mining	13.1	16.1%
Utilities	4.5	21.7%
Manufacturing	200.8	51.2%
Food Products	16.6	58.8%
Chemicals	65.4	65.9%
Primary Metals	11.3	46.2%
Machinery	13.6	10.7%
Other Manufacturing	52.0	40.7%
Wholesale	65.7	57.2%
Information	38.2	70.9%
Banking	32.1	60.7%
Finance (ex. Banks)	96.0	39.3%
Services	19.7	51.4%
Other	326.7	62.6%

Note: Historical-cost basis, 2002
Source: Bureau of Economic Analysis

Figure 4

Europe's FDI Roots in the U.S.

US$ Billions	US FDI from Europe	% of US Total
Total from Europe	1006.5	74.7%
Manufacturing	383.5	81.5%
Food Products	11.4	75.3%
Chemicals	107.9	95.8%
Primary Metals	14.0	75.5%
Machinery	30.7	86.5%
Other Manufacturing	121.1	71.5%
Wholesale	120.7	63.9%
Retail	22.5	79.4%
Banking	58.9	73.0%
Information	165.3	89.2%
Finance & Insurance (ex. Banks)	113.4	69.6%
Real Estate	22.1	43.6%
Services	36.7	91.2%
Other	83.3	59.5%

Note: Historical-cost basis, 2002
Source: Bureau of Economic Analysis

Figure 5

The World's Most Knowledge Competitive Regions, 2004

Rank 2004 and Region	Rank 2003	Change
1. San Francisco, CA US	1	0
2. Boston, MA US	3	+1
3. Grand Rapids–Muskegon-Holland, MI US	9	+6
4. Seattle, WA US	12	+8
5. Hartford, CT US	7	+2
6. San Diego, CA US	10	+4
7. Rochester, NY US	4	−3
8. Sacramento-Yolo, CA US	17	+9
9. Austin-San Marco, TX US	2	−7
10. Minneapolis-St. Paul, MN US	5	−5
11. Los Angeles, CA US	21	+10
12. Detroit-Ann Arbor-Flint, MI US	14	+2
13. New York, NY US	11	−2
14. Denver-Boulder-Greeley, CO US	6	−8
15. Stockholm, Sweden	18	+3
16. Philadelphia, PA US	26	+10
17. Chicago, IL US	19	+2
18. Cincinnati- Hamilton, OH US	28	+10
19. Uusimaa, Finland	37	+18
20. Portland-Salem, OR US	16	−4
21. Dallas-Ft. Worth, TX US	13	−8
22. Raleigh-Durham, NC US	8	−14
23. Washington, DC US	20	−3
24. Salt Lake City-Ogden, UT US	23	−1
25. Houston-Galveston-Brazoria, TX US	32	+7
26. Indianapolis, IN US	24	−2
27. Milwaukee-Racine, WI US	27	0
28. Buffalo-Niagara Falls, NY US	33	+5
29. Columbus, OH US	29	0
30. Phoenix-Mesa, AZ US	36	+6
31. Atlanta, GA US	22	−9
32. Kansas City, KS, US	25	−7
33. Cleveland-Akron, OH, US	34	+1
34. Île de France, France	54	+20
35. Pittsburgh, PA US	38	+3
36. Charlotte-Gastonia-Rock Hill, NC US	30	−6
37. Richmond-Petersburg, VA US	31	−6
38. Tokyo, Japan	15	−23
39. Shiga, Japan	46	+7
40. South East, UK	77	+37
41. Greensboro—Winston-Salem–High Point, NC, US	35	−6
42. St. Louis, MO US	41	−1
43. San Antonio, TX US	43	0
44. West, Sweden	69	+25
45. Switzerland	49	+4
46. London, UK	68	+22
47. Nashville, KY US	42	−5
48. Norfolk-Virginia Beach-Newport Beach, VA US	48	0
49. Louisville, KY US	39	−10
50. Eastern, UK	84	+34

Source: The World Knowledge Competitiveness Index 2004 measures 125 of the world's "knowledge
    regions" according to a variety of criteria. http://www.hugginsassociates.com
© Robert Huggins Associates

Graph 1

The Transatlantic vs. the World Economy

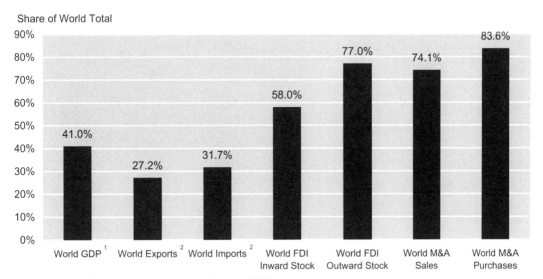

Share of World Total

Source: UN, IMF, Official Government sources, figures for 2002.
1. Based on PPP estimates. 2.Excluding intra-EU trade

Graph 2

Global Engagement: Foreign Affiliate Sales vs. Trade

U.S. $ Billions, 2001	U.S. Foreign Affiliate Sales vs. Trade
Global Affiliate Sales of U.S.	2,929.6
Total U.S. Exports	1,284.9
Total Affiliate Sales in U.S.	2,354.1
U.S. Imports	1,632.1
U.S. Billions, 2001	
U.S. Affiliate Sales in Europe	1,460.0
U.S. Exports to Europe (G&S)	357.7
European Affiliate Sales in U.S.	1,389.0
U.S. Imports from Europe (G&S)	418.9

Source: Bureau of Economic Analysis

Graph 3

U.S. FDI in China and Europe, 1994-2003

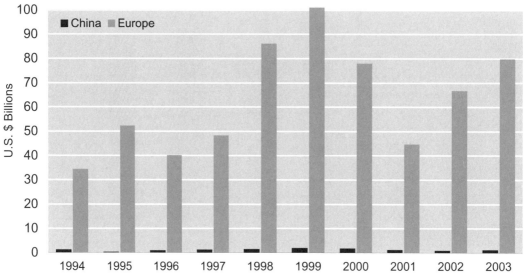

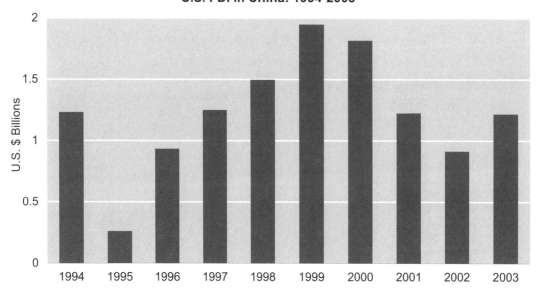

Charts and Maps

Chart 1

Top Five Sectors of U.S. Projects in European Countries, 1997-2003

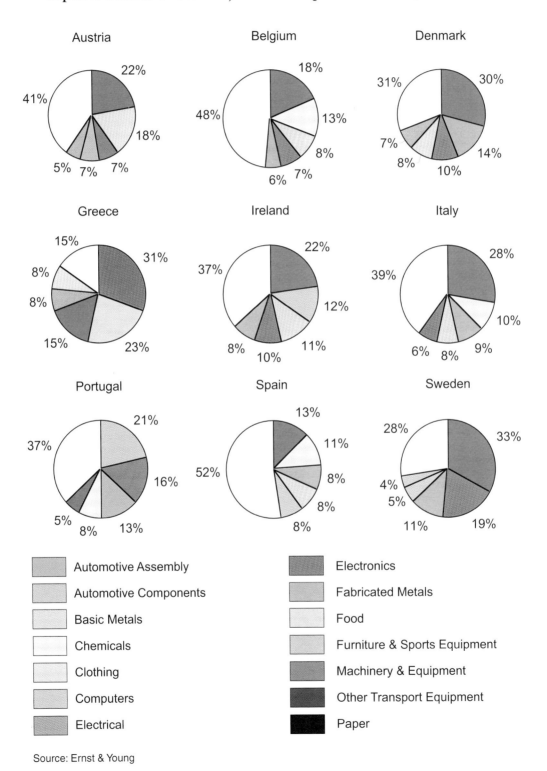

Source: Ernst & Young

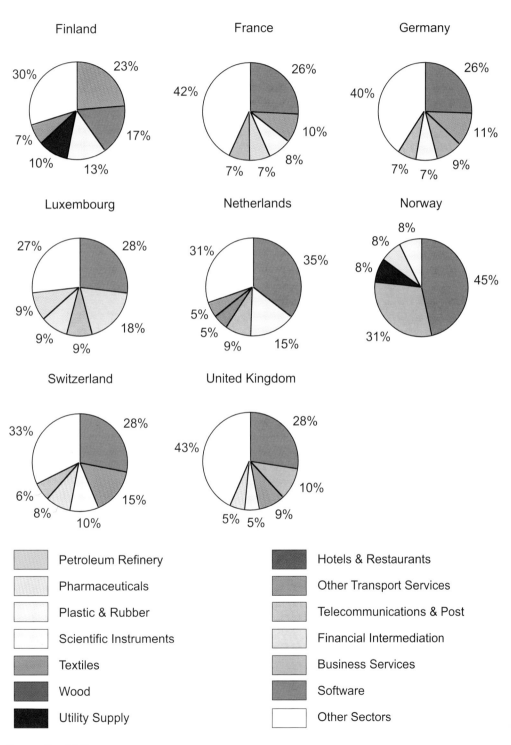

Source: Ernst & Young

Chart 2

Top Five Sectors of U.S. Projects in French Regions, 1997-2003

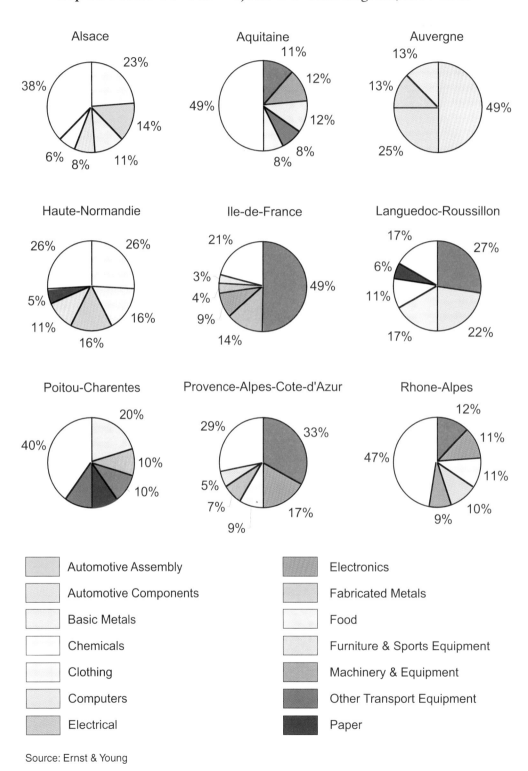

Source: Ernst & Young

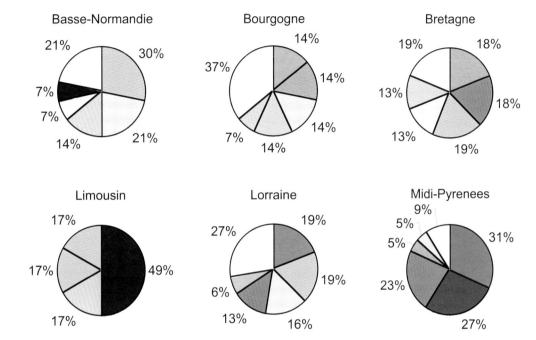

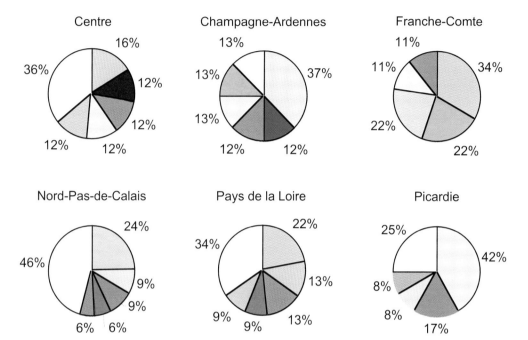

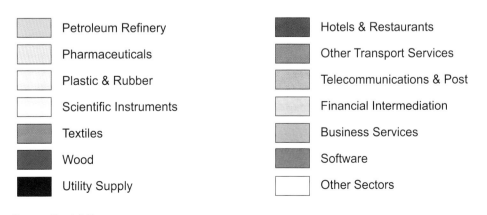

Petroleum Refinery		Hotels & Restaurants
Pharmaceuticals		Other Transport Services
Plastic & Rubber		Telecommunications & Post
Scientific Instruments		Financial Intermediation
Textiles		Business Services
Wood		Software
Utility Supply		Other Sectors

Source: Ernst & Young

Source: Ernst & Young

Chart 3

Top Five Sectors of U.S. Projects in German Regions, 1997-2003

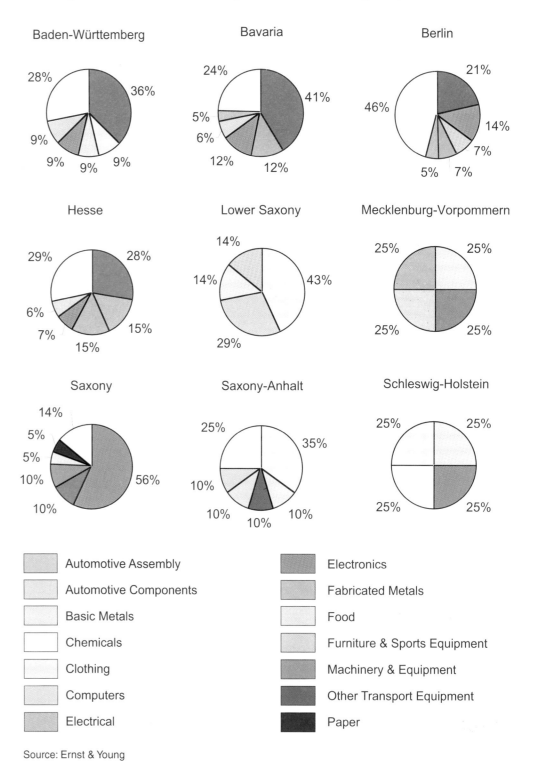

Source: Ernst & Young

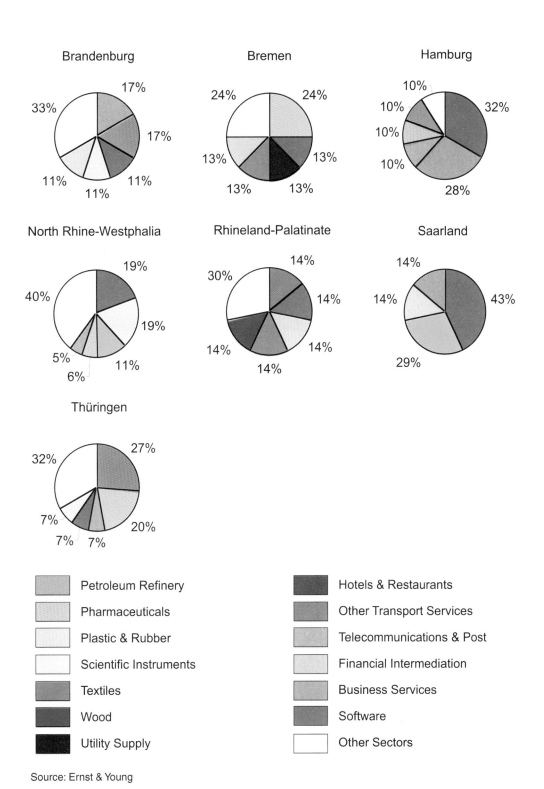

Source: Ernst & Young

Chart 4

Top Five Sectors of U.S. Projects in UK Regions 1997-2003

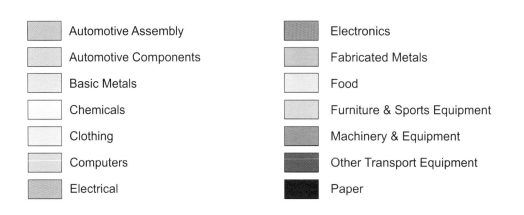

Source: Ernst & Young

Northern Ireland

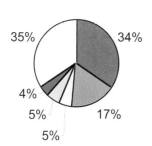

35%   34%
4%
5%   17%
5%

North West

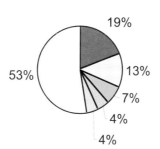

19%
53%   13%
7%
4%
4%

Scotland

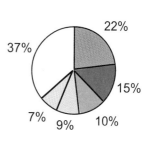

22%
37%
15%
7%   9%   10%

West Midlands

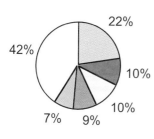

22%
42%
10%
10%
7%   9%

Yorkshire and Humberside

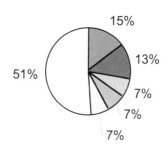

15%
13%
51%
7%
7%
7%

Petroleum Refinery	
Pharmaceuticals	
Plastic & Rubber	
Scientific Instruments	
Textiles	
Wood	
Utility Supply	

Hotels & Restaurants

Other Transport Services

Telecommunications & Post

Financial Intermediation

Business Services

Software

Other Sectors

Source: Ernst & Young

Map 1

Jobs directly supported by European foreign direct investment in the 50 United States and Puerto Rico, 2001 (thousands of jobs)

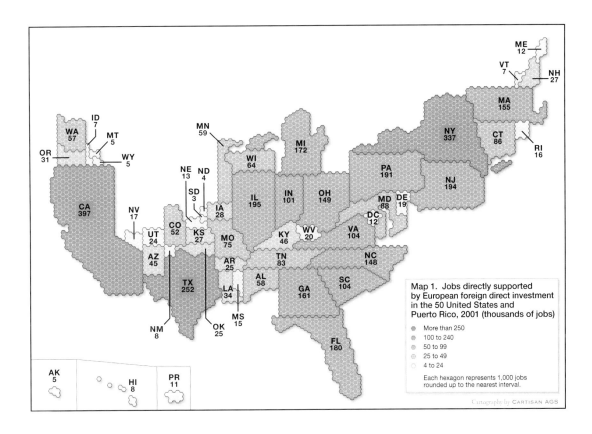

Map 1. Jobs directly supported by European foreign direct investment in the 50 United States and Puerto Rico, 2001 (thousands of jobs)

- More than 250
- 100 to 240
- 50 to 99
- 25 to 49
- 4 to 24

Each hexagon represents 1,000 jobs rounded up to the nearest interval.

Cartography by CARTISAN AGS

Map 2

European foreign direct investment in the 50 United States and Puerto Rico, 2001 (billions of dollars)

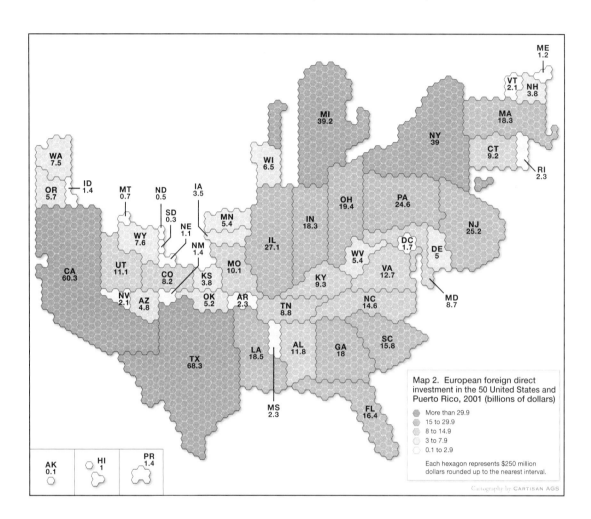

Map 2. European foreign direct investment in the 50 United States and Puerto Rico, 2001 (billions of dollars)

- More than 29.9
- 15 to 29.9
- 8 to 14.9
- 3 to 7.9
- 0.1 to 2.9

Each hexagon represents $250 million dollars rounded up to the nearest interval.

Cartography by CARTISAN AGS

Map 3

Exports by the 50 United States and Puerto Rico to Europe, 2003
(billions of dollars)

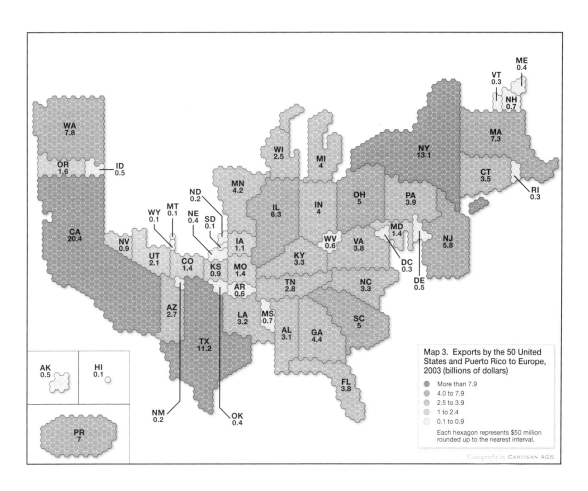

Map 3. Exports by the 50 United States and Puerto Rico to Europe, 2003 (billions of dollars)

- More than 7.9
- 4.0 to 7.9
- 2.5 to 3.9
- 1 to 2.4
- 0.1 to 0.9

Each hexagon represents $50 million rounded up to the nearest interval.

Cartography by CARTISAN AGS

Map 4

U.S. foreign direct investment in the EU15, Norway and Switzerland, 2002
(billions of dollars)

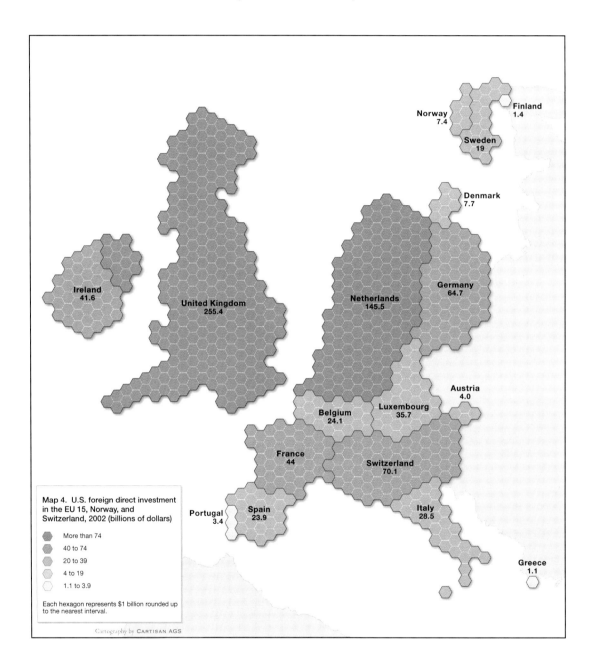

Map 4. U.S. foreign direct investment in the EU 15, Norway, and Switzerland, 2002 (billions of dollars)

More than 74
40 to 74
20 to 39
4 to 19
1.1 to 3.9

Each hexagon represents $1 billion rounded up to the nearest interval.

Cartography by CARTISAN AGS

Map 5

European sources of foreign direct investment in the United States, 2002 (EU 15, Norway and Switzerland; billions of dollars)

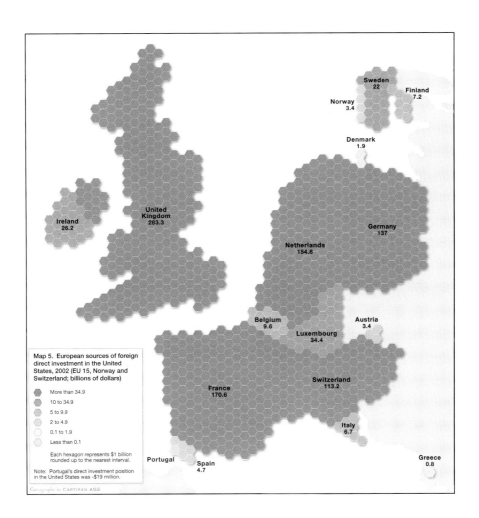

Map 5. European sources of foreign direct investment in the United States, 2002 (EU 15, Norway and Switzerland; billions of dollars)

- More than 34.9
- 10 to 34.9
- 5 to 9.9
- 2 to 4.9
- 0.1 to 1.9
- Less than 0.1

Each hexagon represents $1 billion rounded up to the nearest interval.

Note: Portugal's direct investment position in the United States was -$19 million.

Cartography by CARTISAN AGS

Map 6

European exports to the United States on a country-by-country basis, 2002 (EU 15, Norway and Switzerland; billions of dollars)

Map 6. European exports to the United States on a country-by-country basis, 2002 (EU 15, Norway and Switzerland; billions of dollars)

- More than 34.9
- 20 to 34.9
- 5.5 to 19.9
- 1.5 to 5.4
- 0.5 to 1.5

Each hexagon represents $250 million dollars rounded up to the nearest interval.

Cartography by CARTISAN AGS

Map 7

European imports from the United States on a country-by-country basis, 2002 (EU 15, Norway and Switzerland; billions of dollars)

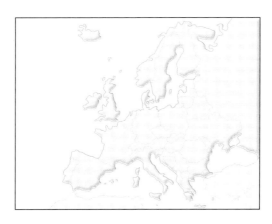

Map 8

The French Regions: Trade with the United States, 2001
(millions of dollars)

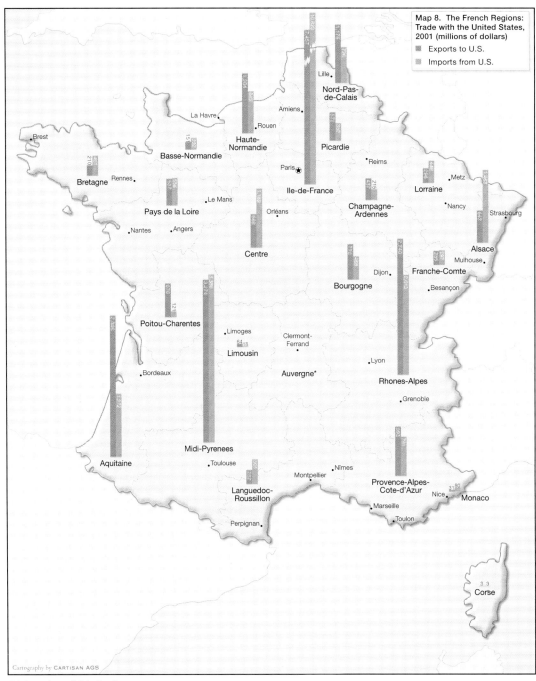

Map 8. The French Regions: Trade with the United States, 2001 (millions of dollars)

Exports to U.S.
Imports from U.S.

*data not available for Auvergne

Map 9

The German *Länder*: Commerce with the United States, 2001 and 2002 (millions of dollars)

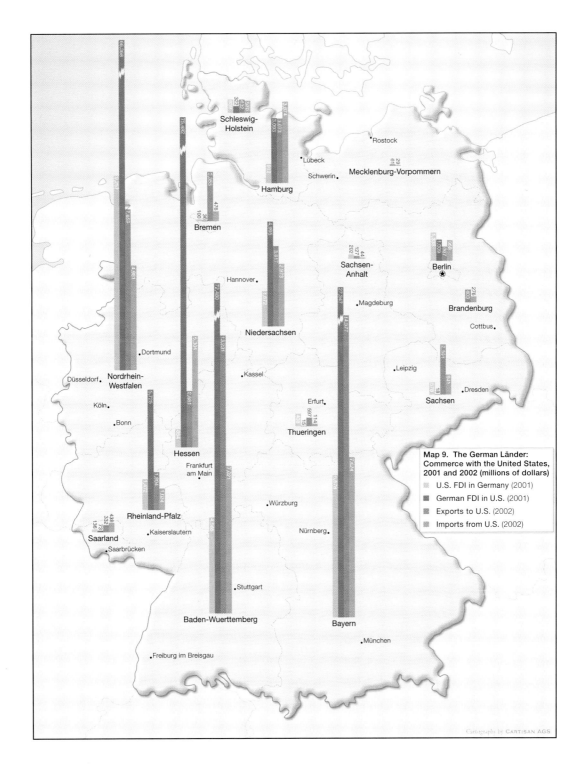

Map 9. The German Länder:
Commerce with the United States,
2001 and 2002 (millions of dollars)

- U.S. FDI in Germany (2001)
- German FDI in U.S. (2001)
- Exports to U.S. (2002)
- Imports from U.S. (2002)

Map 10

The British Regions: Exports to the United States, 2003
(millions of dollars)

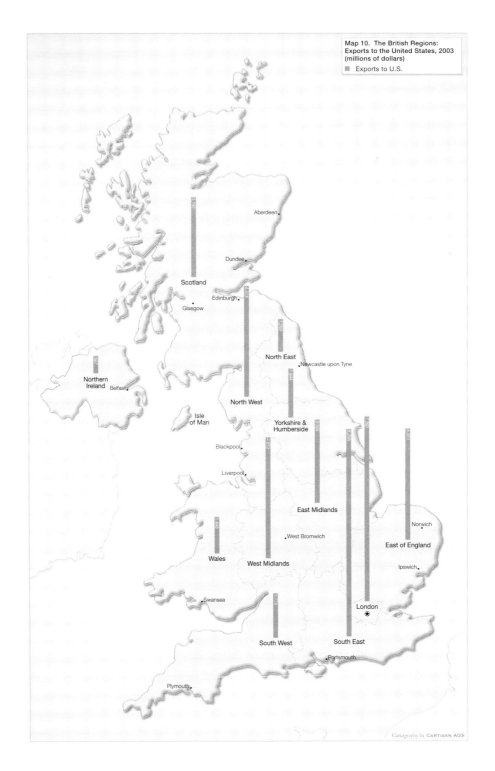

Map 10. The British Regions:
Exports to the United States, 2003
(millions of dollars)
■ Exports to U.S.

Cartography by CARTISAN AGS

Notes on Data and Sources

Employment, Investment, and Trade Linkages for the 50 U.S. States and Europe

Data for investment as well as investment-related jobs are from the U.S. Commerce Department's Bureau of Economic Analysis. Investment data measure gross property, plant, and equipment of affiliates. Europe includes Belgium, France, Germany, Italy, Netherlands, Sweden, Switzerland, and the United Kingdom. Trade data are from the International Trade Administration's Office of Trade and Economic Analysis at the U.S. Commerce Department. Europe includes Andorra, Austria, Belgium, Bosnia-Herzegovina, Croatia, Cyprus, Denmark, Faeroe Islands, Finland, France, Germany, Gibraltar, Greece, Iceland, Ireland, Italy, Liechtenstein, Luxembourg, Macedonia, Malta and Gozo, Monaco, Netherlands, Norway, Portugal, San Marino, Slovenia, Spain, Sweden, Switzerland, Turkey, United Kingdom, Vatican City, Yugoslavia. The top ten exports to Europe bar chart employs a logarithmic scale to facilitate cross state comparisons.

Investment and Trade for the EU 15, Norway and Switzerland and the United States

Investment data are from the Bureau of Economic Analysis. Trade data are from the IMF Trade Statistics. Data for the top ten U.S. imports bar charts are from the Office of Trade and Economic Analysis of the International Trade Administration. They employ logarithmic scales to facilitate cross-country comparisons. Capital expenditure data are from Ernst & Young's European Investment Monitor. They describe the number of foreign inward investment projects, but do not assign values to these projects.

Investment and Trade Figures for the EU Accession Countries and the United States

Investment data are from the Bureau of Economic Analysis. Trade data are from the IMF Trade Statistics. Data for the top ten U.S. imports bar charts are from the International Trade Administration's Office of Trade and Economic Analysis at the U.S. Department of Commerce. They employ logarithmic scales to facilitate cross-country comparisons. Capital expenditure data are from Ernst & Young's European Investment Monitor. They describe the number of foreign inward investment projects, but do not assign values to these projects.

Appendix

Maps one through seven are skewed to reflect concentrations of transatlantic commerce. Data for investment as well as investment-related jobs for maps one and two are from the U.S. Commerce Department's Bureau of Economic Analysis. Europe includes Belgium, France, Germany, Italy, the Netherlands, Sweden, Switzerland, and the United Kingdom. Trade data for map three are from the International Trade Administration's Office of Trade and Economic Analysis at the U.S. Department of Commerce. Europe includes Andorra, Austria, Belgium, Bosnia-Herzegovina, Croatia, Cyprus, Denmark, Faeroe Islands, Finland, France, Germany, Gibraltar, Greece, Iceland, Ireland, Italy, Liechtenstein, Luxembourg, Macedonia, Malta and Gozo, Monaco, the Netherlands, Norway, Portugal, San Marino, Slovenia, Spain, Sweden, Switzerland, Turkey, United Kingdom, Vatican City, Yugoslavia. Respective outward and inward U.S. direct investment position data in maps four and five are from the Bureau of Economic Analysis and are calculated on a historical-cost basis. Respective European export and import data are from IMF Trade Statistics.

Maps eight through ten display the transatlantic commerce of the French, German, and British regions. French trade data are from the French Ministry of the Economy, Finance and Industry. German trade data are from the Federal Statistical Office Germany. German foreign direct investment data are from the Deutsche Bundesbank. British export data are from HM Customs & Excise.

The pie charts display the sector breakdown of project-based foreign inward investments in the European countries and the regions of France, Germany, and the United Kingdom. The data are from Ernst & Young's European Investment Monitor.

Bibliography

Barba Navaretti, G., J.I. Haaland, and A. Venables, *Multinational Corporations and Global Production Networks: The Implications for Trade Policy* (London: CEPR, 2002)

Brawly, Mark. R., *The Politics of Globalization* (Peterborough, Ont.: Broadview Press, 2003).

Dunning, J., "Location and the Multinational Enterprise: A Neglected Factor? *Journal of International Business Studies*, Vol, 29, No. 1 (1998), pp. 45-66.

Dunning, J., (ed.), *Regions, Globalization and the Knowledge Economy* (Oxford: Oxford University Press, 2000)

Friedman, T., *The Lexus and the Olive Tree* (New York: Simon and Shuster, 2001)

Ghemawat, P., "Distance Still Matters: The Hard Reality of Global Expansion," *Harvard Business Review*, Vol. 79:8 (September 2001), pp. 137-147.

Ghemawat, P., "Semiglobalization and International Business Strategy," *Journal of International Business Studies*, doi:10.1057/palgrave.jibs.8400013.

Hirst, Paul, and Grahame Thompson, *Globalization in Question: The International Political Economy and the Possibilities of Governance*, 2nd ed. (Cambridge: Polity Press, 1999).

Krugman, P. R., *Geography and Trade* (Cambridge, MA: MIT Press, 1991)

Morrison, A.J., Ricks, D.A. and Roth, K., "Globalization Versus Regionalization: Which Way for the Multinational? *Organizational Dynamics*, 19(3): 17-29.

Nye, J. S. and Donahue, J. (eds.), *Governance in a Globalizing World* (Cambridge, MA: Visions of Governance for the 21st Century, 2000)

Ohmae, K., *Triad Power: The Coming Shape of Global Competition* (New York: The Free Press, 1985).

Porter, M., *The Competitive Advantage of Nations* (New York: Free Press, 1990)

Quinlan, J.P., *Global Engagement: How American Companies Really Compete in the Global Economy* (New York: McGraw Hill, 2000)

Rugman, A.M., *The End of Globalization* (London: Random House and New York: Amacom-McGraw Hill, 2000)

Rugman, A. and D'Cruz, J., *Multinationals as Flagship Firms: Regional Business Networks* (Oxford: Oxford University Press, 2000)

Scott, Allen J. (ed.), *Global City-Regions: Trends, Theory, Policy* (Oxford: Oxford University Press, 2001).

Scott, Alan J., *Regions and the World Economy: The Coming Shape of Global Production, Competition, and Political Order* (Oxford: Oxford University Press, 1998)

Scott, Alan J., *The Limits of Globalization. Cases and Arguments* (New York and London: Routledge, 1997).

Slaughter, M., *Host-Country Determinants of U.S. Foreign Direct Investment into Europe*, available at http://www.dartmouth.edu/~mjs/Papers/Kap01_Slaughter.pdf

United Nations. UNCTAD. *World Investment Report*. Annual editions, 1995-present.

About the Authors

Daniel S. Hamilton is the Richard von Weizsäcker Professor and Director of the Center for Transatlantic Relations at the Paul H. Nitze School of Advanced International Studies, Johns Hopkins University. He also serves as Executive Director of the American Consortium on EU Studies (ACES), a five-university partnership of national capital area universities designated by the European Commission as the EU Center Washington, DC. He is the publisher of the bimonthly magazine *Transatlantic: Europe, America & the World*. He previously served as Deputy Assistant Secretary of State for European Affairs, U.S. Special Coordinator for Southeast European Stabilization, Associate Director of the Policy Planning Staff, Senior Associate at the Carnegie Endowment for International Peace, and Deputy Director of the Aspen Institute Berlin. He has also taught at the University of Innsbruck and the Free University of Berlin, is a regular media commentator on international relations, and has published many works, most recently *Transatlantic Transformations: Equipping NATO for the 21st Century* (2004).

Joseph P. Quinlan is a Fellow at the Center for Transatlantic Relations at the Paul H. Nitze School of Advanced International Studies, Johns Hopkins University. He specializes in global capital flows, international trade and multinational strategies. He has extensive experience on Wall Street and in the U.S. corporate sector. He lectures at New York University and was appointed as an Eisenhower Fellow in 1998. His publications have appeared in such venues as *Foreign Affairs*, the *Financial Times* and the *Wall Street Journal*. He is the author of the Center's 2003 study, *Drifting Apart or Growing Together? The Primacy of the Transatlantic Economy* and is the author of three other books, the most recent being *Global Engagement: How American Companies Really Compete in the Global Economy* (2000).